Godot 4 for Beginners

Develop engaging 2D and 3D games with Godot 4's scripting and design features

Robert Henning

‹packt›

Godot 4 for Beginners

Copyright © 2025 Packt Publishing

All rights reserved. No part of this book may be reproduced, stored in a retrieval system, or transmitted in any form or by any means, without the prior written permission of the publisher, except in the case of brief quotations embedded in critical articles or reviews.

Every effort has been made in the preparation of this book to ensure the accuracy of the information presented. However, the information contained in this book is sold without warranty, either express or implied. Neither the author, nor Packt Publishing or its dealers and distributors, will be held liable for any damages caused or alleged to have been caused directly or indirectly by this book.

Packt Publishing has endeavored to provide trademark information about all of the companies and products mentioned in this book by the appropriate use of capitals. However, Packt Publishing cannot guarantee the accuracy of this information.

Portfolio Director: Rohit Rajkumar
Relationship Lead: Neha Pande
Program Manager: Sandip Tadge
Content Engineer: Shreya Sarkar
Technical Editor: Tejas Mhasvekar
Copy Editor: Safis Editing
Indexer: Tejal Soni
Proofreader: Shreya Sarkar
Production Designer: Prashant Ghare
Growth Lead: Lee Booth

First published: August 2025
Production reference: 1250725

Published by Packt Publishing Ltd.
Grosvenor House
11 St Paul's Square
Birmingham
B3 1RB, UK.

ISBN 978-1-83620-309-4

www.packtpub.com

This book is dedicated to
encouragement, you can

Creating games like Godot. How
engines like a divers
mastering ones
obvious ones
workin

Foreword

...is accessible, thanks in large part to powerful yet approachable ..., diving into engines like Godot—while user-friendly—still involves ... of skills, from the obvious ones like programming and math to the less ... software architecture and game design. Even if you already know the inner ... a game engine, transitioning to another can be tedious.

... book, written by professional game development tutor Robert Henning, addresses exactly this issue and eases readers into the vast field of game development. The cultivation of new skills will be much easier through Robert's teaching methods. Moreover, you will even enjoy the process, as the book includes exercises and projects that offer early wins to boost your motivation.

Although I have never met Robert in person, he helped me become a professional game developer in a very direct way—by creating tutorials and Godot Engine-related content on YouTube that both aided and motivated me. At the time of writing this foreword, his channel has over 50,000 subscribers, which is a testament to the usefulness of his videos and his prolific will to help people get started with game development in Godot.

Reading through these pages and doing the exercises transports me back to when I was a beginner—a blank slate—and makes me excited to try out new things. Because if there is one thing that is most important, it is this: always keep a beginner's mindset and experiment. Every time you learn something or do an exercise, take it to its limits. Change a value here and there until it breaks, and then take a step back. It's only when we leave the path that we see clearly why the path is there in the first place.

So, I will hold you no longer. Go explore the path laid out by Robert in this excellent book. Look at it as an adventure. Experiment freely, explore the possibilities, and find your own style. You won't regret it.

Sander Vanhove,

Lead Game Developer and Technical Artist, and Author of the bestselling book Learning GDScript by Developing a Game with Godot 4

Contributors

About the author

Robert Henning has over 20 years of computer science education experience, specializing in game development. He has taught game development using Scratch, Java with Greenfoot, Delphi, Construct 3, Unity, and Godot. A passionate advocate for Godot, Robert has promoted this platform since the early versions.

Robert also runs a popular YouTube channel (`https://www.youtube.com/@GameDevJourney`) offering tutorials and showcasing games made with Godot. His hands-on approach and dedication to accessible learning have earned him a reputation as a trusted educator. *Godot 4 for Beginners* is a culmination of his expertise, designed to guide newcomers through creating their own games with clear, step-by-step instructions.

About the reviewers

Deepak Jadhav is an experienced professional with extensive experience in game development and project management, particularly in extended reality (XR) technologies. He excels in creating immersive augmented reality (AR) and mixed reality (MR) experiences, delivering innovative solutions across various industries. His expertise spans game programming, game engines (Godot, Unity, and Unreal), AI system implementation, and applying these skills to enterprise applications. Deepak holds a Master's degree in Game Development and Project Management and a Bachelor's degree in Computer Technology, equipping him with technical and managerial skills for leading complex XR and game development projects.

Ural, a game developer based in Turkey, holds a PhD in veterinary medicine. His journey in game development began in high school with Python, leading him to work on diverse projects using engines such as Godot, Unity, and Unreal Engine. He started using Godot as his first game engine in 2018 and has solo-developed various games with it. Since 2021, he has been a lead developer at Harmonia Games. Ural is passionate about exploring different workflows and game architectures. He led the development of the PC game *REM the Dreamer*, released on Steam, and engineered his own custom game engine from the ground up using C++.

Henrique "Ludonaut" Campos is an indie game developer and game designer working in the industry for years. Started as a University teacher in 2015 in the Computer Graphics and Artificial Intelligence chairs and working in the GDQuest team from 2018 to 2022, Henrique is also an independent consultant for studios and schools. Under the alias of **Ludonaut**, Henrique creates game development content on his YouTube channel creating games, assets, ebooks, and courses that can be found in his `itch.io` profile. Being the author of the *Game Development Patterns with Godot 4* book, Henrique paved the way for Godot users to make reusable and scalable code libraries for Godot Engine projects.

Table of Contents

Preface   xvii

Part 1: Learning How the Godot Engine Works   1

Chapter 1: Let's Get Godot-ing!   3

Getting the most out of this book – get to know your free benefits 4
- Next-gen reader • 4
- Interactive AI assistant (beta) • 5
- DRM-free PDF or ePub version • 5

Technical requirements 6
What is Godot? 6
- What makes Godot so special? • 7

Setting up Godot 4 8
Creating a new project 12
- Making the scene dynamic • 23
  - *Delta* • 24
- Continuing the bouncing label project • 25

Summary 28

Chapter 2: Exploring the Godot Engine Interface   29

Technical requirements 29
Important terms 30

Editing an existing Godot project 31
Creating an additional scene 35
Reacting to player input 39
    Scripting player reactions to input • 49
        Hiding the label until the user provides input • 49
        Input handling • 50
Summary 52

Chapter 3: Introduction to 3D   55

Technical requirements 55
Creating 3D objects 56
    Moving around the scene • 59
Creating a material for your object 62
    Creating a material • 62
    Applying a material • 65
    Challenge yourself • 67
Creating lighting for the scene 72
    Directional light • 73
    Omni light • 74
    Spotlight • 78
Summary 81

Chapter 4: Scripting with GDScript   83

Technical requirements 84
Understanding GDScript 84
Creating scripts 84
Understanding functions 89
    Understanding the game loop • 90
        _ready() • 90
        _process(delta) • 90
        _physics_process(delta) • 91

Understanding variables **93**

Creating a variable • 93

Data types • 95

Naming conventions • 96

Understanding operators **98**

Order of operations • 99

Practice exercise • 100

Relational and comparison operators **101**

Practice exercise • 103

Using custom functions **104**

Arguments and parameters or function inputs • 105

Functions can return output • 106

Summary **108**

Part 2: Working with the Godot Engine 111

Chapter 5: Understanding Vectors 113

Technical requirements **113**

What are vectors? **114**

Coordinates in Godot • 118

Using vectors in Godot **119**

Movement and positioning • 122

Vector addition • 123

Vector subtraction • 124

Vector multiplication • 125

Vector length • 127

Distance • 128

Normalization • 128

Summary **129**

Chapter 6: Creating a 2D Mini-Game in Godot – Part 1   131

Technical requirements 132
Building the level with a TileMap 132
Creating and controlling the player 136
  Adding the background • 136
  Setting up the player animations • 139
  Detecting collisions • 142
  TileMap collisions • 143
  Collision layers and collision masks • 144
  Painting the tiles • 148
Adding the CharacterBody2D template for the Player script 149
Cleaning the code 154
Summary 155

Chapter 7: Creating a 2D Mini-Game in Godot – Part 2   157

Technical requirements 158
Controlling player animations with code 158
  Helper variables • 159
Wall-sliding and double-jumping mechanics 160
  Double-jump function • 160
  Wall-slide function • 161
    Checking conditions • 162
    Detecting input • 162
    Resetting the wall slide • 162
    Limiting downward speed • 162
  Animate function • 163
Falling through platforms 165
Adding collectible items 166
  Strawberry scene (our collectible item) • 166
  Implementing the Strawberry script • 170

Adding a patrolling enemy 175

Mushroom stomping • 180

Implementing level completion 183

Summary 186

Part 3: Building and Beyond — Your Game Development Journey 189

Chapter 8: Creating a 3D Mini-Game in Godot — Part 1   191

Technical requirements 192
Working in 3D: a new dimension in Godot 192
Building a 3D character 192
Creating a level design 196

Creating a level component • 197

Example: creating a grass platform • 197

Handling irregular collision shapes • 199

Creating the level layout • 201

Organizing the level scene • 202

Working with a Character Controller script 203
Using variables 204

Linking the Player script with the camera • 205

Alternative method for adding reference variables • 207

Exploring functions 208

Creating an input map • 209

Implementing player controls and actions • 211

Handling game events and feedback • 212

Implementing a camera controller 215
Running tests 220
Summary 221

Chapter 9: Creating a 3D Mini-Game in Godot – Part 2   223

Technical requirements 224
Exploring collectibles 224
Creating the Gem scene • 224
Adding the Gem script • 225
Introducing obstacles 230
Creating the Cannon scene • 230
Creating the Ball scene • 231
Writing the Ball script • 233
Writing the Cannon script • 233
Completing our level 235
Creating the Flag scene • 235
Changing scenes • 236
Polishing our level 237
Setting the background color • 238
Adding particle effects • 238
Creating the smoke scene • 238
Adding audio to our level • 242
Using the sine function • 246
Summary 247

Chapter 10: Adding Game Juice   249

Technical requirements 250
Understanding game juice 250
Foundations of juicing: animation and audio • 251
Visual feedback (animation and particle effects) • 251
Audio feedback (music and sound effects) • 251
Implementing a health bar HUD 251
Developing a heart-based health system • 252
Updating the HUD in the Level script • 255

Adding a hit animation 257

Creating a confetti cannon effect 262

    Scripting the confetti cannon • 268

Adding audio and sound effects 270

    Implementing a sound effect • 272

Summary 275

Chapter 11: Understanding Game Design   277

Technical requirements 277

Understanding the foundations of game design 278

    Introducing the game design document • 279

    Why is documentation necessary for your game design? • 279

    Understanding the guiding principles for the GDD • 280

        Think visually • 281

        Keep it brief and clear • 281

        Stay organized • 281

        Learn by example • 282

Exploring the Game Design Document 282

    Title: what will you call your game? • 282

    Team: who will build or develop the game? • 282

    Status: what is the status of the project? • 282

    Statement of concept: what is your game about in one sentence? • 283

    Expanded concept paragraph and USP: what makes your game unique, and how can you describe it in more detail? • 283

    Genre: what type of game are you making? • 284

    Audience: who is this game for? • 284

    Experience: what should the player feel or experience while playing? • 284

    Anchor points: what are the core ideas, inspirations, or reference points? • 285

    Platform: which platforms will the game be released on? • 285

    Review competition: what similar games exist, and how will yours stand out? • 285

Assets: what art, sound, and other resources will your game need? • 285

Monetization: how will the game generate revenue, if at all? • 286

Describing game elements of the GDD in detail 286

Player progression and objectives • 286

Game world and background • 287

User interface • 288

Audio and visual style • 290

Game systems and features • 291

Software requirements • 292

Game objects • 294

Detailed asset list • 295

Prototypes • 296

Playtesting • 297

Archive • 298

Current concerns and considerations • 298

Implementation details • 299

Summary 300

Chapter 12: Where to Next? 301

Technical requirements 302

Utilizing educational resources 302

YouTube • 302

Blogs • 303

Exploring opportunities for practice 304

Participating in game jams • 305

Community and networking 306

Why networking matters • 306

Where to build your network • 306

People to follow • 307

Utilizing tools and assets 307

Tools • 307

Resources • 308

Building your portfolio 309

Developing game ideas 310

Design guide for your next project 311

Further reading 313

Summary 315

Chapter 13: Unlock Your Book's Exclusive Benefits   317

How to unlock these benefits in three easy steps 317

Step 1 • 317

Step 2 • 318

Step 3 • 318

Need help? • 319

Other Books You May Enjoy   323

Index   327

Preface

Hello and welcome to *Godot 4 for Beginners*! My name is Robert Henning, and I was once a Godot beginner myself, so I know how it feels to be searching for resources to help you learn how to make games with the Godot Engine. It was specifically because of the lack of good Godot resources for beginners that I wrote this book.

This book takes a hands-on, step-by-step approach to teaching game development, beginning with the basics of downloading and installing the Godot 4 game engine and gradually building your knowledge through a series of progressively more complex topics. Each chapter is designed to be practical and interactive, allowing you to immediately apply what you've learned through real-world examples and projects. The book is structured to ensure that even those with no prior programming or game development experience can follow along and succeed.

Throughout this book, you will get familiar with the Godot 4 interface and the tools it provides, while also learning the foundational game development philosophy behind Godot's unique system of nodes, scenes, signals, and scripts. You will use GDScript, Godot's scripting language, and explore both 2D and 3D workflows. Along the way, you'll build character controllers, design interactive elements such as enemies and hazards, implement scoring systems and collectibles, and discover how to polish your projects for a more professional finish. The book also guides you through the fundamentals of game design, helping you understand not only how to build a game but also how to craft a fun and engaging experience.

By the end of this book, you will have a solid understanding of the Godot 4 game engine and its interface and be able to create both 2D and 3D games, manipulate lighting, script with GDScript, and implement key game elements such as players, enemies, and collectibles. You will also be skilled in designing and constructing engaging game levels, tracking scores, and managing game-over states, empowering you to bring your own game ideas to life.

Now it's your turn to get started. With curiosity, patience, and practice, you will be building your very own games before you know it. Let's begin your journey into game development!

Who this book is for

This book is ideal for anyone new to game development who wants to explore the powerful and accessible Godot engine. Whether you're an aspiring game developer, an indie creator looking for a free and open source tool, a student eager to build interactive projects, or an artist curious about bringing your ideas to life, this book will provide you with a solid foundation in using Godot 4. With clear explanations and hands-on projects, it's designed to help you make the transition from curiosity to creation—no prior experience required.

Additionally, students wanting to learn game development fundamentals, educators seeking a comprehensive resource to teach the basics, and aspiring game developers aiming to bring their game ideas to life using the open source, beginner-friendly Godot game engine will find this book invaluable.

Whether you're starting completely from scratch or already know a few basics, this book walks you through Godot 4 with clear, step-by-step guidance. No prior coding experience is required—although a rudimentary grasp of concepts such as variables, loops, and conditionals can help, every essential programming idea is explained from the ground up within these pages.

What this book covers

Chapter 1, Let's Get Godot-ing!, explores the history and core features of Godot 4.0 and aims to provide you with the knowledge to install, launch, and create your first project in the engine.

Chapter 2, Exploring the Godot Engine Interface, explores the fundamental features of the interface and helps you to edit your first project in Godot 4. You will also understand the node and scene design philosophy that underscores Godot.

Chapter 3, Introduction to 3D, explains how to build and illuminate a simple 3D environment and helps you to gain confidence in navigating Godot's 3D workspace.

Chapter 4, Scripting with GDScript, provides the foundational knowledge to script essential game mechanics and confidently control the logic and flow of your game.

Chapter 5, Understanding Vectors, explains what vectors are and why they play a vital role in game mechanics. You'll learn how to use vectors effectively within the Godot engine.

Chapter 6, Creating a 2D Mini-Game in Godot – Part 1, details the creation of an interactive, fully playable platformer level and explains how these components work together to form the foundation of many platformer games. This chapter includes creating the level design with TileMap, developing the player character, scripting the player character, and learning about clean code.

Chapter 7, Creating a 2D Mini-Game in Godot – Part 2, explores how to bring your game mechanics to life with code and create a more dynamic and engaging platformer experience. This chapter includes animating the player and programming platform game mechanics, collectible items, patrolling enemies, and level completion.

Chapter 8, Creating a 3D Mini-Game in Godot – Part 1, explains how to create reusable 3D scenes, control your player character, and design levels that are both visually appealing and functional. This chapter includes creating a 3D character, designing a level, working with a character controller script, and implementing a camera controller.

Chapter 9, Creating a 3D Mini-Game in Godot – Part 2, continues the work started in the previous chapter and includes final touches, including adding a power-up, introducing obstacles, and polishing the level.

Chapter 10, Adding Game Juice, details how small changes can dramatically improve the feel of your game. You'll gain practical experience in implementing visual and audio feedback that enhances player immersion, making your game more enjoyable and satisfying to play.

Chapter 11, Understanding Game Design, expounds on the value of thoughtful game design in streamlining development, reducing costly errors, and improving player satisfaction.

Chapter 12, Where to Next?, provides a curated list of resources to deepen your knowledge, expand your skills, and connect with other developers. You'll also discover how to stay motivated, stay informed about the latest trends, and build your presence in the game development community.

To get the most out of this book

To fully engage with the exercises and examples provided in this book, you will need to download and install **Godot Engine 4.3**. This version of the engine introduces key features and updates that are essential for understanding and implementing the techniques we cover. *Whether you're new to Godot or have experience with earlier versions, it's important to work with version 4.3 to ensure compatibility with the projects and concepts discussed throughout this book.*

Software/hardware covered in the book	Operating system requirements
Godot Engine 4.3	Windows, macOS, or Linux

You can easily download Godot Engine 4.3 from the official website at godotengine.org. While version 4.4.1 is now available, using 4.3 is recommended for full compatibility with the examples in this book. That said, everything should continue to work as expected in the latest version.

The installation process is straightforward, and the engine is available on Windows, macOS, and Linux. Be sure to follow the instructions for your operating system, and once it is installed, familiarize yourself with the interface using *Chapter 1*. By using the same tools and environment that we explore in this book, you will have the best learning experience and will be able to follow along with the code examples smoothly.

If you are using the digital version of this book, we advise you to type the code yourself or access the code from the book's GitHub repository (a link is available in the next section). Doing so will help you avoid any potential errors related to the copying and pasting of code.

Note that the author acknowledges the use of cutting-edge AI, such as ChatGPT, with the sole aim of enhancing the language and clarity within the book, thereby ensuring a smooth reading experience for readers. It's important to note that the content itself has been crafted by the author and edited by a professional publishing team.

Download the example code files

The code bundle for the book is hosted on GitHub at https://github.com/PacktPublishing/Godot-4-for-Beginners.

We also have other code bundles from our rich catalog of books and videos available at https://github.com/PacktPublishing. Check them out!

Download the color images

We also provide a PDF file that has color images of the screenshots/diagrams used in this book. You can download it here: https://packt.link/gbp/9781836203094

Code in Action

The Code in Action videos for this book can be viewed at https://packt.link/cFyK6

Logo attribution

Note that the Godot logo is used under the **CC BY 4.0** license. Copyright © Godot Engine developers. Used with credit, not endorsement.

Conventions used

There are a number of text conventions used throughout this book.

`CodeInText`: Indicates code words in text, database table names, folder names, filenames, file extensions, pathnames, dummy URLs, user input, and X handles. For example: "Now press *Ctrl + S* to save the scene as `player.tscn` in our `Scenes` folder."

A block of code is set as follows:

```
extends Node2D

@onready var update_health_hud = $HUD
@onready var player = $Player
@onready var strawberries = $Collectibles

func _ready():
    player.level_strawberries = strawberries.get_child_count()

func _process(delta):
    update_health_hud.frame = player.get_hearts()
```

When we wish to draw your attention to a command-line input or output in a set of steps, the relevant lines or items are set in bold:

```
extends Node2D
var health : int = 100
var jump_strength : float = 220.5
var is_dashing : bool = true
var player_name : String = "Riptide"
var player_level : int = 23
var player_exp : float = 123.45
var has_key : bool = false
var spike_damage : int = 10
```

On Linux, run the following command in the terminal:

```
Unzip Godot_v4.3-stable_linux.x86_64.zip -d Godot
```

Bold: Indicates a new term, an important word, or words that you see on the screen. For instance, words in menus or dialog boxes appear in text like this. For example: "Enable **Rotate Y** and **Disable Z** in the **Particle Flags** settings."

> Warnings or important notes appear like this.

> Tips and tricks appear like this.

Get in touch

Feedback from our readers is always welcome.

General feedback: If you have questions about any aspect of this book or have any general feedback, please email us at customercare@packt.com and mention the book's title in the subject of your message.

Errata: Although we have taken every care to ensure the accuracy of our content, mistakes do happen. If you have found a mistake in this book, we would be grateful if you reported this to us. Please visit http://www.packt.com/submit-errata, click **Submit Errata**, and fill in the form.

Piracy: If you come across any illegal copies of our works in any form on the internet, we would be grateful if you would provide us with the location address or website name. Please contact us at copyright@packt.com with a link to the material.

If you are interested in becoming an author: If there is a topic that you have expertise in and you are interested in either writing or contributing to a book, please visit http://authors.packt.com/.

Share your thoughts

Once you've read *Godot 4 for Beginners*, we'd love to hear your thoughts! Scan the QR code below to go straight to the Amazon review page for this book and share your feedback.

https://packt.link/r/1836203098

Your review is important to us and the tech community and will help us make sure we're delivering excellent quality content.

Join our community on Discord

Join our community's Discord space for discussions with the author and other readers:

https://packt.link/godot-4-game-dev

Part 1

Learning How the Godot Engine Works

In this first part of the book, you'll build a strong foundation in using the Godot game engine. We'll begin by exploring Godot's origins and what makes it a unique and powerful tool for game development. Then, you'll get hands-on with the engine's interface, learning how scenes, nodes, and the editor all work together. You'll also take your first steps into 3D game development and dive into scripting with GDScript, Godot's intuitive, Python-like language. By the end of this part, you'll be ready to begin creating interactive games with confidence.

This part of the book includes the following chapters:

- *Chapter 1, Let's Get Godot-ing!*
- *Chapter 2, Exploring the Godot Engine Interface*
- *Chapter 3, Introduction to 3D*
- *Chapter 4, Scripting with GDScript*

1

Let's Get Godot-ing!

In this chapter, we'll explore the history and core features of **Godot 4.0**, a game development engine renowned for its versatility and accessibility. Whether you're an aspiring indie developer or a seasoned creator looking for a new tool, understanding what makes Godot unique will set the foundation for your journey into game development.

This chapter serves two main purposes. The first is to introduce you to Godot's background and key capabilities, showing why it has become a popular choice in the game development community. Next is to guide you through setting up Godot 4.0 and creating your first project, ensuring you have the tools and confidence to begin crafting your own games.

In this chapter, we're going to cover the following main topics:

- What is Godot?
- Setting up Godot 4
- Creating a new project

By the end of this chapter, you'll not only have grasped the essential features that make Godot stand out, but also have the knowledge to install, launch, and create your first project in the engine. These are fundamental steps that lay the groundwork for everything we'll accomplish in later chapters.

Getting the most out of this book — get to know your free benefits

Unlock exclusive **free** benefits that come with your purchase, thoughtfully crafted to supercharge your learning journey and help you learn without limits.

Here's a quick overview of what you get with this book:

Next-gen reader

Our web-based reader, designed to help you learn effectively, comes with the following features:

Multi-device progress sync: Learn from any device with seamless progress sync.

Highlighting and notetaking: Turn your reading into lasting knowledge.

Bookmarking: Revisit your most important learnings anytime.

Dark mode: Focus with minimal eye strain by switching to dark or sepia mode.

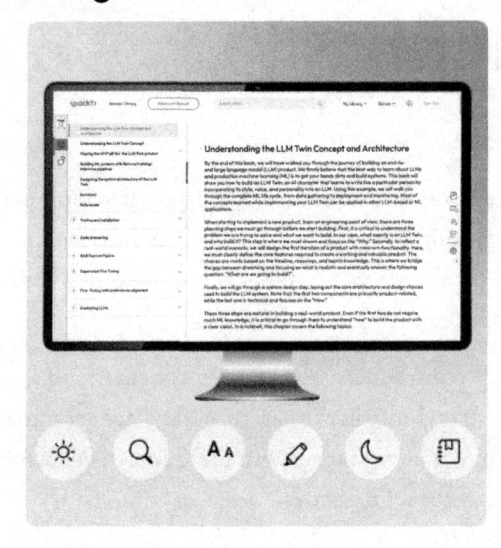

Figure 1.1: Illustration of the next-gen Packt Reader's features

Interactive AI assistant (beta)

Our interactive AI assistant has been trained on the content of this book, to maximize your learning experience. It comes with the following features:

✦ Summarize it: Summarize key sections or an entire chapter.

✦ AI code explainers: In the next-gen Packt Reader, click the Explain button above each code block for AI-powered code explanations.

Note: The AI assistant is part of next-gen Packt Reader and is still in beta.

Figure 1.2: Illustration of Packt's AI assistant

DRM-free PDF or ePub version

Learn without limits with the following perks included with your purchase:

📕 Learn from anywhere with a DRM-free PDF copy of this book.

📗 Use your favorite e-reader to learn using a DRM-free ePub version of this book.

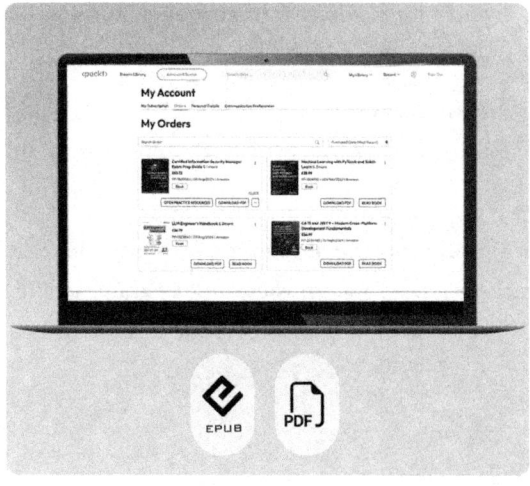

Figure 1.3: Free PDF and ePub

> **Unlock this book's exclusive benefits now**
>
> Scan this QR code or go to packtpub.com/unlock, then search for this book by name. Ensure it's the correct edition.
>
> Note: Keep your purchase invoice ready before you start.

Technical requirements

You can find the example project and code for this book in the GitHub repository:

https://github.com/PacktPublishing/Godot-4-for-Beginners

This chapter's code files are available here: https://github.com/PacktPublishing/Godot-4-for-Beginners/tree/main/ch1/godotintro

Visit this link to check out the video of the code being run: https://packt.link/RjbW3

What is Godot?

The short answer is that Godot is a game engine. It was originally created in 2007 by Juan Linietsky and Ariel Manzur as an in-house tool for various Argentinian studios. Your next questions might be, "What exactly is a game engine?" and "What makes Godot so special?"

Well, making a game is hard—really hard! There are countless moving parts that all need to work together perfectly. While it's possible to build everything from scratch, most developers rely on a game engine to handle the heavy lifting.

So, a **game engine** is a software framework that simplifies game development. It provides the core tools and systems for building a game—such as rendering, physics, input handling, and asset management—so that developers can focus more on gameplay, story, and design, rather than low-level technical code.

What makes Godot so special?

There are many reasons why Godot has become a popular choice for both beginner and experienced game developers. Here are some of the core features that make this engine stand out from the rest:

- **Open source and free**: In 2014, Godot was released as open source under the MIT license. That means it's completely free to use—even for commercial projects—and developers have full access to the source code. This makes Godot highly customizable and community-driven.
- **Versatile scene system**: One of Godot's most defining features is its scene system. Everything in Godot is a scene—and scenes are made up of nodes. Scenes can also be nested inside other scenes, making it easy to build complex, reusable, and modular components. This structure makes organizing and scaling a game project incredibly intuitive.
- **Powerful 2D and 3D support**: Godot includes dedicated tools for both 2D and 3D development. Whether you're making a pixel-art platformer or a fully-fledged 3D experience, Godot provides specialized workflows for both dimensions. While other engines also support both, Godot's 2D system in particular is often praised for its precision and flexibility.
- **Resources—the other side of the coin**: Alongside scenes and nodes, Godot uses something called **resources**—and they're everywhere. A texture on a sprite is a resource. The audio you play is a resource. Even the path in a **Path2D** node is a resource. Resources are data containers that can be reused across your project, edited in the inspector, or saved and loaded from disk. They promote consistency, reduce duplication, and keep your projects lightweight and organized.
- **Lightweight and cross-platform**: Godot is lightweight and quick to install and runs smoothly even on older machines. This low system requirement is a huge win for accessibility and inclusion—anyone can start making games without needing a high-end PC. Plus, when your game is finished, you can export it to a wide variety of platforms, including Windows, macOS, Linux, Android, iOS, and HTML5.
- **Thriving community and active development**: Godot has a friendly, growing community of developers and educators. Whether you're just starting out or are an experienced coder, there's plenty of support through forums, Discord channels, tutorials, and documentation. The engine is under continuous development with regular updates and an open roadmap.

Now that you've learned about the key features that make Godot such a powerful and beginner-friendly game engine—from its flexible node and scene system to its vibrant open-source community—you have a strong understanding of why it is a great choice for your game development journey.

It's time to move from theory to practice!

In the next section, we'll guide you through downloading and installing Godot, and help you run the engine for the very first time. Soon, you'll be setting up your own projects and building your first games step by step. Let's get started!

Setting up Godot 4

To download the latest version of Godot 4, follow these steps:

1. Go to Godot's website (https://www.godotengine.org) and click on the **Download Latest** button, shown in *Figure 1.4*. Note that version 4.3 was the version in use at the time of writing (see *Preface* for details).

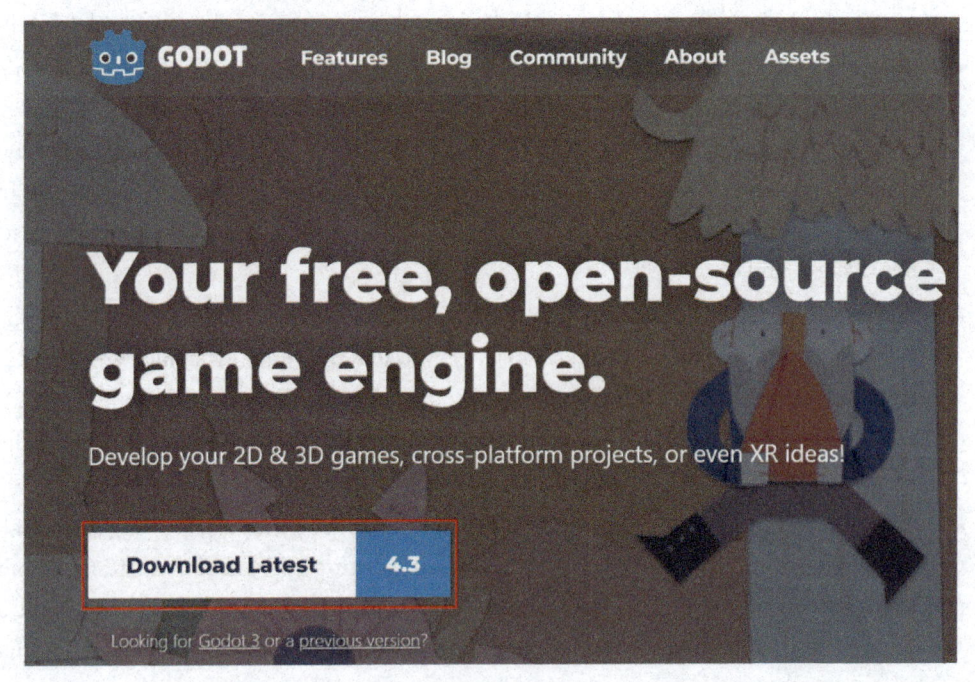

Figure 1.4 – The download page for Godot Engine 4 for Windows

2. The website should detect your operating system platform and take you to the correct download. Click on the **Godot Engine** button rather than the **.NET** one:

Figure 1.5 – The browser has detected the Windows operating system

3. If your platform cannot be detected, you can choose from one of the supported platforms by scrolling further down the page:

Figure 1.6 – Choose your own platform from the available options

4. Once the download is complete, it's time to create our folder structure.
5. On Windows, open the ZIP file. The main executable will be named something such as Godot_v4.3-stable_win64.exe.

    - On macOS, double-click the ZIP file
    - On Linux, run the following command in the terminal:

    ```
    Unzip Godot_v4.3-stable_linux.x86_64.zip -d Godot
    ```

6. Extract this file to a folder on your PC. I recommend naming the folder `Godot4`.
7. Within this folder, create another folder called `Godot 4 Projects`. This is the folder where you will store all your projects made with Godot 4:

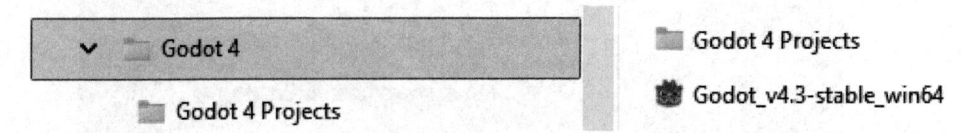

Figure 1.7 – Godot folder structure

8. Time to launch Godot! *Right-click* on the `.exe` file and choose **Pin to Start** to have Godot available in the **Start** menu:

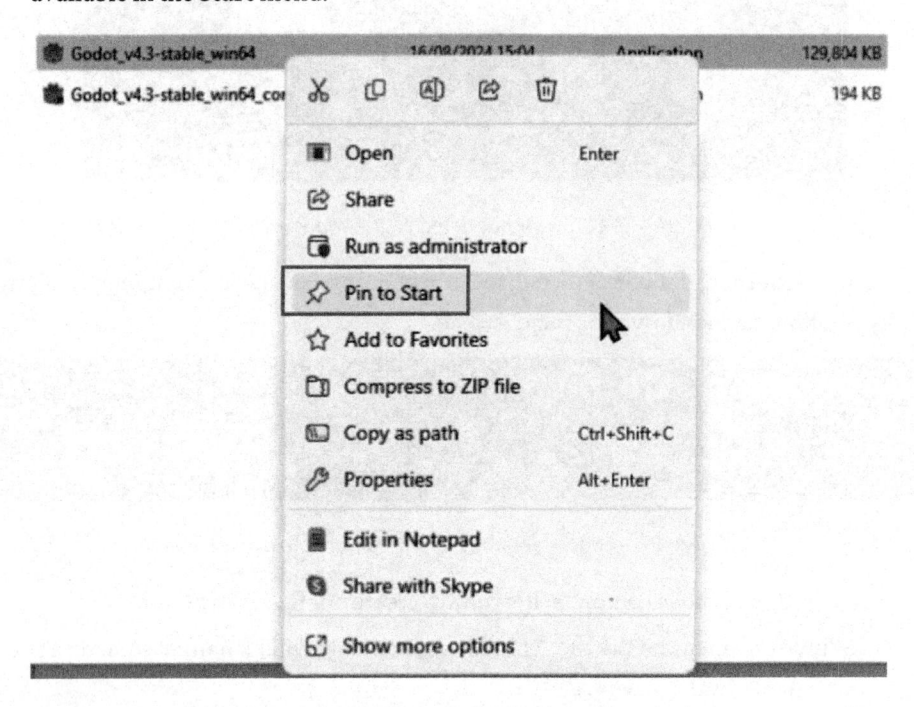

Figure 1.8 – How to pin to Start

9. You can also click on **Show more options** and then choose **Pin to taskbar** so that Godot is always ready and waiting at the bottom of your screen:

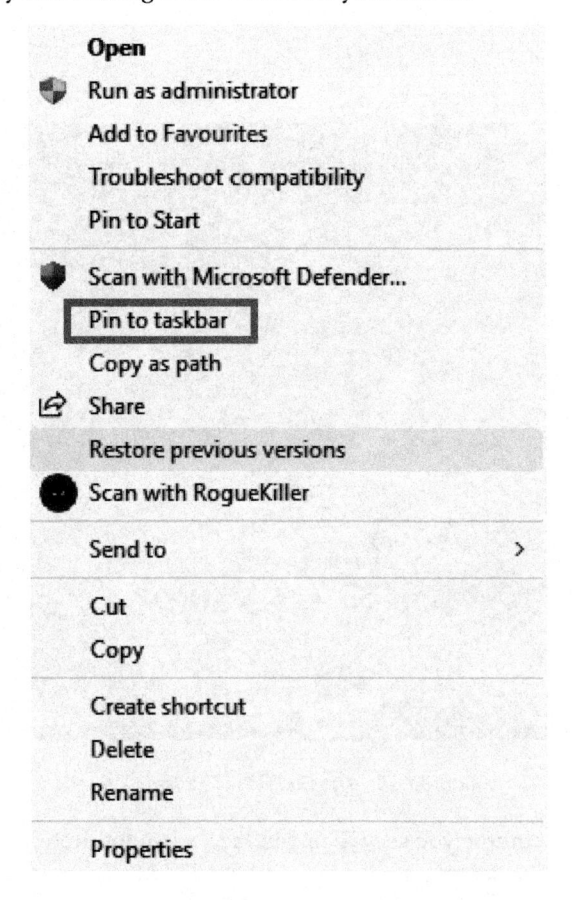

Figure 1.9 – Show more options and Pin to taskbar

10. Double-click on the extracted .exe file within the Godot 4 folder to launch Godot 4!

Godot is up and running. Our next step is to create our first project—our wonderful adventure in game development starts now!

Creating a new project

Having followed the steps in the previous section, you are now presented with the Godot **Project Manager**:

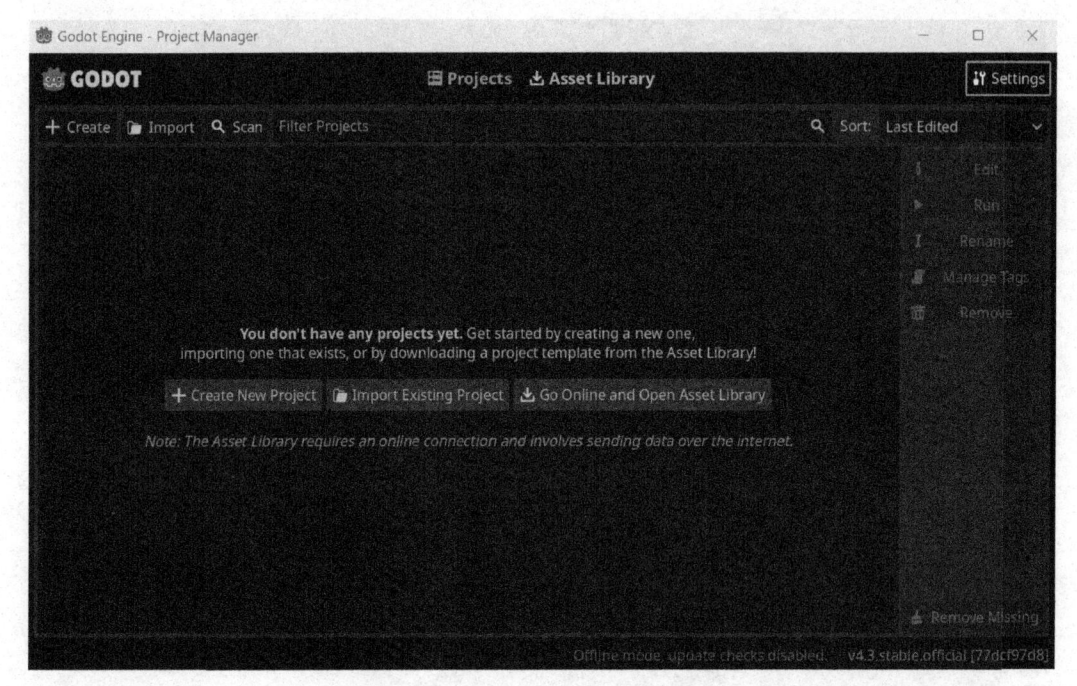

Figure 1.10 – The Godot Project Manager

This is always the first window you see when you launch Godot. Here, you can create, remove, import, edit, and play game projects.

Chapter 1

Because of all the black ink needed to print images in dark mode, we will do our bit to save the planet by switching to light mode. There is no difference other than appearance. To do that, follow these steps:

1. Click on the **Settings** button in the top-right corner:

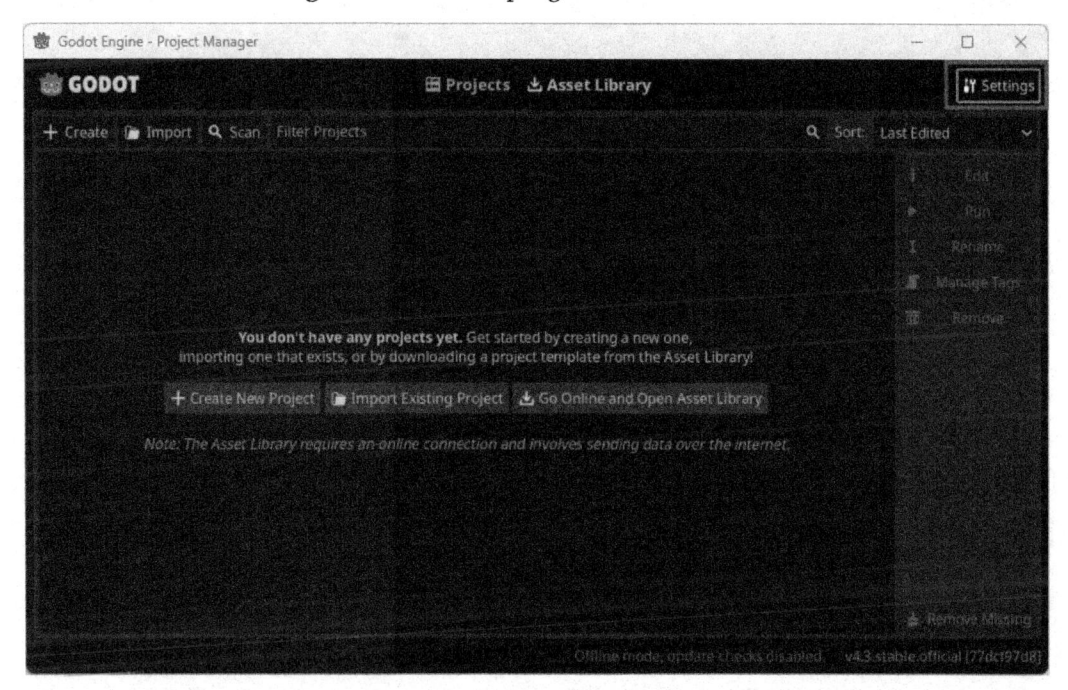

Figure 1.11 – The Project Manager Settings button

2. Now, change the **Interface Theme** dropdown to **Light**:

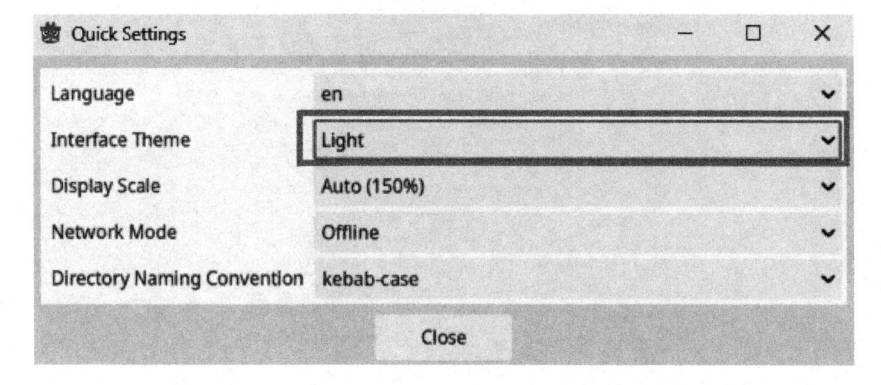

Figure 1.12 – Changing to the Light theme in the Quick Settings menu

Now, let's now walk through the steps to set up a new project in Godot 4:

1. Click on the **+ Create** button in the top-left corner to create a new project:

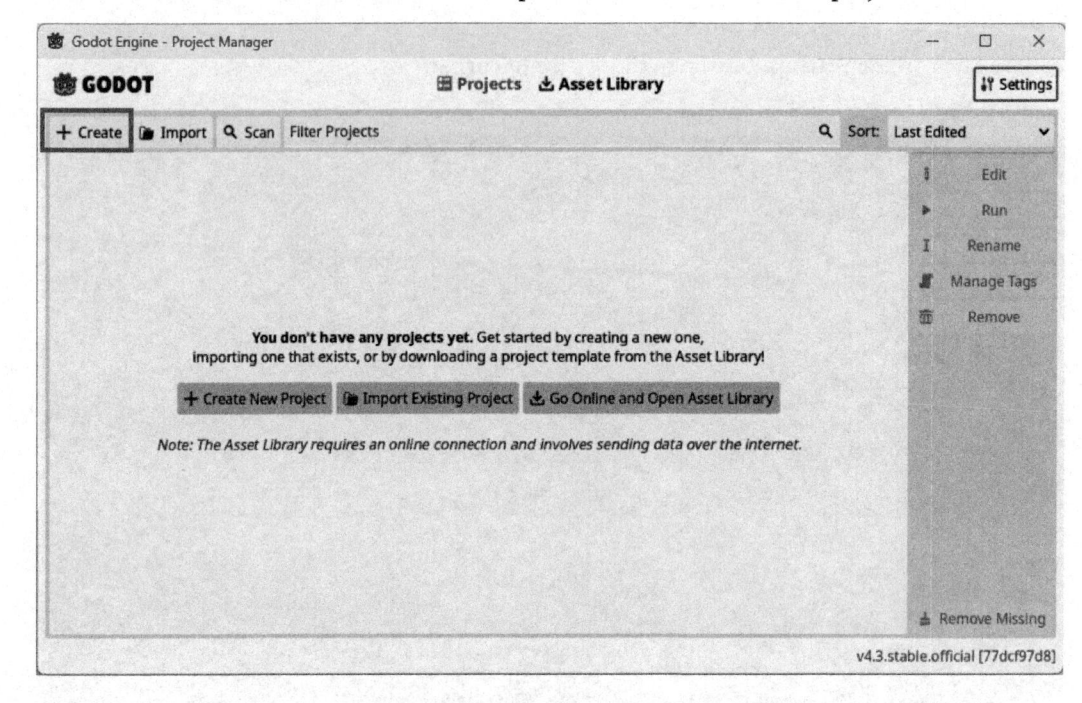

Figure 1.13 – How to create a new project in the Godot Project Manager

2. We are now presented with a new window in which we can adjust the details of the project:

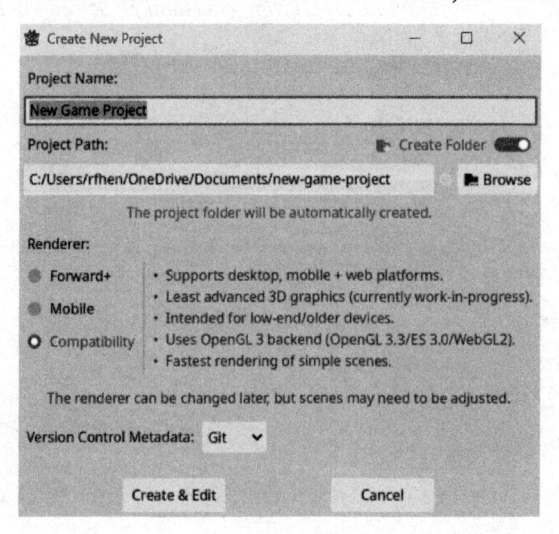

Figure 1.14 – The Create New Project sub-menu

3. The next step is to give our project a name. Let's call it `GodotIntro`.

   Also, ensure that **Project Path** points to the `Godot 4 Projects` folder we created earlier and that the **Create Folder** button is toggled on:

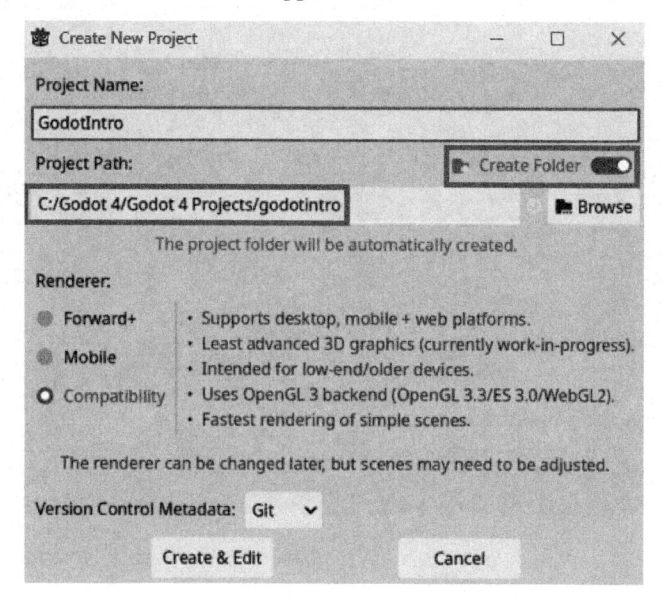

   Figure 1.15 – Initial settings for our new Godot project

4. This will create a new folder within `Godot 4 Projects` named `GodotIntro`. Creating a new folder for each new project in Godot will help us keep everything organized.

   You can leave **Renderer** in **Compatibility** mode. Each renderer option is explained here:

   - **Forward+** is a renderer that is aimed at improving the rendering of lights on desktop platforms. This is not recommended for mobile development as it is not efficient.
   - **Mobile** uses a more efficient approach for lighting that is intended for mobile platforms, but can also run on a desktop. However, this renderer does not provide high-end graphical features.
   - **Compatibility** has even fewer high-end graphical features than **Mobile**, but it will run on most hardware.

5. Click on **Create & Edit**, and you will be presented with the following window:

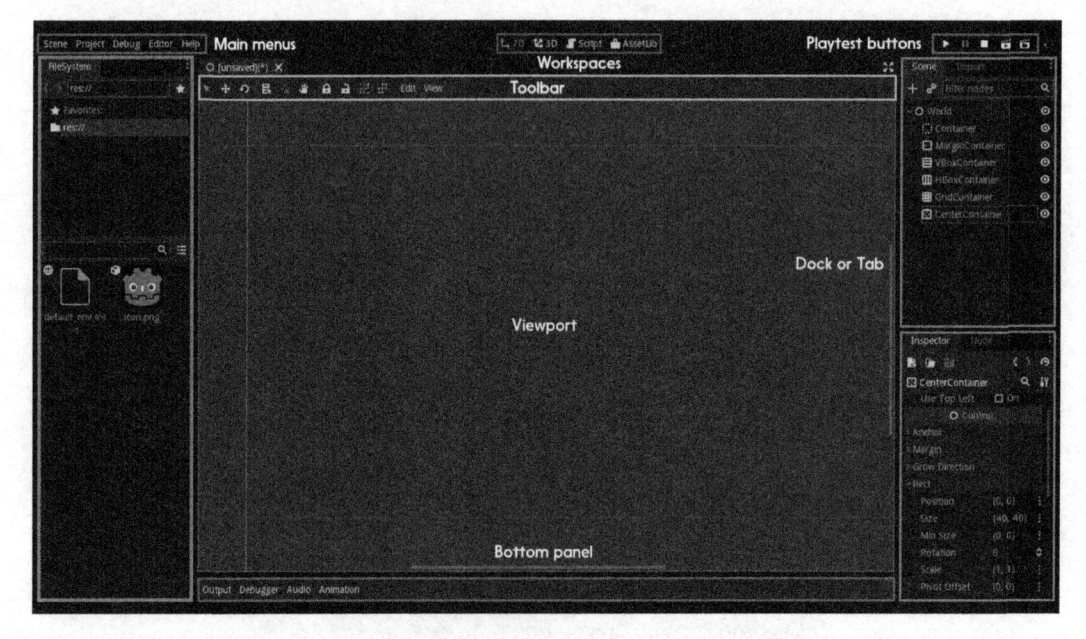

Figure 1.16 – The main Godot engine editor interface

6. By default, Godot opens in 3D view. We can change this using the view menu at the top; however, Godot will change the view automatically once we add our first node.

Figure 1.17 – The context menu to switch views

From here, we will create our first little project and then take a closer look at the interface in the next chapter:

1. Click on **2D Scene** in the top left of the screen:

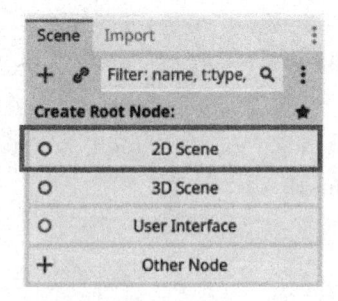

Figure 1.18 – The Scene window

Chapter 1　　　17

2. Clicking this button creates **Node2D** as the root node of our scene. You can see it in the **Scene** window on the left-hand side. We will rename it by selecting it and pressing *F2*. Name it Main as it will be our main node for now:

Figure 1.19 – Renaming Node2D to Main

3. It's important to get into the habit of being organized from the beginning. In the **FileSystem** window at the bottom left of the editor, create a new folder and call it Scenes. Do this by right-clicking anywhere in the **FileSystem** window and selecting **New Folder…**:

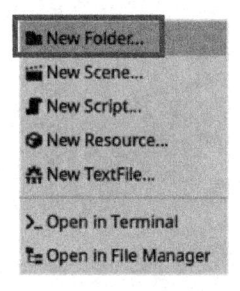

Figure 1.20 – Creating a new folder in the FileSystem window

4. Now, save the scene as main.tscn by pressing *Ctrl + S* and choosing the Scenes folder that you just created:

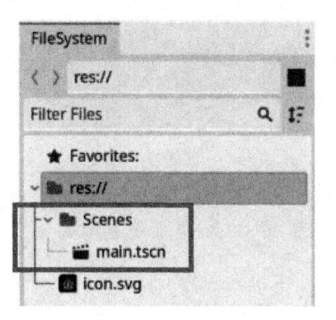

Figure 1.21 – Saving the main scene in the Scenes folder

5. Add a **Label** node as a child of **Main** (which is the **Node2D** we created earlier):

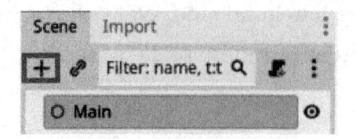

Figure 1.22 – Click the + button to add a new node

6. Now, search for the **Label** node:

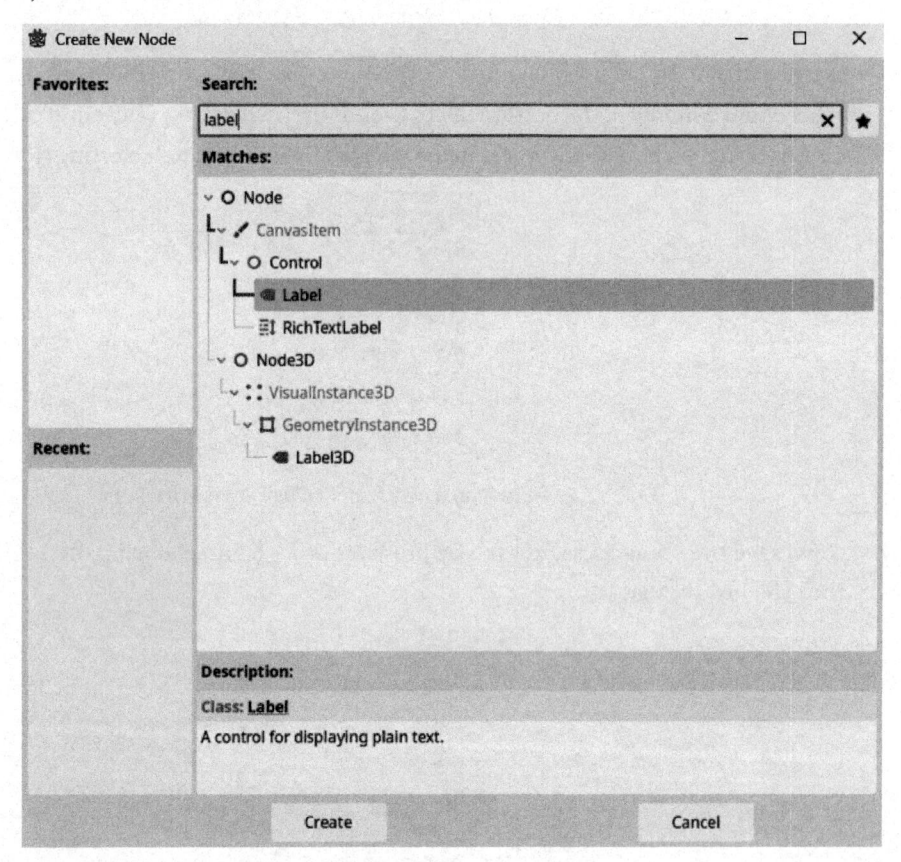

Figure 1.23 – Searching for the Label node

Chapter 1

7. Select it once found, and you will see it added to your scene tree:

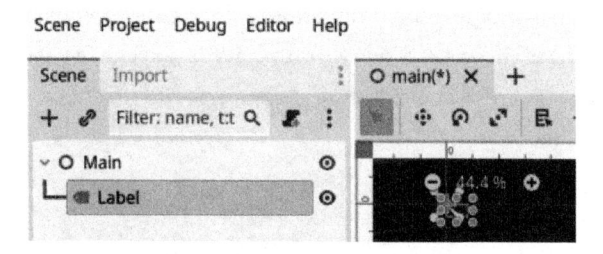

Figure 1.24 – The Label node in the editor

8. Now, rename the **Label** node to GreetingsLabel:

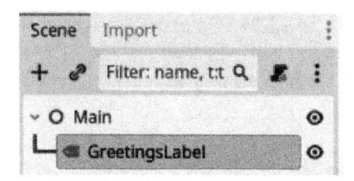

Figure 1.25 – Renaming the Label node

9. With **GreetingsLabel** selected, on the right-hand side of the inspector, we can see the properties of the **Label** node. Enter your greeting in the **Text** property:

Figure 1.26 – Editing the Text property of the Label node in the inspector

We can now run our scene to see the output by pressing *F6* as this will run the current scene. Another way to launch the project is to press *F5*. A window will appear asking us to choose the main scene. Since we only have one scene, we will press the **Select Current** button. However, if we have multiple scenes, we could choose which one we want as the first scene that runs:

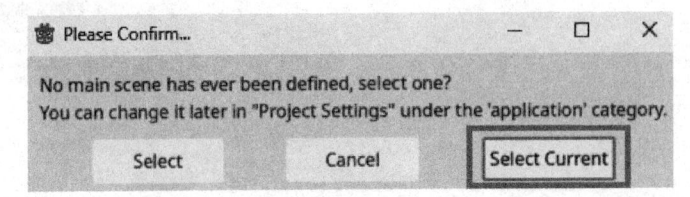

Figure 1.27 – Selecting the main scene of the project

10. When the project launches, you will see your greeting in the top-left corner of the screen:

Figure 1.28 – The output of our project

11. We can change the value of the **Text** property of the **Label** node in the inspector or using code.

A script allows us to program custom behavior for our nodes. We use it to add logic to our node, such as playing sound effects, moving a character, or changing text.

12. Before we add a script to our **Label** node, let's create a folder for scripts in **FileSystem**. *Right-click* in **FileSystem**, select **New Folder**, and call it `Scripts`:

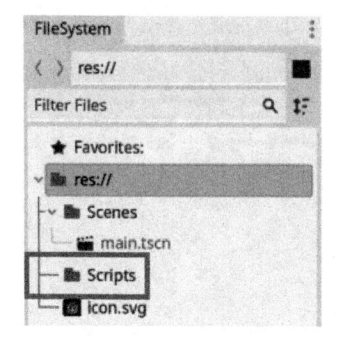

Figure 1.29 – Adding a Scripts folder to our project

13. *Right-click* **GreetingsLabel** and select **Attach Script...**:

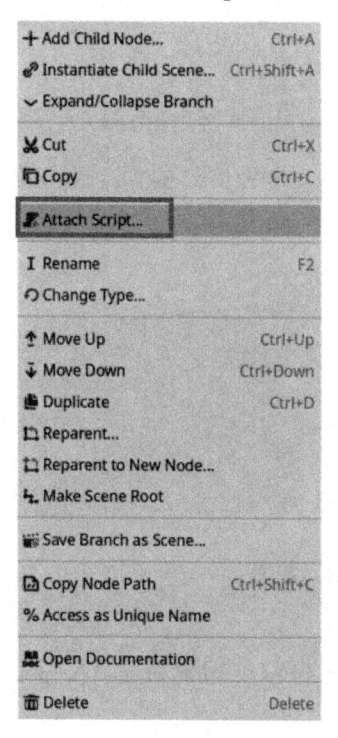

Figure 1.30 – Attaching a script to a node

14. A window pops up. Don't change anything for the moment or worry too much about all the options. Just take note that the language is **GDScript** and the script name is created for us. Check the path and, if necessary, change it to your **Scripts** folder:

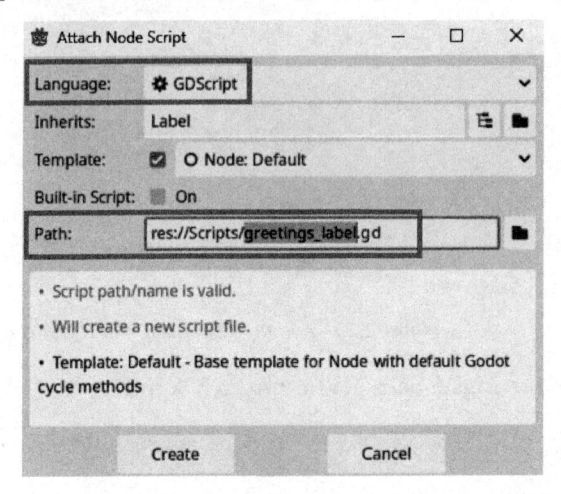

Figure 1.31 – The Attach Node Script menu

15. Edit the script so that it matches the following code and launch the project again by hitting the play button:

```
extends Label

# Called when the node enters the scene tree for the first time.
func _ready():
    text = "Go Go Godot!"

# Called every frame. 'delta' is the elapsed time since the previous frame.
func _process(delta):
    pass
```

Note that now, the output of the project has changed from **Hello World!** to: **Go Go Godot!**.

> 💡 **Quick tip**: Enhance your coding experience with the **AI Code Explainer** and **Quick Copy** features. Open this book in the next-gen Packt Reader. Click the **Copy** button **(1)** to quickly copy code into your coding environment, or click the **Explain** button **(2)** to get the AI assistant to explain a block of code to you.
>
> ```
> function calculate(a, b) {
>   return {sum: a + b};
> };
> ```
>
> 📕 **The next-gen Packt Reader** is included for free with the purchase of this book. Scan the QR code OR go to `packtpub.com/unlock`, then use the search bar to find this book by name. Double-check the edition shown to make sure you get the right one.

Finally, we can make the scene more dynamic by making the label bounce around the screen like the famous DVD screensaver!

Making the scene dynamic

To do this, we need to break the problem into smaller parts:

1. Give the label an initial velocity (speed and direction).
2. Find out the dimensions of the screen.
3. Find out the size of the label.
4. Test whether the label has reached the left or right edge and reverse direction.
5. Test whether the label has reached the top or bottom edge and reverse the direction.
6. Repeatedly update the label's position so that it moves.

The `velocity` variable controls both the speed and direction of movement. Because it is a `Vector2`, we can pass through both the *x* and *y* values in one container.

In this example, we're setting the initial speed to 150 pixels per second along the *x* axis (to the right, because it's positive) and 120 pixels per second along the *y* axis (downward, since Godot's coordinate system starts from the top-left corner).

Add these lines starting from the second line in the program:

```
var xVelocity = 150 #150 pixels per second to the right
var yVelocity = 120 #120 pixels per second downwards
var velocity = Vector2(xVelocity, yVelocity)  #Initial speed and direction
```

To make the label move, we need to continuously update its position at each frame. The `_process(delta)` function runs every frame, making it the perfect place to handle updates like this. By adding a line of code that adjusts the label's position inside `_process()`, we can create smooth, ongoing movement.

Add the following code as the first line inside the `_process()` function and run the game. You will see the label move diagonally down and to the right!

```
position = position + velocity * delta
```

In the preceding line, we repeatedly add the current position to the value of the velocity multiplied by `delta`. Here, `delta` is the amount of time that has passed since the previous frame and is a way to make sure that movement is smooth and consistent on all hardware.

You've now taken the first steps toward making your text move—just like the classic DVD logo!

Before we go any further and make the motion smooth and consistent, it's important to understand a key concept that controls how things behave over time in Godot: delta.

Let's take a moment to explore what `delta` is and why it's so important.

Delta

When we make something move in a game, we usually want it to move at a consistent speed—such as 150 pixels per second. But here's the tricky part: not all computers run games at the same speed. Some may run at 60 frames per second, while others might run slower or faster, depending on their hardware.

This is where delta comes in.

delta is a small number that tells us how much time has passed since the last frame was drawn. If your game is running fast, delta might be something such as 0.016 (about 1/60th of a second). If it's running slower, delta will be a bit bigger, such as 0.03.

By multiplying the movement speed by delta, we're saying the following:

"Move this object based on how much time has actually passed, not how many frames have gone by."

This means the object will move at the correct speed per second, no matter how many frames your computer is managing to draw.

So, instead of moving 150 pixels every frame (which would be way too fast!), we move 150 × delta pixels per frame, which adjusts automatically based on performance.

Continuing the bouncing label project

Bringing this back to our bouncing label project, the next step is to set up some important information about the screen and the label itself. This will let us detect when the label hits the edges and needs to bounce.

Now, we should add variables to store the screen size and the size of the label. It's important to understand that we cannot determine these values until the scene has loaded.

The first function to run once the scene is ready is the _ready() function. So, we should initialize (assign values to) our variables there. First, add the variables to our collection at the top and then assign them as the first lines in the _ready() function after setting the text:

```
var xVelocity = 150 #150 pixels per second to the right
var yVelocity = 120 #120 pixels per second downwards
var velocity = Vector2(xVelocity, yVelocity) # Initial speed and direction
var screen_size_x #screen horizontal dimension
var screen_size_y #screen vertical dimension
var label_size_x #label width
var label_size_y #label height
```

Now, assign values to these variables in the _ready() function as follows:

```
func _ready():
    text = "Go Go Godot!"
    # Get the screen size (viewport size)
    screen_size_x = get_viewport_rect().size.x
    screen_size_y = get_viewport_rect().size.y
    label_size_x = size.x
    label_size_y = size.y
```

All that is left to do now is test to see whether the label has reached the left, right, top, or bottom edge of the screen, and if it has, turn it around.

We do this in the _process() function after setting the direction. Begin with a test for the left and right screen edges, as follows:

```
# Bounce off left/right edges
if position.x < 0 or position.x + label_size_x > screen_size_x:
    velocity.x *= -1
```

This line checks whether the label has hit the left or right edge of the screen, and if so, it makes the label *bounce* by reversing its horizontal direction.

Technically, our bouncing works and we could leave it there, but there are rare edge cases in which the label could move past the edge of the screen in one frame and the direction reverses, but we are already beyond the edge, so the label could get stuck or jitter. To prevent this, we can use a built-in method that clamps a value between a minimum and maximum value:

```
# Bounce off left/right edges
if position.x < 0 or position.x + label_size_x > screen_size_x:
    velocity.x *= -1
    position.x = clamp(position.x, 0, screen_size_x - label_size_x)
```

The check is similar for the top and bottom edges:

```
# Bounce off top/bottom edges
if position.y < 0 or position.y + label_size_y > screen_size_y:
    velocity.y *= -1
    position.y = clamp(position.y, 0, screen_size_y - label_size_y)
```

The full code for the bouncing label is presented here:

```
extends Label
var xVelocity = 150 #150 pixels per second to the right
var yVelocity = 120 #120 pixels per second downwards
var velocity = Vector2(xVelocity, yVelocity) # Initial speed and direction
var screen_size_x #screen horizontal dimension var screen_size_y
#screen vertical dimension
var label_size_x #label width
var label_size_y #label height

func _ready():
    text = "Go Go Godot!"
    # Get the screen size (viewport size)
    screen_size_x = get_viewport_rect().size.x
    screen_size_y = get_viewport_rect().size.y
    label_size_x = size.x
    label_size_y = size.y

func _process(delta):
    position = position + velocity * delta
    # Bounce off left/right edges
    if position.x < 0 or position.x + label_size_x > screen_size_x:
        velocity.x *= -1
        position.x = clamp(position.x, 0, screen_size_x - label_size_x)

    # Bounce off top/bottom edges
    if position.y < 0 or position.y + label_size_y > screen_size_y:
        velocity.y *= -1
        position.y = clamp(position.y, 0, screen_size_y - label_size_y)
```

And there you have it — your own version of the classic bouncing DVD logo! Now that you've built your first simple animation in Godot, you're ready to dive even deeper into creating interactive and dynamic games.

Summary

In this chapter, we learned about the history of Godot and its node and scene design philosophy. We downloaded Godot and ran it. We created our first project and produced our first output to the game window. We also made the scene dynamic by working with the position and velocity of the label. We also learned about screen dimensions and how to clamp them between a range, as well as the important role played by the `delta` variable.

In the next chapter, we will take a closer look at the Godot editor interface and how to use the tools provided by it.

> **Unlock this book's exclusive benefits now**
>
> Scan this QR code or go to packtpub.com/unlock, then search this book by name.
>
> *Note: Keep your purchase invoice ready before you start.*

2

Exploring the Godot Engine Interface

In this chapter, you will edit your first project in Godot 4 and explore the fundamental features of the interface. You will also gain a deeper understanding of the node and scene design philosophy that underscores Godot. It is fundamental to using Godot day in and day out to understand how it is intended to be used.

In this chapter, we're going to cover the following main topics:

- Important terms
- Editing an existing Godot project
- Creating an additional scene
- Reacting to player input

By the end of the chapter, you'll be able to create new projects, build scenes, and navigate the interface with ease—essential skills for any game developer.

Technical requirements

This chapter's code files are available here in the book's GitHub repository: https://github.com/PacktPublishing/Godot-4-for-Beginners/tree/main/ch2/godotintro

Visit this link to check out the video of the code being run: https://packt.link/2R1xc

Important terms

This is an important section. Before we dive into the chapter and come across terms that are unknown to us, let's take a quick look at them:

- **Nodes**: Nodes are the basic building blocks of Godot 4 scenes. Each node represents a single object in your game world, such as a sprite, a sound effect, a UI element, and so on. Multiple nodes usually form a hierarchy, often with parent nodes controlling the behavior of their child nodes.

    When working with nodes, we can press *Q*, *W*, *E*, and *S* to use the different tools:

    - *Q* – **Select tool**: Allows us to select a node and position it in the Viewport
    - *W* – **Move tool**: Allows us to move the node along the various axes
    - *E* – **Rotate tool**: Allows us to rotate an object on the various axes
    - *S* – **Scale tool**: Allows us to resize an object on the various axes

    Each node has properties that determine its behavior and appearance. For example, a sprite node has properties such as **Texture**, **Position**, and **Scale**, as shown in *Figure 2.1*:

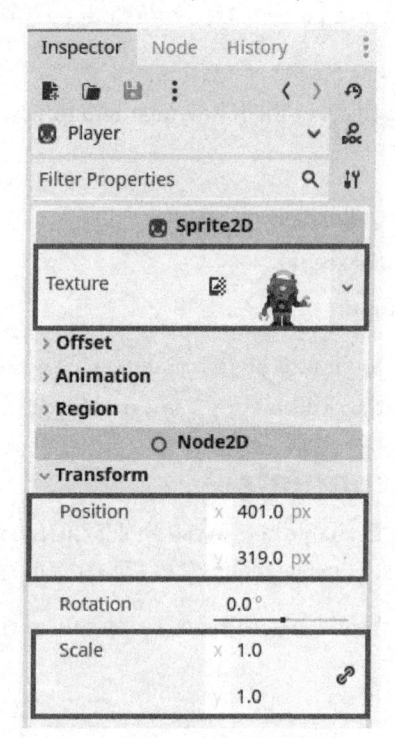

Figure 2.1 – Some of the properties of a Sprite2D node

Chapter 2

- **Scenes**: Scenes are collections of nodes. They could make up a level, menu, character, enemy, or any other part of a game. A scene can be saved as a separate file and loaded into your game as needed using instancing.
- **Scripts**: Scripts are an essential part of game development. They allow you to create custom actions and interactions that make your game unique.

To visualize how nodes are combined to form scenes, look at *Figure 2.2*, which shows **Strawberry**, which is a collectible item. It is made up of an **Area2D** node, a **CollisionShape2D** node, and an **AnimatedSprite2D** node. Together, they make the **Strawberry** scene.

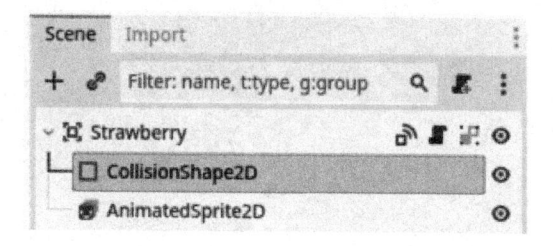

Figure 2.2 – A combination of nodes forming a scene

Let's get into the chapter!

Editing an existing Godot project

We created a Godot project in the previous chapter, and when we launch Godot, we can see it in the **Project Manager** window, and we can reopen it by selecting **Edit** or pressing *Ctrl + E* and then double-clicking on the name of our project: GodotIntro:

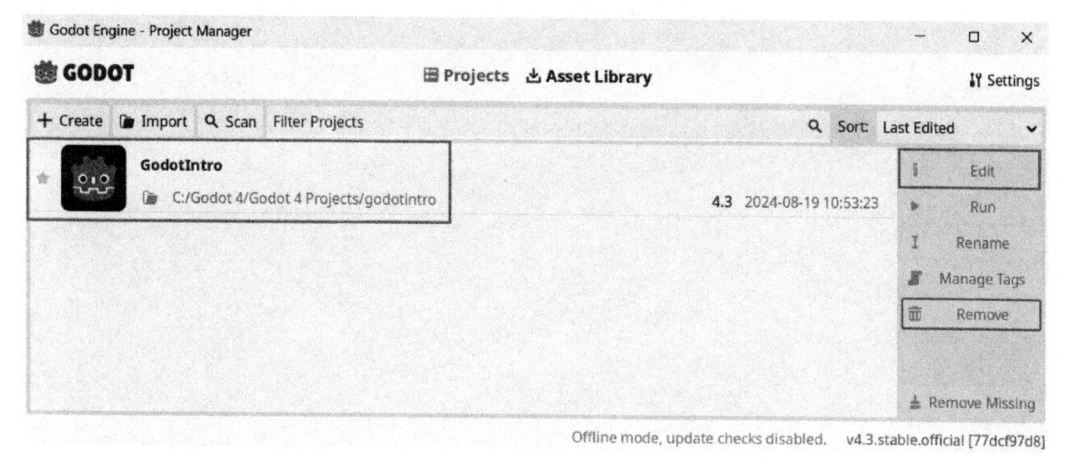

Figure 2.3 – Our existing Godot project from Chapter 1

The Godot editor will open and display the last thing you were working on. In my case, it is the **Script** view. Change the view to 2D by clicking on **2D** at the top of the screen:

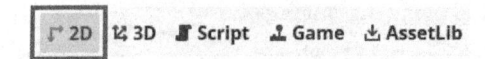

Figure 2.4 – Change to the 2D view by clicking on 2D at the top of the screen

Now we can take a closer look at the main features of the Godot editor. Your screen should now look as it does in *Figure 2.5*:

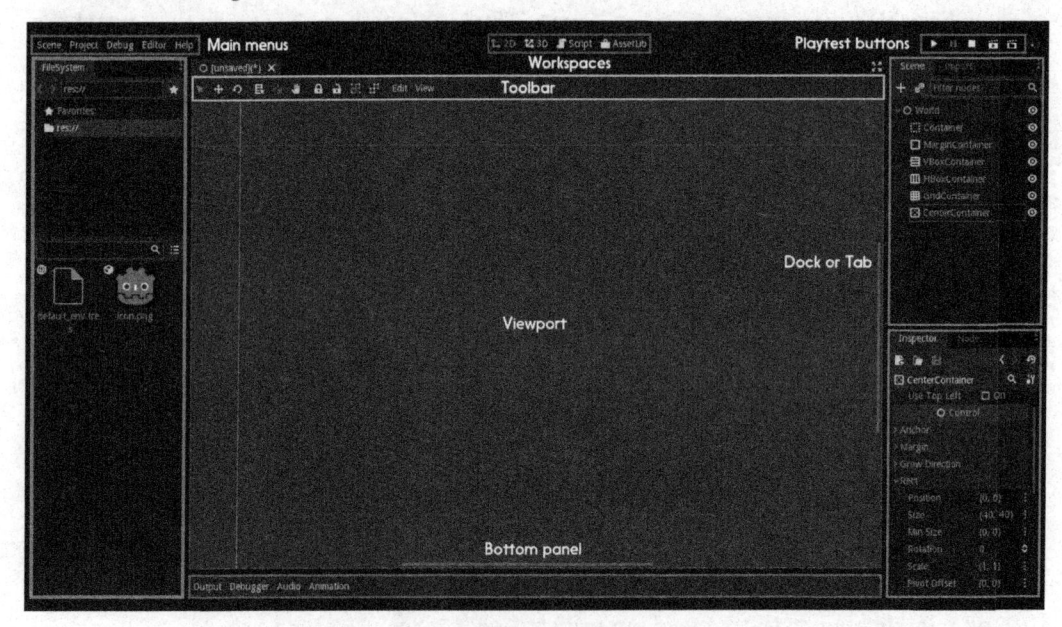

Figure 2.5 – An overview of the Godot Interface

🔍 **Quick tip**: Need to see a high-resolution version of this image? Open this book in the next-gen Packt Reader or view it in the PDF/ePub copy.

🔒 **The next-gen Packt Reader** and a **free PDF/ePub copy** of this book are included with your purchase. Scan the QR code OR visit `packtpub.com/unlock`, then use the search bar to find this book by name. Double-check the edition shown to make sure you get the right one.

The most used parts of the editor are labelled **1** to **4**:

1. The **scene tree** area shows all the nodes that make up the current scene. We can see our **Main** node (**Node2D**) and our **GreetingsLabel** (**Label** node).
2. The **FileSystem** area shows all the files that are part of our project. We can see the `Scenes` and `Scripts` folders that we made.
3. Here, we see the **Viewport**. Think of it as what is within the imaginary camera frame. Here, we will place our nodes within the 2D space in the scene.
4. On the far right is the **Inspector** area. With it, you can view the properties of the currently selected node. You can also find many settings within sub-menus. As an example, you could click on the **Transform** property to unfold settings for **Position**, **Rotation**, and **Scale**.

LEGO – a useful metaphor to understand how Godot works

Building a game in Godot is like constructing a LEGO model. In this analogy, nodes are like individual LEGO bricks. Each brick has a specific function—some are basic, like simple blocks, while others might have specialized purposes, like wheels, windows, or gears.

The real power of Godot's system comes from how flexible it is. Just as you can disassemble and recombine LEGO modules to build something entirely new, you can mix and match scenes in Godot to quickly assemble different parts of your game. This modularity allows you to create complex games in a more manageable, efficient, and creative way.

In Godot, you use *nodes* to represent different elements of your game, such as characters, environments, and behaviors. Just like how you can connect LEGO bricks in various ways to create different structures, you can combine nodes in Godot to build complex game objects and systems.

Now, think of a *scene* as a pre-built section or module made from those LEGO bricks. A scene could be a small part, like a car or a tree, or something larger, like an entire building. In Godot, a scene is a collection of nodes arranged in a specific way to create a meaningful part of your game. You can reuse scenes just like you can attach a pre-built LEGO module to a larger structure.

But there's one more piece to the puzzle: *resources*. If nodes are LEGO bricks and scenes are LEGO modules, then resources are like the stickers, blueprints, and instruction manuals that come with your LEGO sets. Stickers represent visuals such as textures and materials. Blueprints or manuals describe how something behaves or animates—like animation resources, scripts, and audio streams in Godot.

And just like you can apply the same sticker to multiple bricks or use the same manual for several builds, resources in Godot are reusable, customizable, and sharable across your entire game.

They don't build the structure themselves, but they add style, data, and behavior to the pieces you've already put together.

This layered approach—**Nodes** (bricks), **Scenes** (modules), and **Resources** (custom details and instructions)—makes Godot a powerful and intuitive tool for building games, the same way LEGO makes building imaginative creations fun and accessible.

Creating an additional scene

Suppose we want to disconnect one of our LEGO bricks (see the preceding feature on *LEGO – a useful metaphor to understand how Godot works*). Let's remove our **Label** node from our **Main** scene and put it in a scene of its own:

1. We can do this by right-clicking on the **GreetingsLabel** node and choosing **Save Branch as Scene…**. This is shown in *Figure 2.6*:

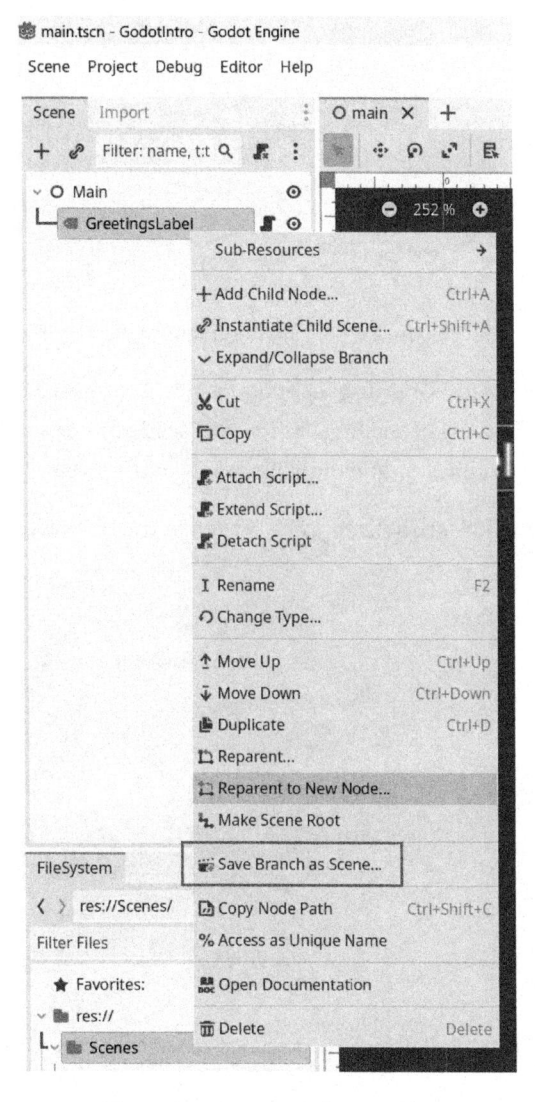

Figure 2.6 – Save Branch as Scene…

2. Save the scene as `greetings_label.tscn` in our `Scenes` folder:

Figure 2.7 – Saving the greetings_label as its own Scene

You will notice that **GreetingsLabel** does not disappear from the scene. However, now that we have a copy of the label as its own scene, we can delete it from our **Main** scene and easily add it back or add multiple labels to the scene.

3. If you double-click `greetings_label.tscn` in the **FileSystem** area, it will open in a new scene window:

Figure 2.8 – Double-click greetings_label.tscn to open it in its own scene tab

Chapter 2   37

4. Now, delete **GreetingsLabel** from the **Main** scene.
5. Then add it back by dragging and dropping `greetings_label.tscn` from the **FileSystem** area into the Viewport:

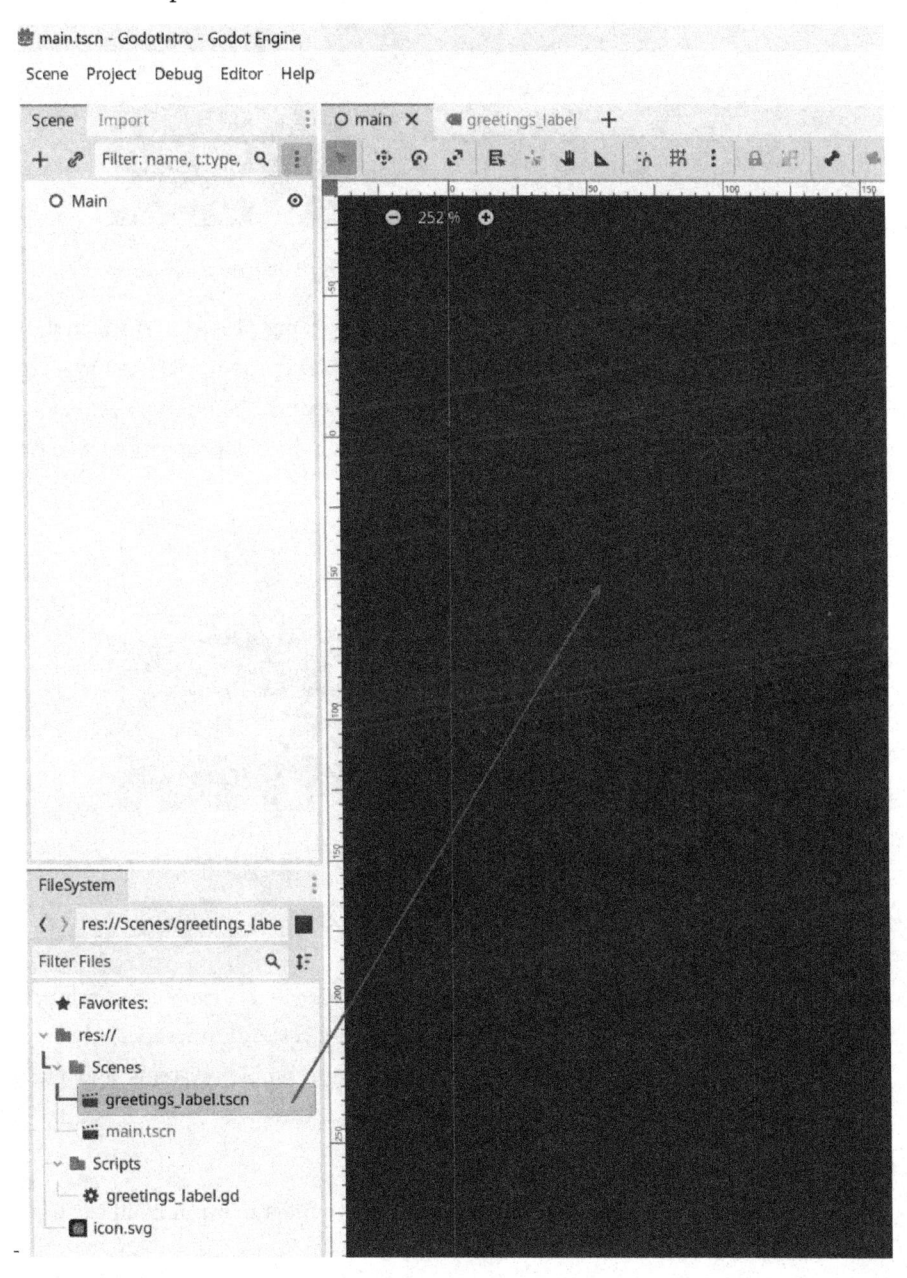

Figure 2.9 – Drag and drop the greetings_label.tscn back into the Viewport

Now we can see how things look with the label returned to the scene:

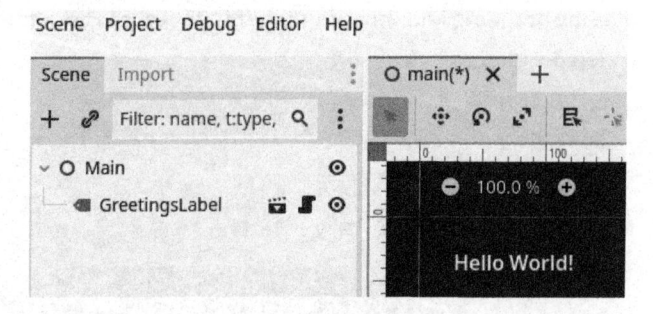

Figure 2.10 – Main Scene with the GreetingsLabel node returned

We can now drag and drop several instances of the `greetings_label` scene into the **Main** scene, and we can change the text property of each one in the **Text** property of the **Inspector**. However, when we run the **Main** scene, each label reverts to **Go Go Godot!**. This is because each instance has the same script attached to it, and we previously changed the text property to read **Go Go Godot!**.

Figure 2.11 – Multiple instances of greetings_label in the Main scene

> What is an instance?
>
> **Instancing** is the process of producing a game object from a blueprint or primary design. Instancing works well with scenes. It gives you the ability to divide your game into reusable components, a tool to structure complex systems, and a language to think about your game structure in a natural way.

We can demonstrate instancing by allowing our game to react to input from the user.

Reacting to player input

Now, we can do an experiment in which we display a different label depending on the input received from the user. In this case, we will add a sprite and place the label above its head. A **sprite** is a 2D image or animation used in a game to represent characters, objects, or other visual elements. In simpler terms, it's the picture or graphic you see in the game that moves or interacts with the environment.

If the player left-clicks on the sprite, we will say **Hello Folks!** If they *right-click* on the sprite, we will say **Godot is Great!**, and if they press *Enter / Return* on the keyboard, we will display **Hello World!**

Firstly, we need a sprite. A great place to get free game assets is from **Kenney**. You can find the website here: https://kenney.nl/. The assets I am using for this experiment can be found here: https://kenney.nl/assets/toon-characters-1.

The sprite I have chosen can be found once you have extracted the folder here: \kenney_toon-characters-1\Robot\PNG\Poses HD \character_robot_interact.

This is what our sprite looks like:

Figure 2.12 – The robot sprite character for our experiment

However, you can use any character you prefer for this experiment. We will now add the sprite to our scene:

1. Create a new folder in **FileSystem** and name it `Sprites`:

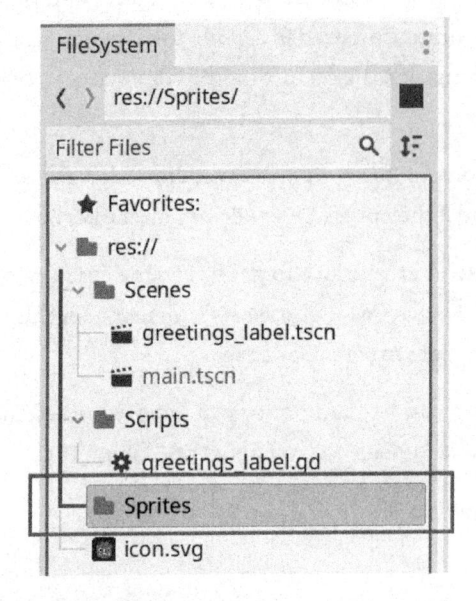

Figure 2.13 – Create the Sprites folder

2. Now drag the character you chose into this `Sprites` folder:

Figure 2.14 – Your chosen image within the Sprites folder in FileSystem

3. Now we will create a new scene for our character. Click on the **Scene** menu and select **New Scene** (press *Ctrl + N*), or click on the + symbol near the **Scene** tabs:

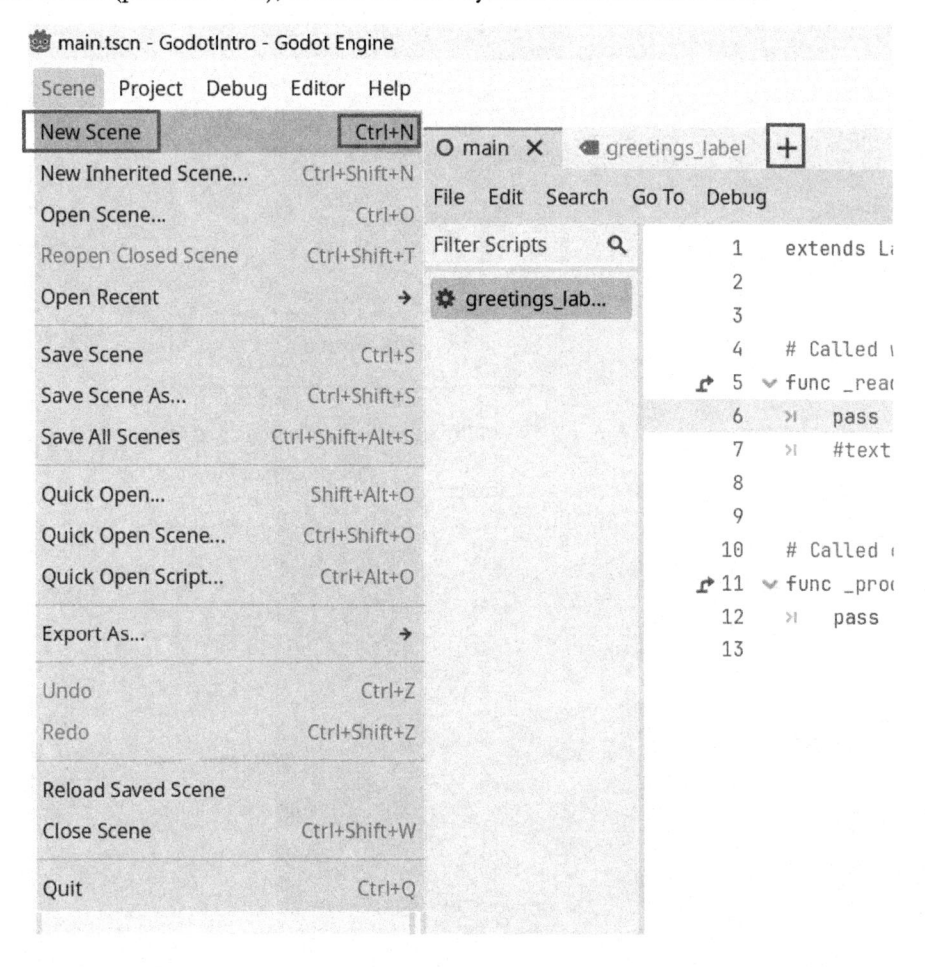

Figure 2.15 – Multiple ways of creating a new scene

4. Now add the parent or primary node for our scene by pressing *Ctrl + A*, clicking on the + icon in the **Scene** view, or clicking on the **Other Node** button:

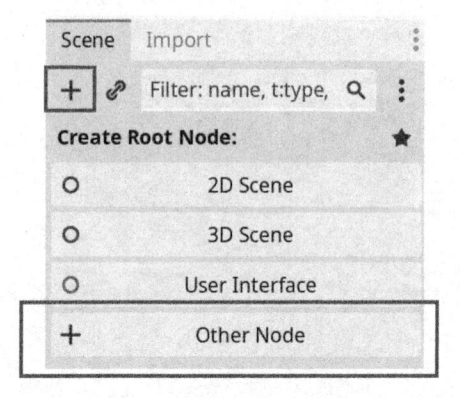

Figure 2.16 – Multiple ways to add a node to a scene

5. Search for a **Sprite2D** node and add it:

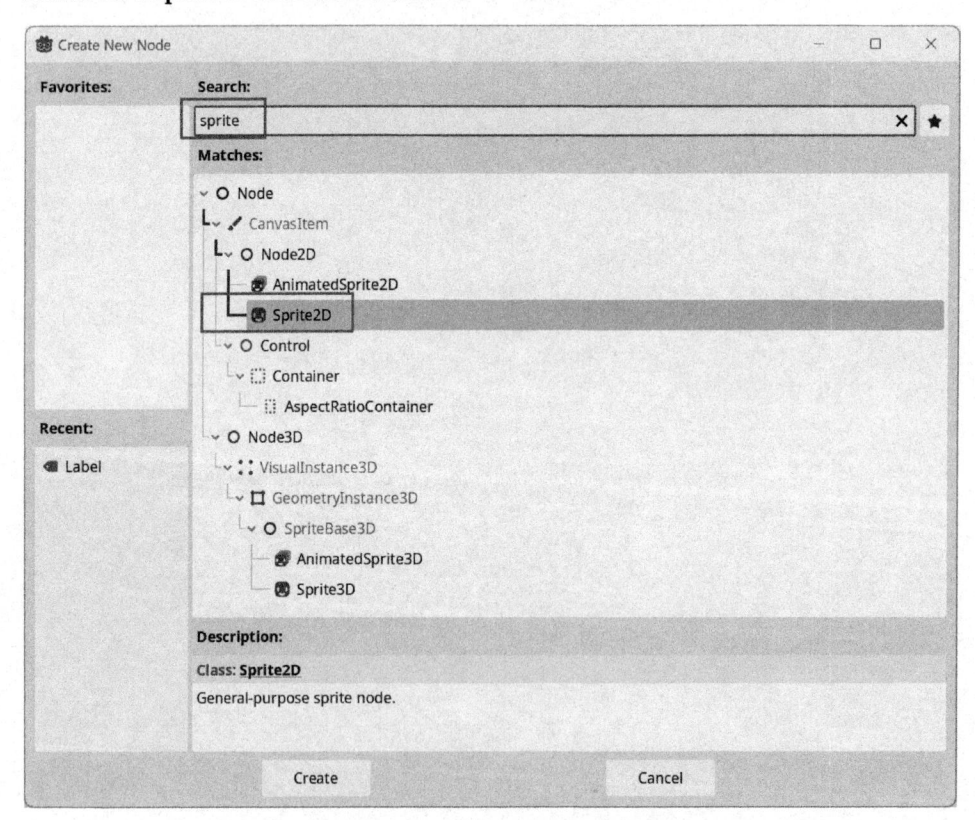

Figure 2.17 – Add a Sprite2D node to the scene

Chapter 2

6. Rename the node to Player:

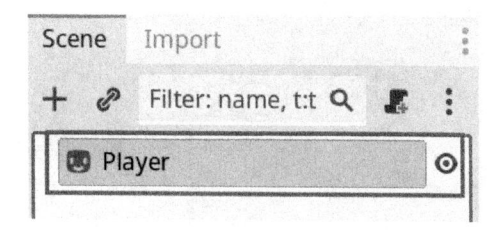

Figure 2.18 – Sprite2D renamed as Player

7. Now press *Ctrl + S* to save the scene as player.tscn in our Scenes folder:

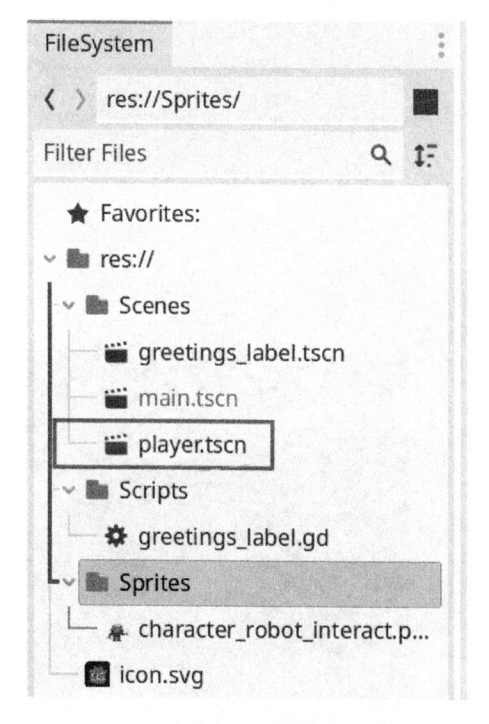

Figure 2.19 – The saved player.tscn scene

8. Make sure that you are in the 2D view. Switch to it if you need to, by clicking on **2D** at the top of the screen.

9. Now drag and drop the character image you selected onto the `<Empty>` **Texture** property of the **Player** node:

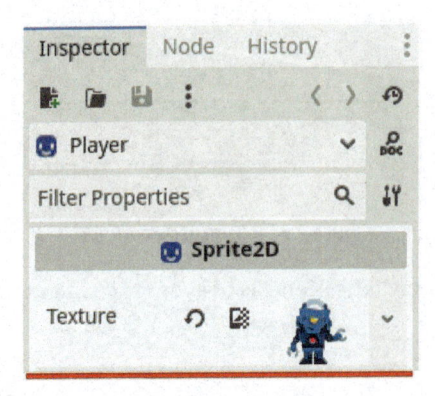

Figure 2.20 - Place your character image in the Texture property of the Player node

10. Now your character is in the **Player** scene:

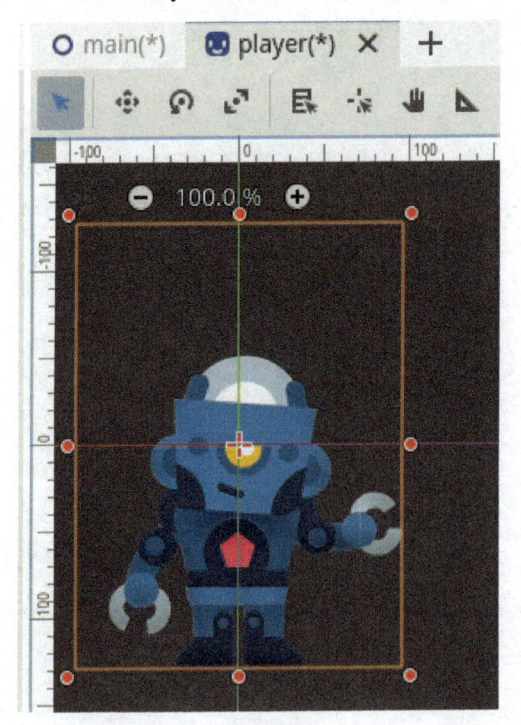

Figure 2.21 – The Player sprite in the Viewport

Chapter 2   45

11. Now we will attach a script to the **Player**. Right-click on the **Player** node and select **Attach Script...** or click on the **Scroll+** icon:

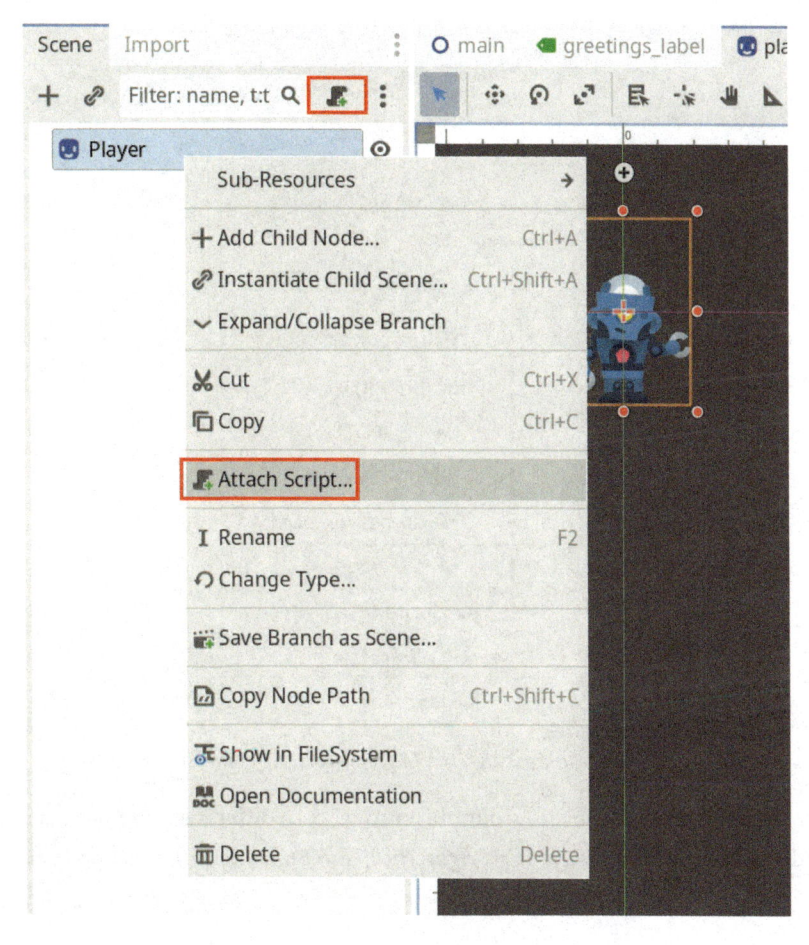

Figure 2.22 – Attach a new script to the Player node

12. Press *Ctrl + S* to save the script and save it in the `Scripts` folder. You will now have a new `player.gd` script in the `Scripts` folder:

Figure 2.23 – The player.gd scripts in the Scripts folder

Before we write some code to allow our player to react to different user input, remember that we want a different greeting for *left-click*, *right-click*, and *Enter/Return* being pressed.

Chapter 2   47

If you remember our LEGO analogy, we need to attach a **GreetingsLabel** brick (Node) to our **Player** brick (Node). We do this by dragging greetings_label.tscn from **FileSystem** to the **Player** node in the **Player** scene:

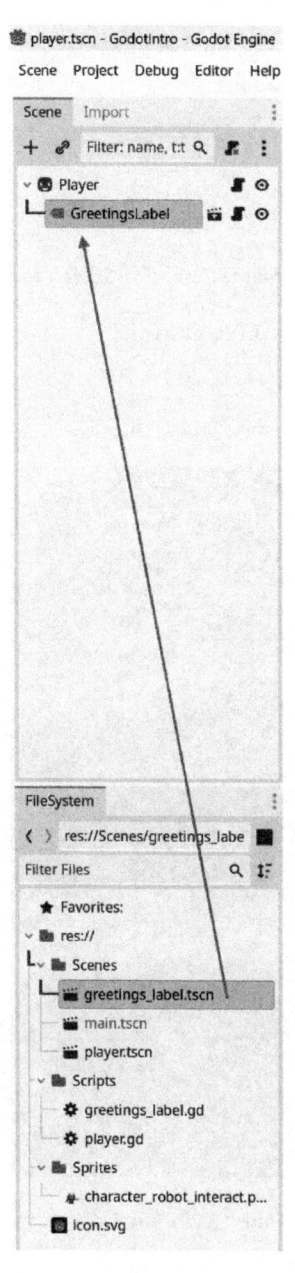

Figure 2.24 – Drag the greetings_label.tscn onto the Player node to make it a child

In Godot, the origin or starting position is measured from the top-left corner of the screen or position 0, 0. Almost always, you will want to leave the origin unchanged, but just for this example, we will move it.

Position **Player** and **GreetingsLabel** in the Viewport using the **Select** tool (which looks like the cursor) or by pressing Q on the keyboard:

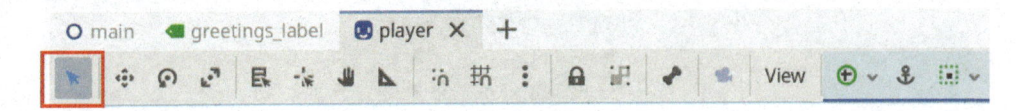

Figure 2.25 – The SELECT tool

Your **Player** scene should look something like this:

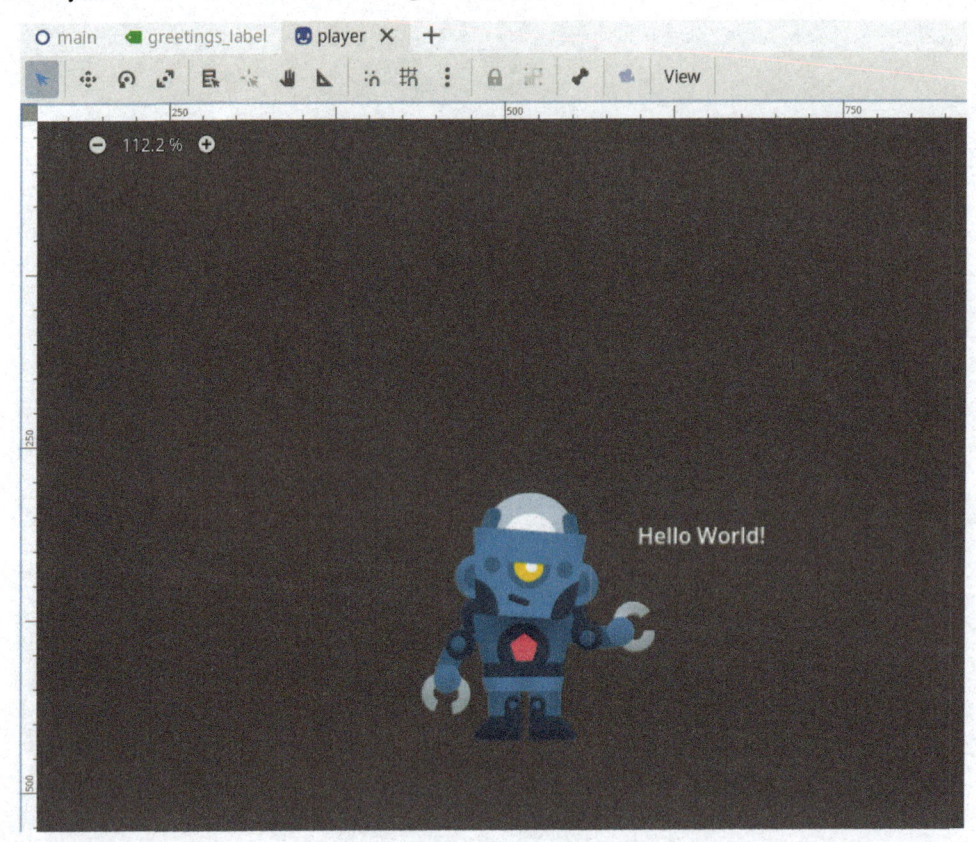

Figure 2.26 – The Player scene

Now that our sprite is somewhere near the center of the scene, we need to write a script to make it respond to user input.

Scripting player reactions to input

Our aim in writing the code for this section is to allow the user to receive a different response from the sprite depending on which mouse button the user is pressing. We'll handle three types of interaction:

- *Left click*: Shows the greeting **Hi Folks!**
- *Right click*: Shows **Godot is Great!**
- *Pressing Enter*: Shows **Hello World!**

Let's begin by making sure the greeting label is hidden at first.

Hiding the label until the user provides input

We don't want the greeting to be visible when the scene first runs. We want to hide the label by calling its hide() function.

Since the _ready() function is the first to run once the node and all its children are loaded into the scene tree, we can access the **GreetingsLabel** node using the Godot shortcut operator $.

Once we have access to the node, we simply call the hide() function:

```
#Called when the node enters the scene tree for the first time.
func _ready() -> void:
    $GreetingsLabel.hide()
```

> **Important note**
>
> Note that GDScript is an indented language. This means that the first line after a function, as in the preceding code, is tabbed in once. The game engine requires this for the code to work correctly. **I advise all those working from the digital version of the book to re-type the code manually or copy the code files from the book's GitHub repository to avoid errors caused by copying and pasting the code.**

With this code, **GreetingsLabel** is no longer visible when you run the game. You can test this scene by pressing *F6* or clicking on the **Run Current Scene** button as shown in *Figure 2.27*:

Figure 2.27 – The Run Current Scene button

You will notice that you can no longer see the greeting.

Input handling

Now, to keep things simple for our experiment, we will be using a built-in method for handling input. A **built-in method** is simply one that has already been created and comes as part of Godot Engine. You can tell that a method is built in because it begins with an underscore. You have seen two so far: _ready() and _process().

For input, we will make use of _unhandled_input(). Don't worry too much about it now, just know that if no other function/method is there to capture user input and handle it, then this method will run.

We declare the _unhandled_input function header and then handle the different types of input inside the function. For our experiment, we are listening out for two types of input: *mouse* and *keyboard*. For the keyboard, we are only listening for one key – *Enter*. For the mouse, we are listening out for *left-click* and *right-click*. Let's look at this in greater detail:

- When we detect input from the mouse, we need to show the label again, so we call the show() function of the label.
    - If we hear a *left click*, we change the text of the **GreetingsLabel** to **Hi Folks!**
    - If it is a *right click*, we set it to **Godot is Great!**
- When we detect input from the keyboard, we need to show the label again, so we call the show() function of the label.
    - If we hear *Enter* pressed, we set the text to **Hello World!**

Now, let's look at the code implementation:

```
extends Sprite2D
# This script is attached to a Sprite2D node.
# It listens for mouse and keyboard input and displays
# different messages on a Label depending on what was pressed.

# Called when the node enters the scene tree for the first time (i.e.,
when the scene starts).
func _ready():
    # Hide the Label at the beginning so it's not visible until an input event happens.
    $GreetingsLabel.hide()
```

```gdscript
# Called every frame. 'delta' is the time in seconds since the last frame.
func _process(delta):
    # We're not doing anything every frame in this example, but the function is here in case we want to later.
    pass


# Called when the player performs an input action that hasn't already been handled.
func _unhandled_input(event):
    # Check if the event was a mouse button press.
    if event is InputEventMouseButton:
        # Show the label whenever a mouse button is pressed.
        $GreetingsLabel.show()
        # Check which mouse button was pressed.
        if event.button_index == MOUSE_BUTTON_LEFT:
            # If the left mouse button was clicked, set the label's text to "Hi Folks!"
            $GreetingsLabel.text = "Hi Folks!"

        elif event.button_index == MOUSE_BUTTON_RIGHT:
            # If the right mouse button was clicked, set the label's text to "Godot is Great!"
            $GreetingsLabel.text = "Godot is Great!"

    # Check if the event was a key press.
    elif event is InputEventKey:
        # Only show the label and set the text if the Enter key was pressed.
        if event.keycode == KEY_ENTER:
            $GreetingsLabel.show()
            $GreetingsLabel.text = "Hello World!"
```

Now we have tested our **Player** scene, and we know that it works as expected. We can return to our **Main** scene and remove the **GreetingsLabel** node and instead drag `player.tscn` onto the **Main** node. Then, run the game again and check that it all works correctly:

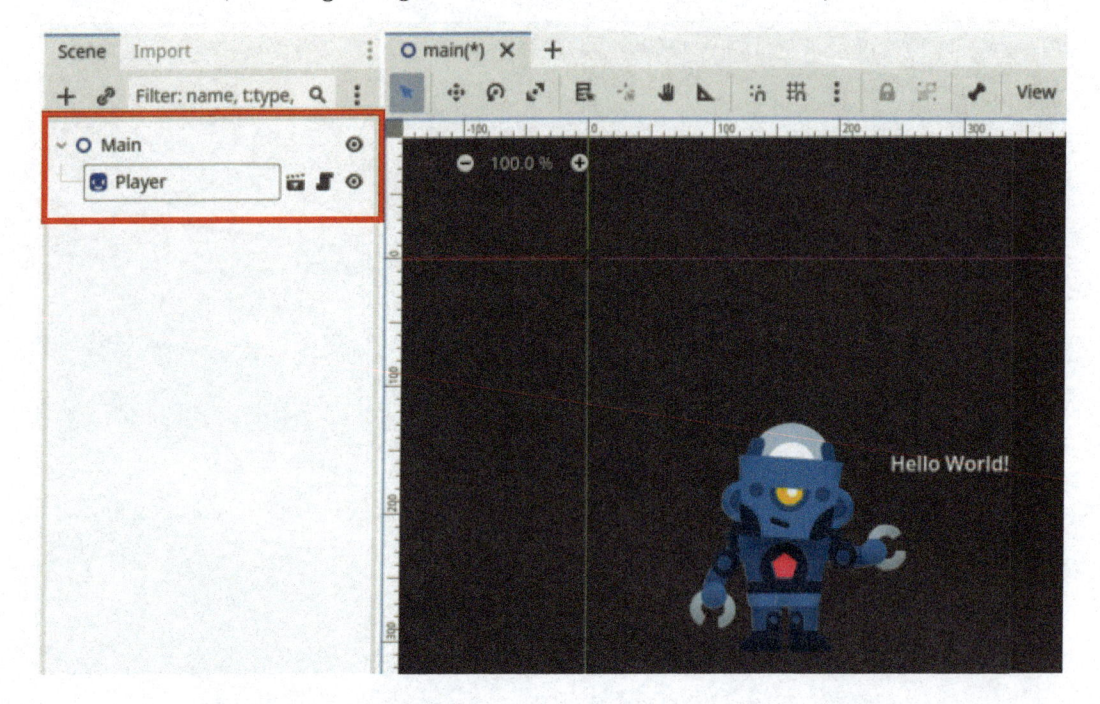

Figure 2.28 – Our new Main scene

This is an important chapter, introducing you to the basic building blocks of Godot. I recommend that you revisit it often or even return to the end-chapter summary to remind yourself of the point and purpose of scenes, nodes, and scripts.

Summary

In this chapter, we explored the foundational features of Godot 4, beginning with editing an existing project and creating an additional scene. You learned how to navigate the interface, save scenes effectively, and grasp the node and scene design philosophy central to Godot. We also covered how to make your projects interactive by reacting to player input. By mastering these core concepts and tools, you've taken the first essential steps toward confidently using Godot to develop games.

In the next chapter, we will get an introduction to 3D and look at how to work with materials and lighting.

Join our community on Discord

Join our community's Discord space for discussions with the author and other readers:

`https://packt.link/godot-4-game-dev`

3

Introduction to 3D

Working with 3D in Godot can feel like stepping into an entirely new dimension of game development—quite literally! This chapter serves as your gateway to understanding the fundamentals of 3D in Godot, guiding you through the essential tools and concepts. Whether you're designing a vast open world or a compact 3D puzzle, these foundational skills will set you up for success.

We'll start by learning how to create 3D objects, the building blocks of any 3D scene. Next, we'll explore how to make these objects visually engaging by applying materials, which give them color, texture, and detail. Finally, we'll introduce you to lighting, a crucial component that brings your 3D environment to life by adding depth, mood, and realism.

In this chapter, we're going to cover the following main topics:

- Creating 3D objects
- Creating a material for your object
- Creating lighting for the scene

By the end of this chapter, you'll not only understand how to build and illuminate a simple 3D environment but also gain confidence in navigating Godot's 3D workspace. These skills are essential for any aspiring game developer and provide a solid foundation for creating immersive 3D experiences.

Technical requirements

This chapter's code files are available here in the book's GitHub repository: https://github.com/PacktPublishing/Godot-4-for-Beginners/tree/main/ch3/introto3d

Visit this link to check out the video of the code being run: https://packt.link/6Se0U

Creating 3D objects

Up until now, we have concentrated on 2D scenes and 2D nodes, along with some scripting using **GDScript**. It's important to know that you are not restricted to 2D though, since Godot is an extremely capable 3D game engine.

We will begin our exploration of 3D by creating a new Godot project in the **Project Manager** window by clicking on the **+Create** button. Remember to create a folder for your project and name it. I have called my project IntroTo3D, as shown in *Figure 3.1*:

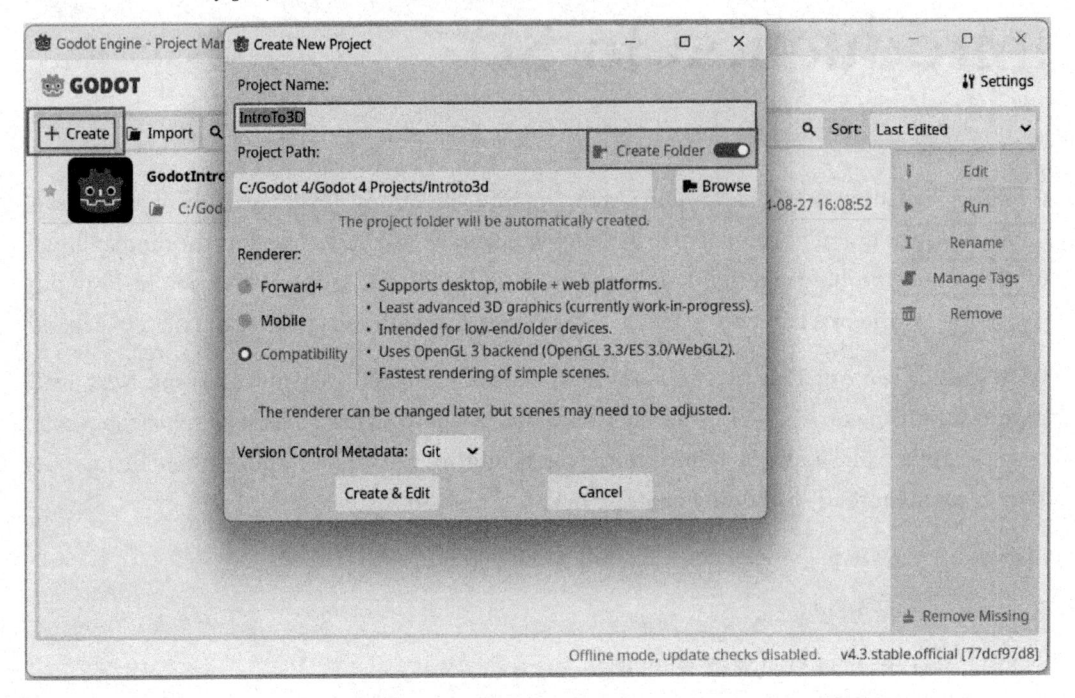

Figure 3.1 – Creating a new Godot project

By default, new Godot projects open in 3D view – that's handy! Now we can create our first 3D scene. Because Godot uses a scene tree structure, we need to choose a root node for the tree. The easiest way to do this is to click on the **3D Scene** button:

Chapter 3

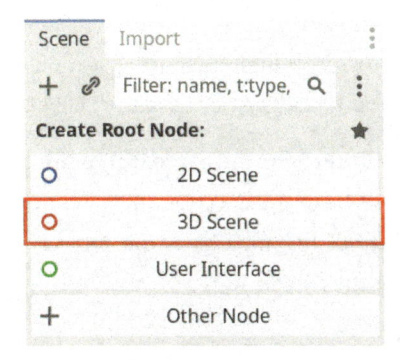

Figure 3.2 – Creating a new 3D scene with Node3D as the root

Your Godot interface should now look like *Figure 3.3*. Take note that we now have an extra dimension – **Z** – representing depth, and we have **Node3D** as the root of our scene tree.

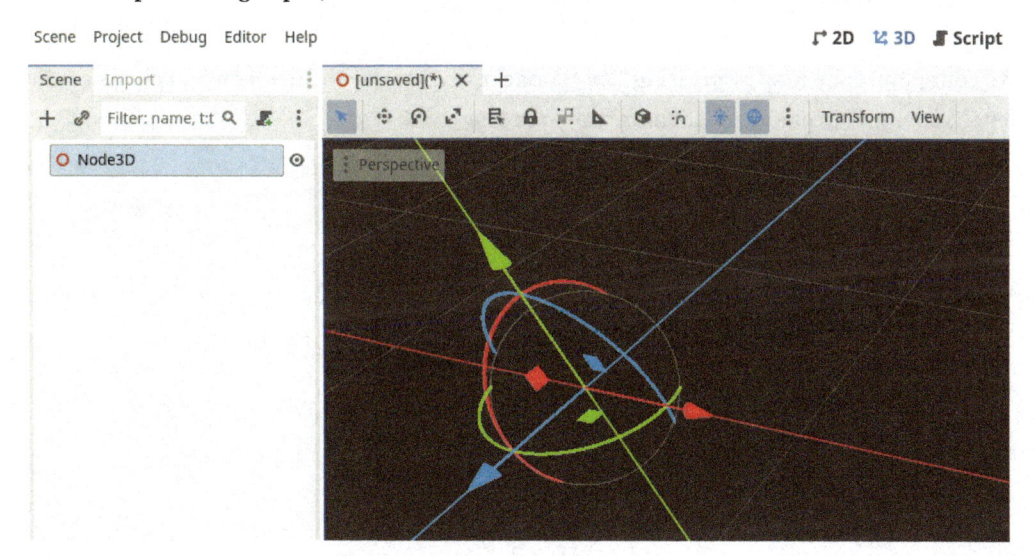

Figure 3.3 – An overview of our first 3D scene

> 🔍 **Quick tip**: Need to see a high-resolution version of this image? Open this book in the next-gen Packt Reader or view it in the PDF/ePub copy.
>
> 🔒 **The next-gen Packt Reader** and a **free PDF/ePub copy** of this book are included with your purchase. Scan the QR code OR visit `packtpub.com/unlock`, then use the search bar to find this book by name. Double-check the edition shown to make sure you get the right one.

Save your new scene now by pressing *Ctrl + S* or clicking on the **Scene** menu and choosing **Save Scene**. Name your scene `main.tscn`, as shown in *Figure 3.4*:

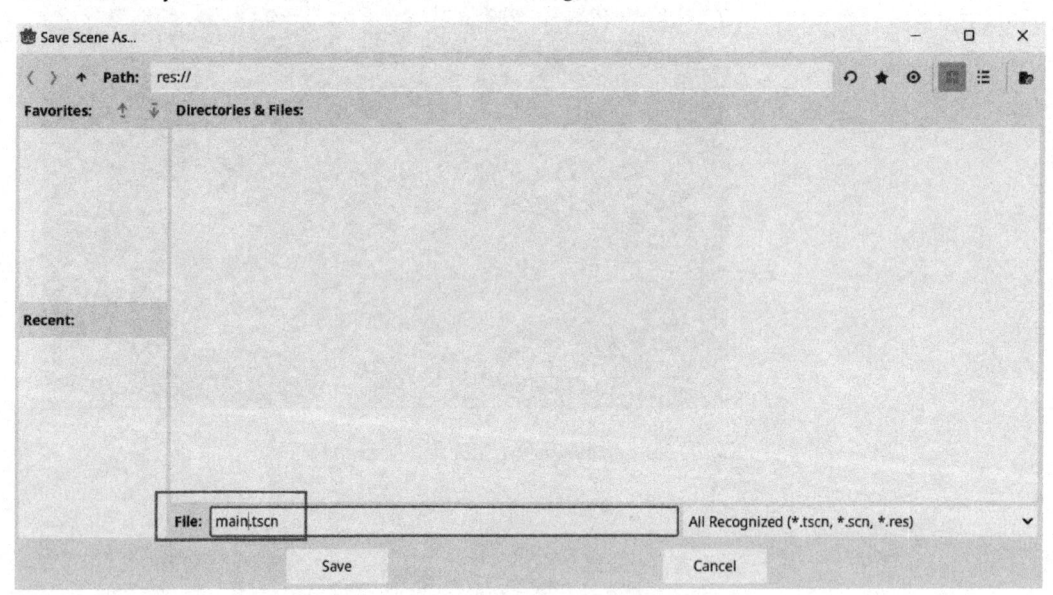

Figure 3.4 – Saving our scene as main

The stage is set for us to explore the scene. We can make use of shortcuts to easily do this.

Moving around the scene

You can move around the 3D scene much like you do in most 3D games:

- Hold down the *right mouse button* to look around
- Use *WASD* to fly around the scene (while holding *right-click*)
- Use *E* to fly up
- Use *Q* to fly down
- Use the *middle mouse button* to fly around the center of whatever is on the screen

In 2D, we made use of **Sprite2D** to visualize things. In 3D, we will use **MeshInstance3D**.

In 3D graphics, a **mesh** is a digital model of a 3D object or shape, created by connecting points (called *vertices*) with lines (*edges*) and flat surfaces (*faces*).

To create a mesh instance in our scene, we can either drag a pre-created 3D model into the scene, or we can use primitive shapes with the **MeshInstance3D**. To do this, add a new **MeshInstance3D** node to the scene tree:

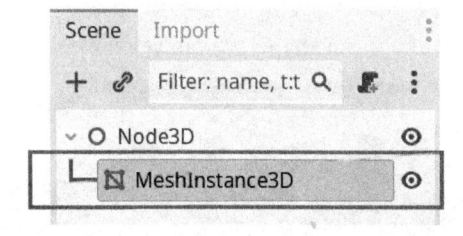

Figure 3.5 – Adding a MeshInstance3D node to our scene

Although we now have a mesh, there is still nothing visible. You could think of it as a sprite with no texture. We need to choose a basic shape. Using the **Inspector** window on the right-hand side, click on the **Mesh** property dropdown and select **New BoxMesh**.

This will create a new cube that you can manipulate with the same **Select**, **Move**, **Rotate**, and **Scale** tools.

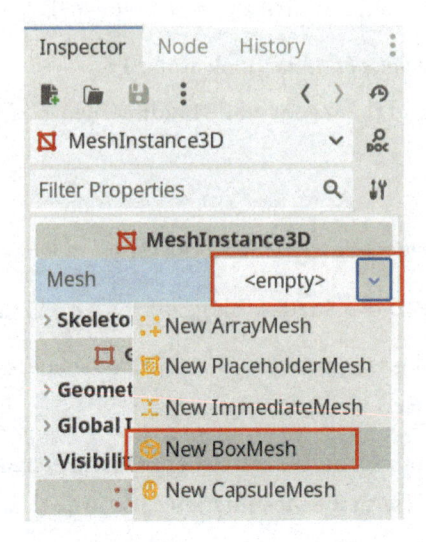

Figure 3.6 – Adding a BoxMesh to our MeshInstance3D

Now that **MeshInstance3D** has a mesh shape, we can see the cube or box in the Viewport:

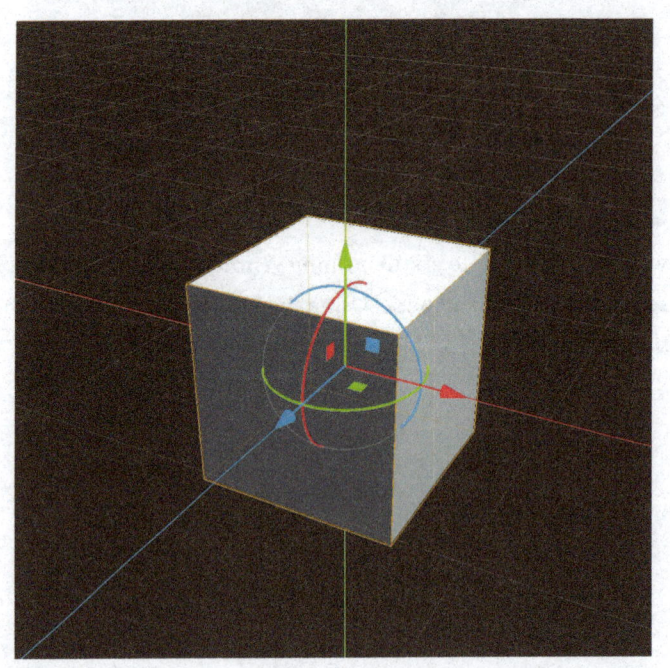

Figure 3.7 – MeshInstance3D is now visible in the Viewport as a 3D cube

Chapter 3 61

> **Note**
>
> In 2D, the positions and sizes of objects are measured in *pixels*, whereas in 3D, Godot uses the *metric system*, so each unit is 1 meter and represents an area of 1 meter by 1 meter.

We could make a 3D stick man using multiple of the simple shapes in **MeshInstance3D**. Have a look at the following result and try to recreate it yourself using the **Selection**, **Move**, **Rotate**, and **Scale** tools. You *do not* have to use the same shapes as I have, so your stick man can look very different from mine, and that is okay.

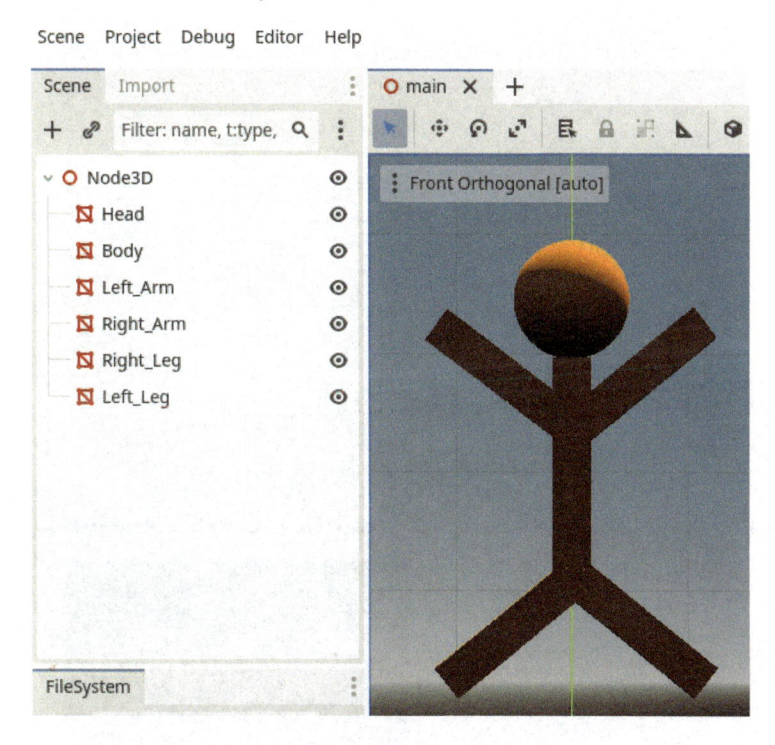

Figure 3.8 – Making a stick man with simple mesh shapes

As you can see in *Figure 3.8*, I have combined different basic shapes to create a stick figure.

Note that if you select the **parent StickMan** node, which is the original **Node3D**, whatever you do to it – such as using **Scale** or **Rotate** – it will do to all of the child nodes.

Creating a material for your object

When working in 2D, we give **Sprite2D** a texture so that we can see it on the screen. In 3D, we use materials.

Materials describe how the game engine should display an object. Once a mesh has material, it can be assigned things such as colors and shadows. It can also interact with the lighting in the scene. Our stick man already has a default material with a gray color, otherwise we wouldn't be able to see it!

Creating a material

Godot saves materials as resources. This means that once we have created one material, we can use it again and again on different objects. Let's create a new folder in **FileSystem** called `Materials`:

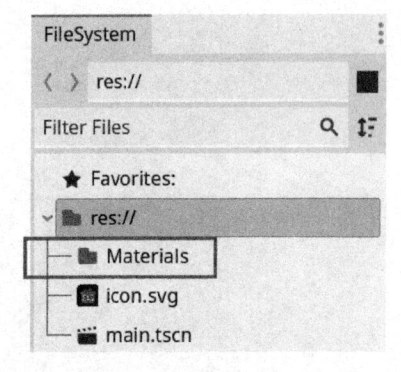

Figure 3.9 – The Materials folder

Now *right-click* on the `Materials` folder, select **Create New**, and then **Resource...**:

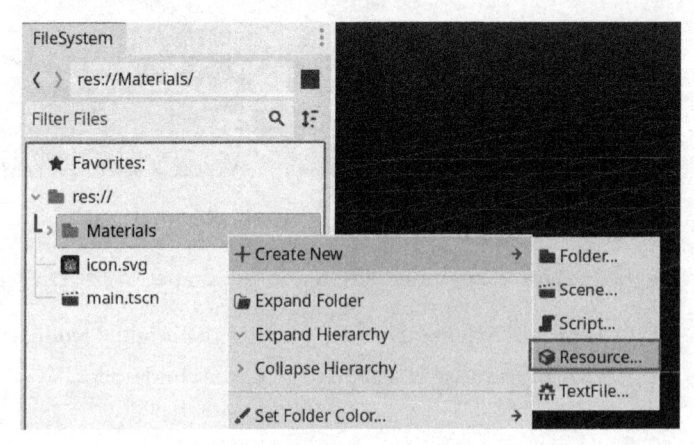

Figure 3.10 – Creating a new resource

Chapter 3

On the **Resource** menu, which is shown next, search for material, choose **StandardMaterial3D**, and give it a name. I have named mine stick_material.tres:

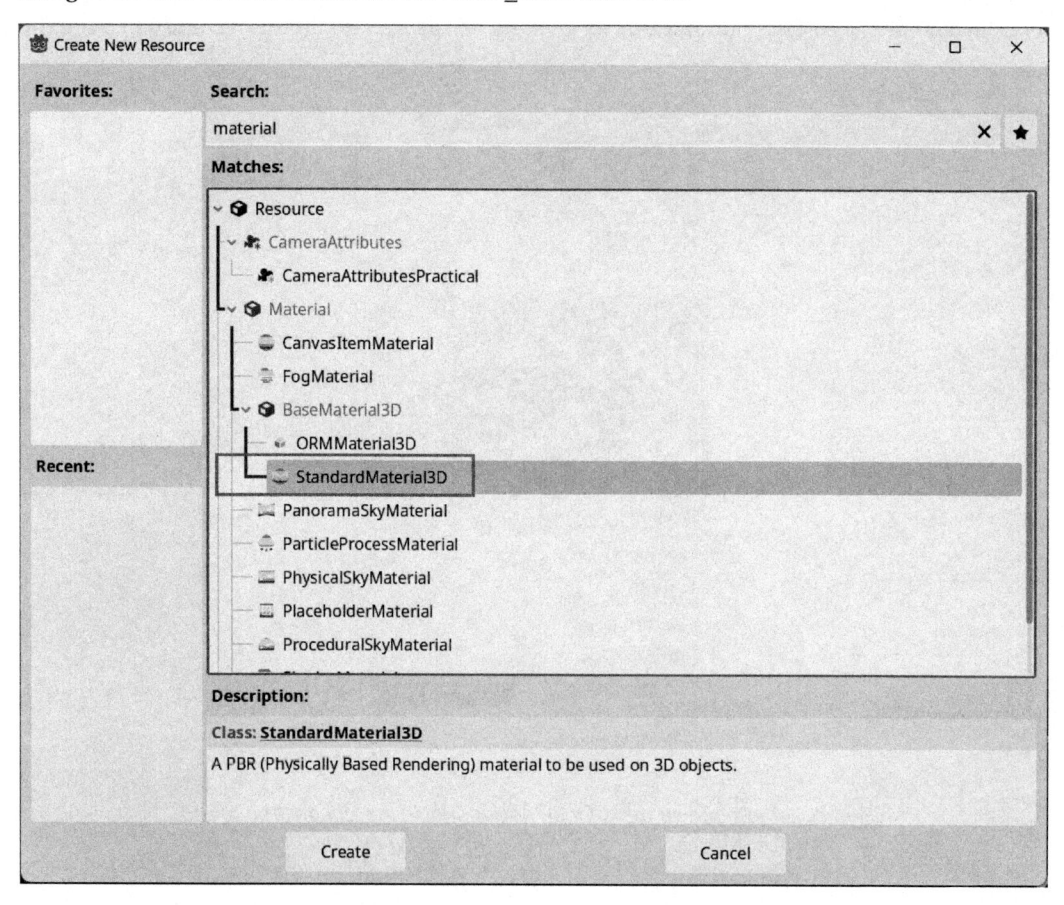

Figure 3.11 – Adding StandardMaterial3D

Once the material has been created, it can be modified in the **Inspector** window. Materials have a lot of changeable properties, such as texture, roughness, shininess, color, and transparency. We can change the color of our material by clicking on the **Albedo** dropdown and selecting the one we like:

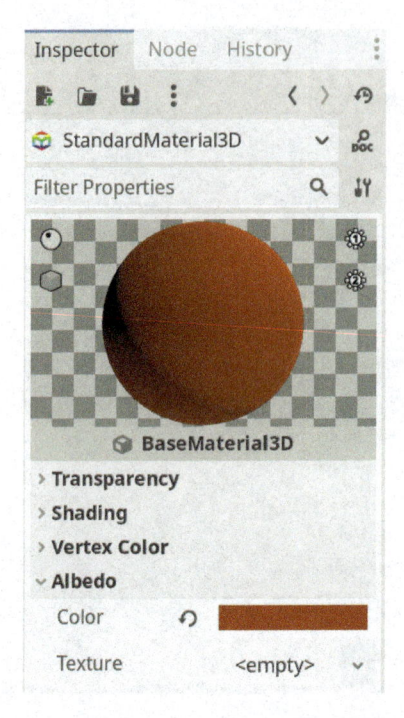

Figure 3.12 – Changing the color of the material in the Albedo dropdown

The word **albedo** comes from the Latin word *albus*, which simply means *white*. Albedo has traditionally been used to change the color and transparency of a material.

I have chosen a *brown* color to make the material look more like wood. Now play with the **Roughness** value to improve the look further:

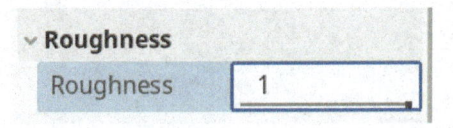

Figure 3.13 – Roughness has a value from 0 to 1

Chapter 3　　　　　　　　　　　　　　　　　　　　　　　　　　　　　　　　　65

There are so many options to experiment with for materials. However, if you really want to create materials that look like the object you are trying to replicate, I suggest using a tool such as **Material Maker**, which is free and made using the Godot Engine:

https://rodzilla.itch.io/material-maker

Applying a material

Actually, putting the material onto the mesh is as simple as dragging the material resource file onto the mesh in Viewport!

You can see the effect of this in *Figure 3.14*:

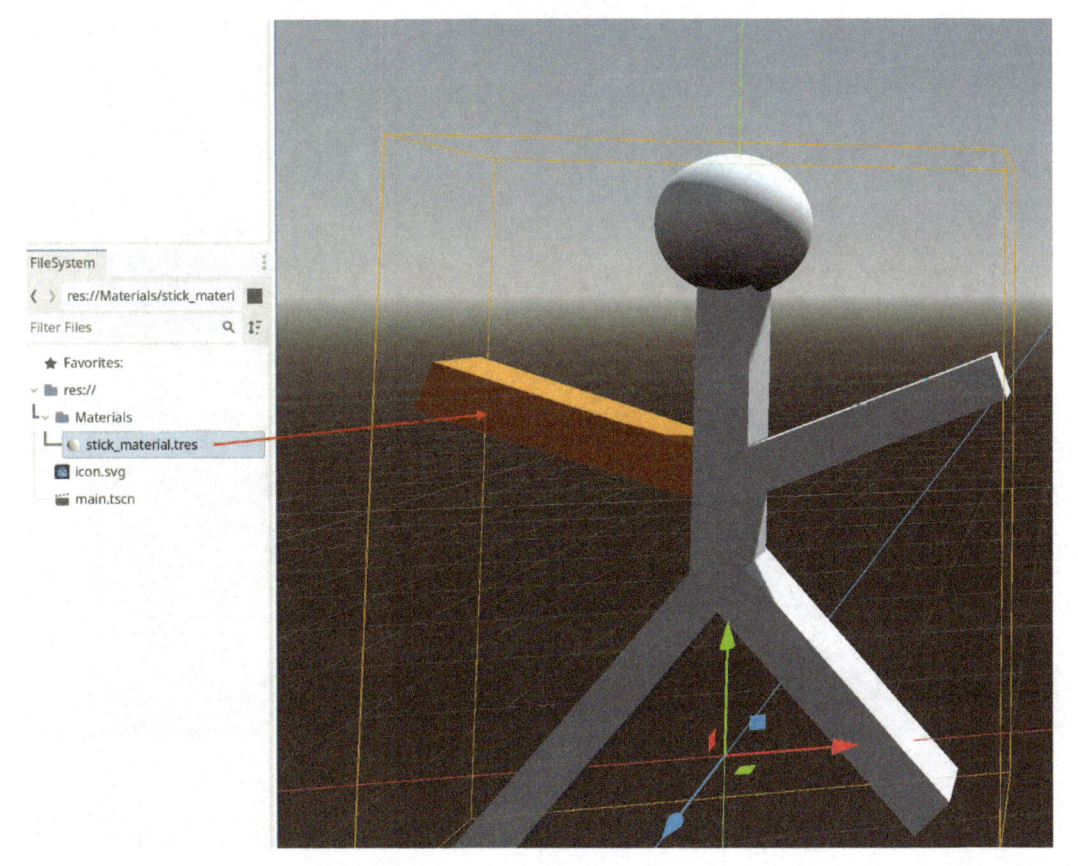

Figure 3.14 – Drag and drop your material onto your mesh

As you see in *Figure 3.14*, when you place your material on one of the mesh shapes, the mesh immediately adopts the color and texture of the material.

If you change any of the properties of the material, any of the meshes to which the material has been applied will update in real time too. I suggest that you try this right now to see the effect.

You can see this effect in *Figure 3.15* – all the meshes have been updated with the new material:

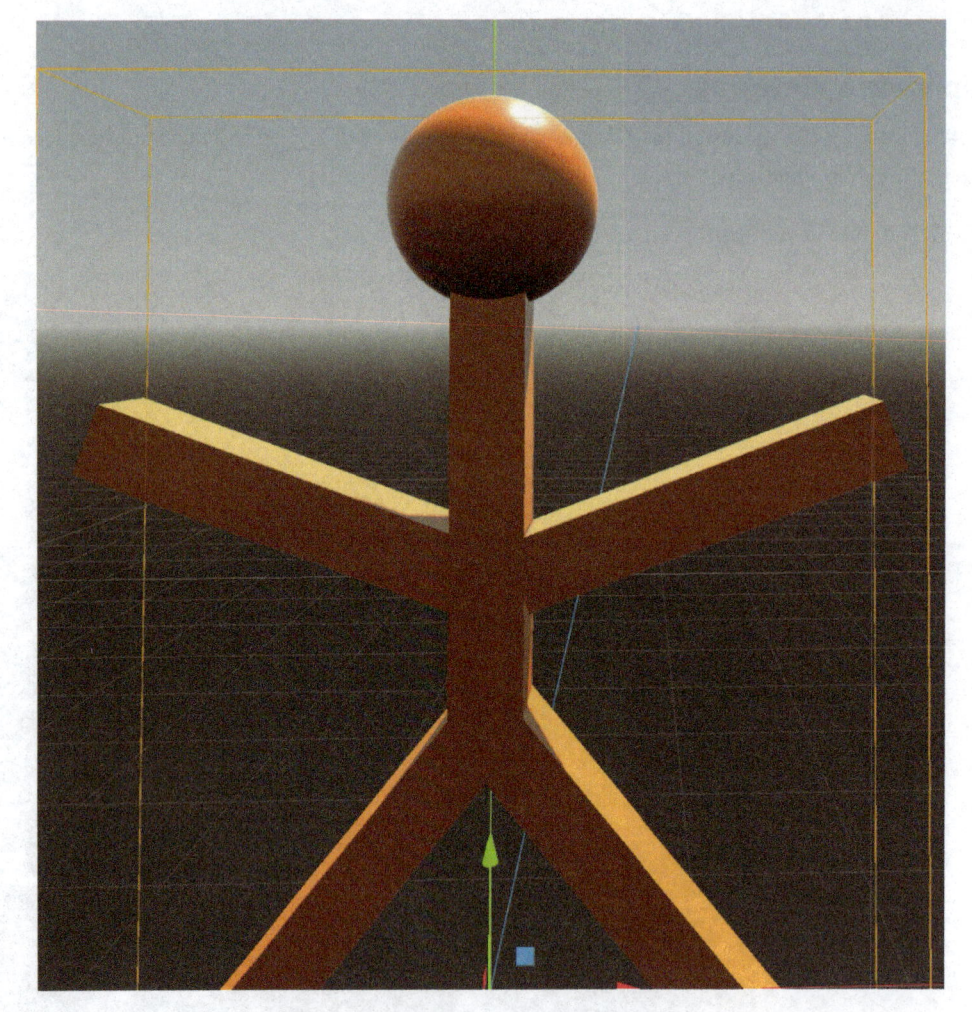

Figure 3.15 – Changing the roughness updated the material on all meshes

Did you notice how the roughness of the material changed the way the stick man looks?

Challenge yourself

In this subsection, we will challenge ourselves to practice using the skills that we have just learned.

Try to replicate the three materials shown in *Figure 3.16*. The first simply uses **Albedo** with low roughness and a high **Metallic** value. The second uses **Transparency**, and the third one has a **Texture** value.

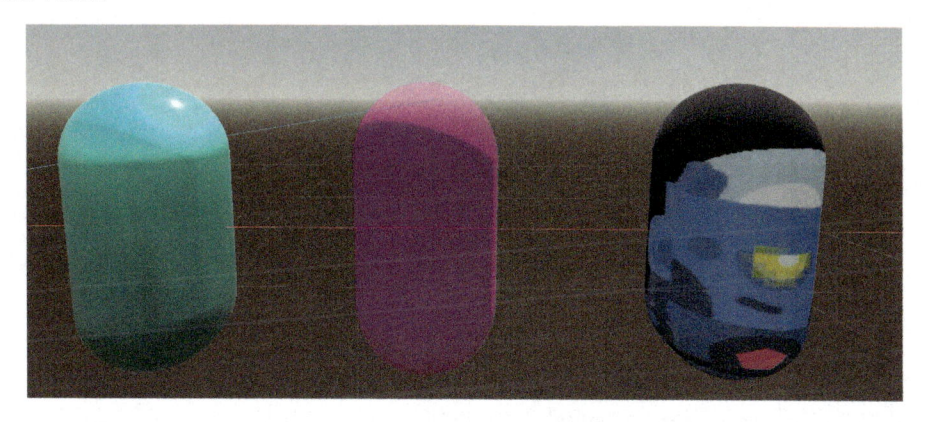

Figure 3.16 – Metallic (left), transparent (center), and textured (right) materials

To walk through the challenge, first, add three **MeshInstance3D** nodes to the scene. In the **Inspector** window, choose a basic **CapsuleMesh** and duplicate it by pressing *Ctrl + D*.

The expected outcome of these steps is shown in *Figure 3.17*:

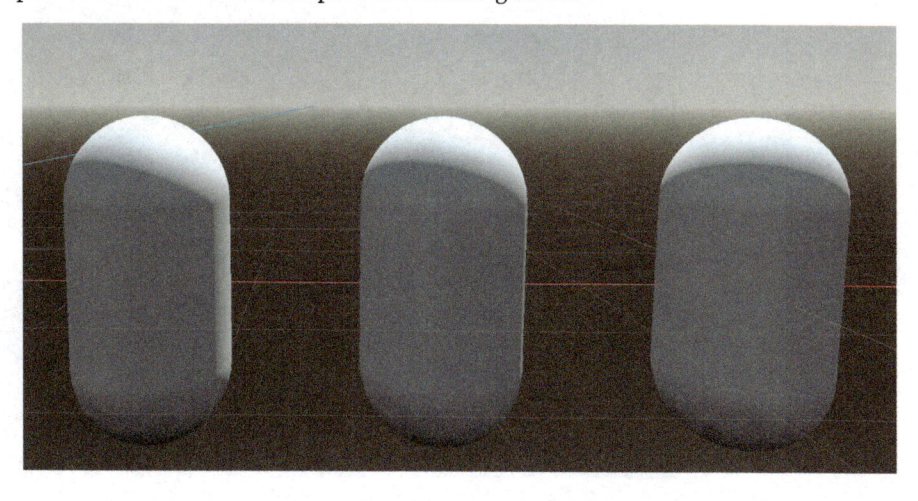

Figure 3.17 – Three MeshInstance3D meshes with CapsuleMesh shapes

The next step of the challenge is to create the first material.

First material

Now we need to create three new resources in the **Materials** folder. We will use the **StandardMaterial3D** resource for each material. To identify them easily, name the materials `metal_material.tres`, `transparent_material.tres`, and `textured_material.tres`:

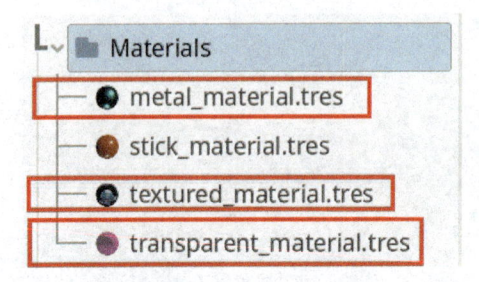

Figure 3.18 – Our new materials

You can click and drag each material onto each capsule so that if we begin changing the material properties, we will see our meshes update in real time:

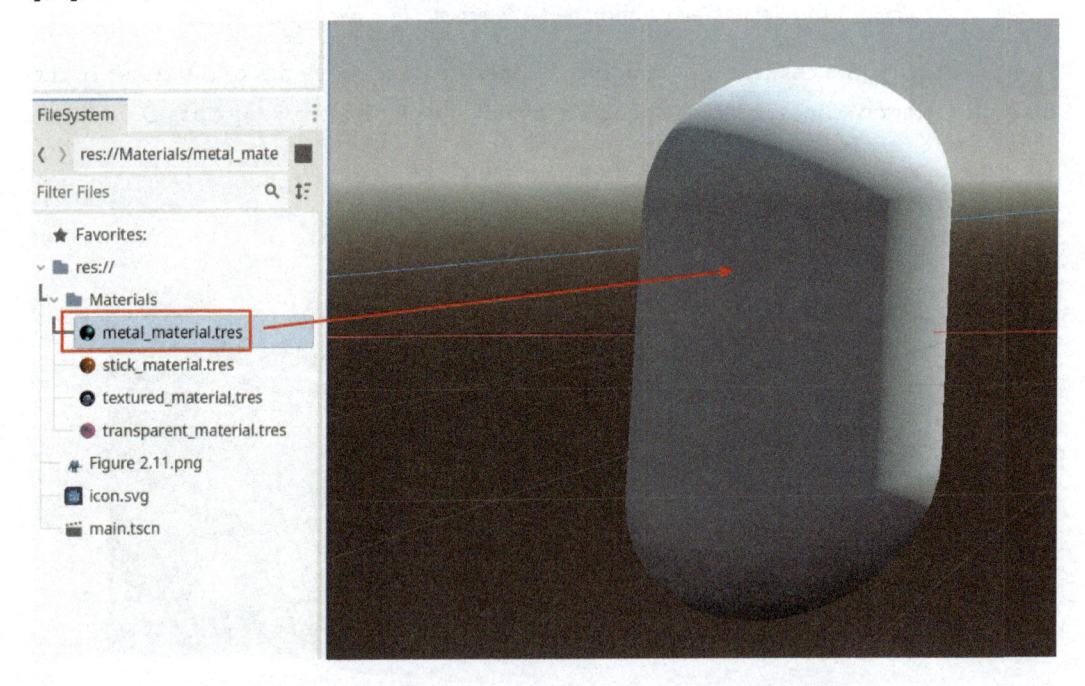

Figure 3.19 – Drag and drop your materials onto the capsules

Chapter 3

On your metal material, open the **Albedo** property and change the color to be like that of the challenge (*sky blue*). Also, adjust the roughness and the **Metallic** property till you are satisfied that it looks shiny and reflective, like metal.

Figure 3.20 – Creating a shiny metal material

Notice the properties you should adjust in *Figure 3.20* to create the metallic effect you want.

Second material

Begin again by changing the **Albedo** property of the material to a bright pink to match the challenge. Take the **Alpha** channel down to around halfway as well. You will notice this has no effect now. This is because we need to adjust the **Transparency** property to use **Alpha**.

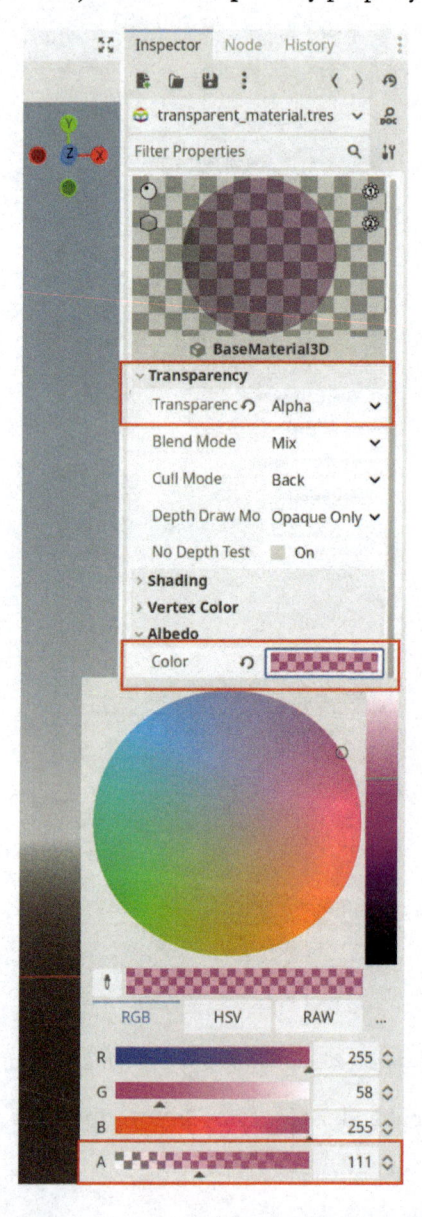

Figure 3.21 – Creating a transparent pink capsule

Chapter 3

Note the properties of the material in *Figure 3.21*, which you need to adjust to create the transparent effect you are after.

Third material

The final material has a texture instead of color. The texture is simply an image that is wrapped around the capsule shape. We can simply use the same robot image that we used for the sprite when we were working in 2D in *Chapter 2*. Expand the **Albedo** dropdown and drag an image onto the empty **Texture** property:

Figure 3.22 – Adding a texture to a material

You can clearly see the flat 2D image of a robot has been applied to the capsule shape and is being stretched around it.

Another fundamental part of any 3D scene is the lighting. In the next section, we'll explore different types of lights and how to use them effectively in your 3D scenes.

Creating lighting for the scene

To influence the mood and atmosphere, and visually enhance a game, **lighting** is crucial. Good lighting adds depth, highlights details, and can guide the players' attention, which all makes the game world more immersive and engaging.

Godot has several lighting nodes available. We will look at a few of the primary ones now. We will add these nodes to the current scene and examine their effects on the three capsules.

Click on the + in the **scene tree** to add a new node to the scene. Search using the keyword `light`. You will see that there are three types of nodes related to light in Godot, as shown in *Figure 3.23*:

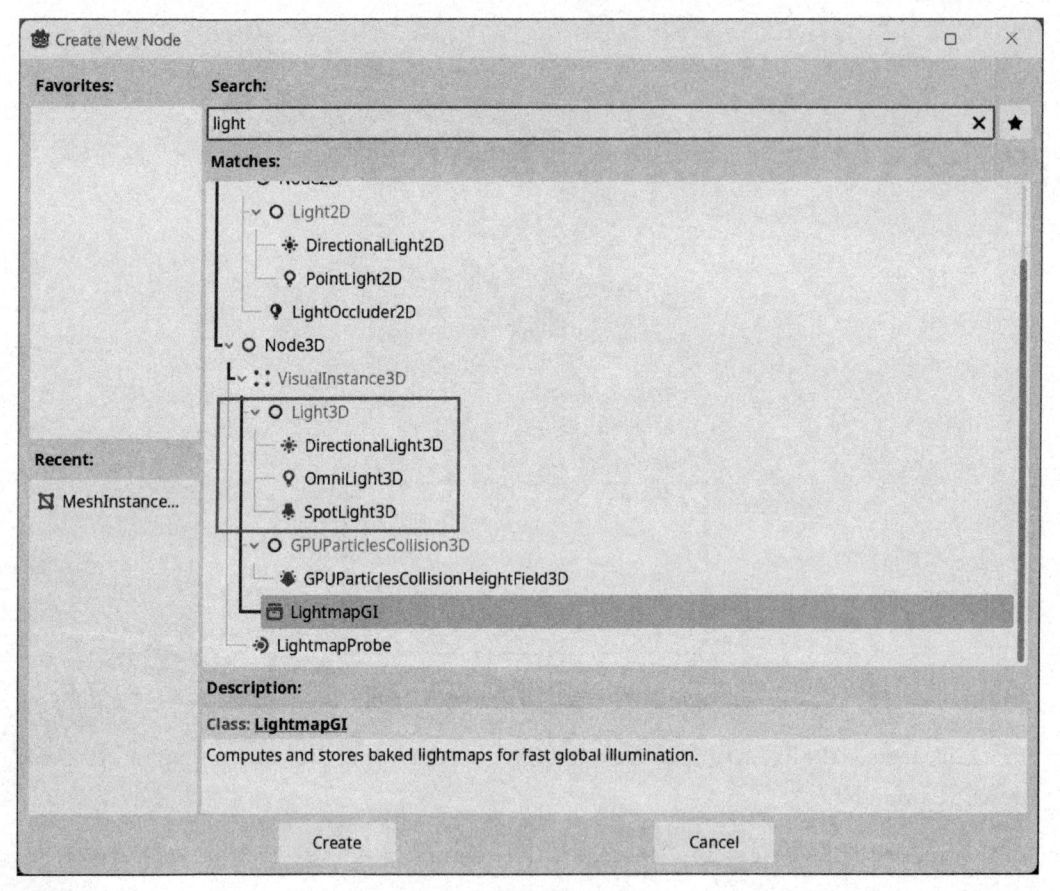

Figure 3.23 – Three primary light nodes in Godot

Chapter 3

Directional light simulates sunlight by casting parallel rays over your entire 3D scene, providing consistent illumination from a specific direction, making it ideal for outdoor environments. Now is the time to implement directional light in Godot.

Directional light

Add a **DirectionalLight3D** node to the scene. This type of light mimics the sun and sends out infinite light in a single direction as parallel rays. It is used for lights with high intensity that are far away from the scene.

In the Viewport, the node is a white arrow pointing in the direction the light comes from. You can *rotate* this node to change the direction of the light. The position of this node will not affect the scene as the light is coming from everywhere.

Try rotating the light to see the effect it has on the scene. You can also change the **Color** and **Energy** properties of the light in the **Inspector** window.

You can see the direction the light is coming from displayed as a large *white arrow* in *Figure 3.24*:

Figure 3.24 – Note the reflection in the metal capsule is as if the sun were directly overhead

Metallic surfaces will reflect the light, as shown in *Figure 3.24*.

In *Figure 3.25*, you can see the **Color** and **Energy** properties, which can be adjusted to change the color of the light and its intensity:

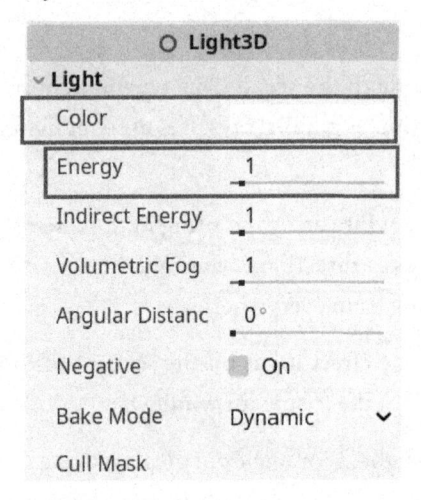

Figure 3.25 – The Color and Energy properties of DirectionalLight3D

Before we add a new light to the scene, click on the **eye** icon to toggle the visibility of the **DirectionalLight3D** node to off so that we can see the effects of the next light:

Figure 3.26 – Toggle the visibility of the DirectionalLight3D node to off

Click on the + in the scene tree to add a new node to the scene. Search using the keyword `light` (see *Figure 3.23*).

Omni light

Add an **OmniLight3D** node to the scene. This node emits light from a single point in all directions, like a light bulb. Like a light bulb in real life, it is brighter as you get closer to it. You can adjust the range of the light by clicking on the orange circle that appears at the edge of its wireframe, as shown in *Figure 3.27*:

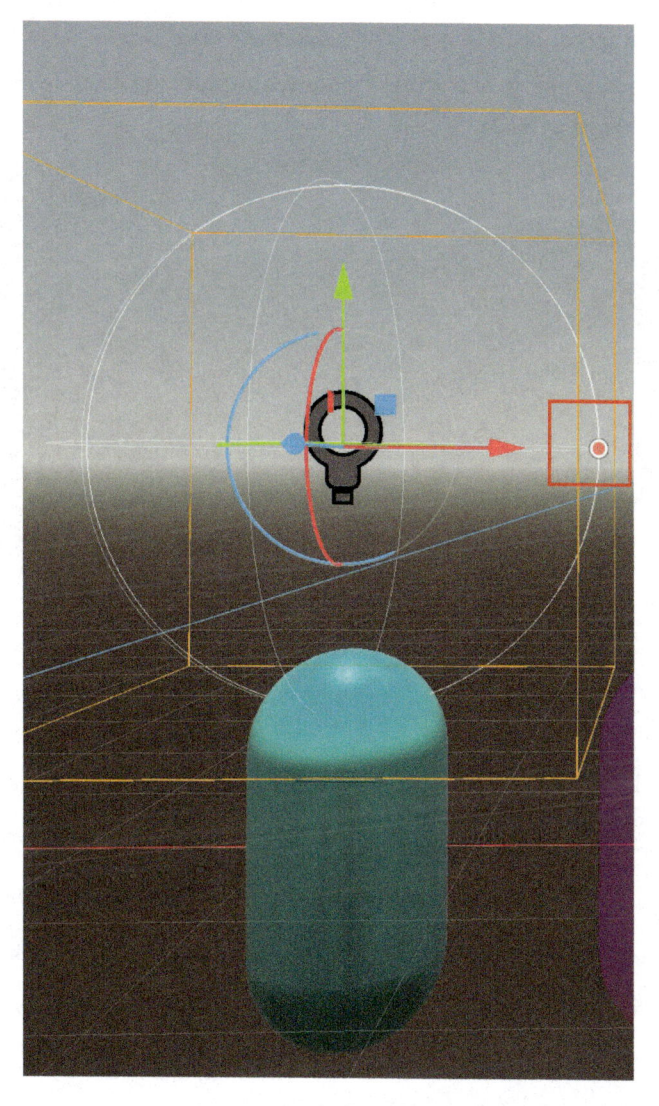

Figure 3.27 – The OmniLight3D range handle

You can also change the **Color** and **Energy** properties of **OmniLight3D**. However, it is hard to see with no surface to reflect off. Follow these steps to fix this:

1. Use your new skills to add a ground surface to the scene by adding another **MeshInstance3D** node. Rename it to Ground.
2. Give it the **PlaneMesh** shape. Scale and move the plane so that it looks like a large floor under the capsules.

3. Create a new material and save it as ground_material.tres.
4. Set the **Albedo** property of the material to **white** and apply it to **Ground**. It should look something like *Figure 3.28*:

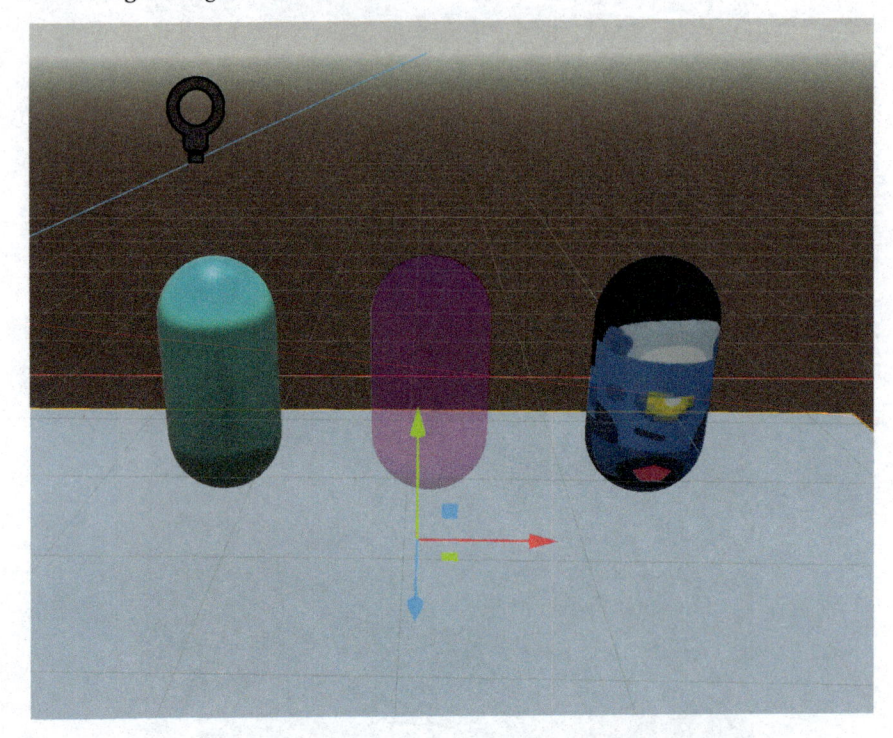

Figure 3.28 – The Ground plane mesh added with a white material applied

Go ahead and experiment with changing the **Color** and **Energy** properties of **OmniLight3D**. Notice how it changes the mood of the scene.

Do you see the *reddish* glow of the light on the floor in *Figure 3.29*?

Chapter 3   77

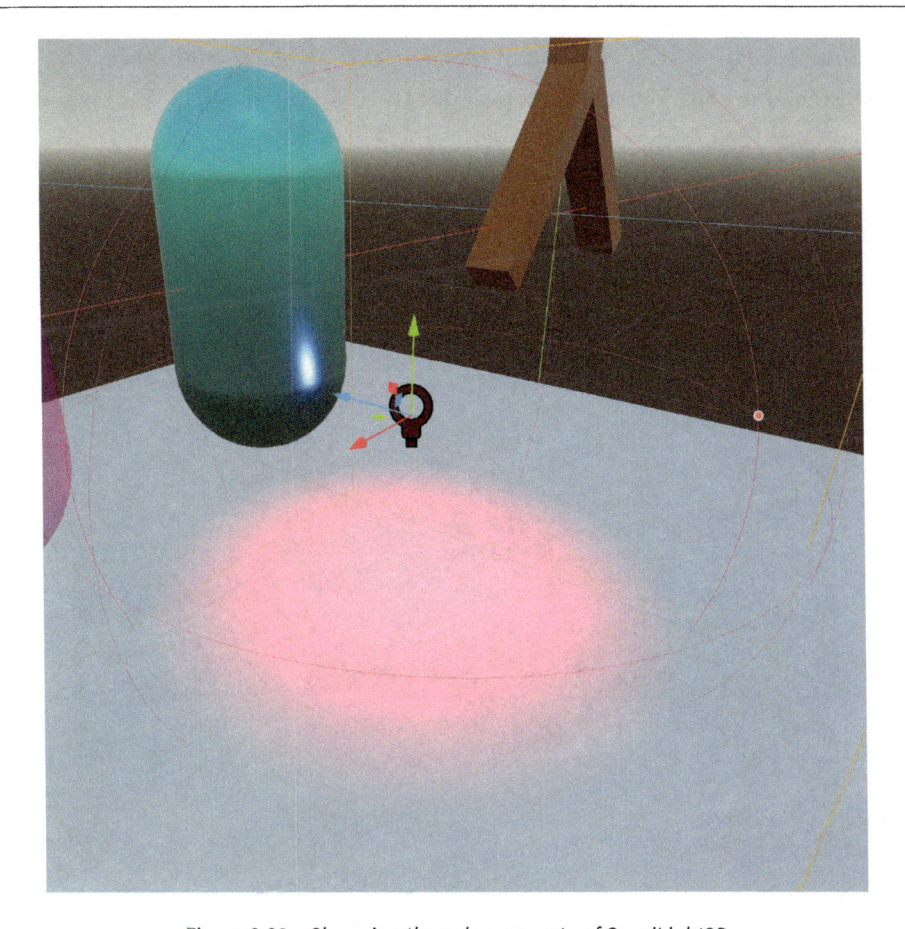

Figure 3.29 – Changing the color property of OmniLight3D

You can also enable shadows with **DirectionalLight3D**. However, to see the shadows, you would need to set the **Energy** property of **DirectionalLight3D** to 0 to turn it off. The shadow will then be cast by **OmniLight3D**. Open the **Shadow** property dropdown and enable it:

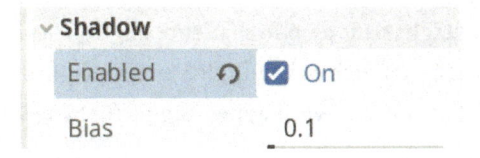

Figure 3.30 – Enabling shadows on DirectionalLight3D

Once shadows have been enabled, you can see them cast by objects in the scene, as shown in *Figure 3.31*. Sometimes shadows do not appear due to a bug in Godot 4. In that case, you should save your work and restart the engine.

Figure 3.31 – Shadows cast by DirectionalLight3D

Now we just have one more light to experiment with.

Spotlight

Just like at the theatre, **SpotLight3D** is a node that emits light in a single direction in the shape of a cone. This works well for lights such as headlights or streetlights. Disable **OmniLight3D** and **DirectionalLight3D** by clicking on the eye visibility toggle to the right of them in the scene tree.

Now add a **Spotlight3D** node to the scene. You will see the cone wireframe of the light, and again we can use the little orange circles to change the range and the angle of the light.

Chapter 3

You can see the cone of light that the spot will cast shown as a *white* cone in *Figure 3.32*:

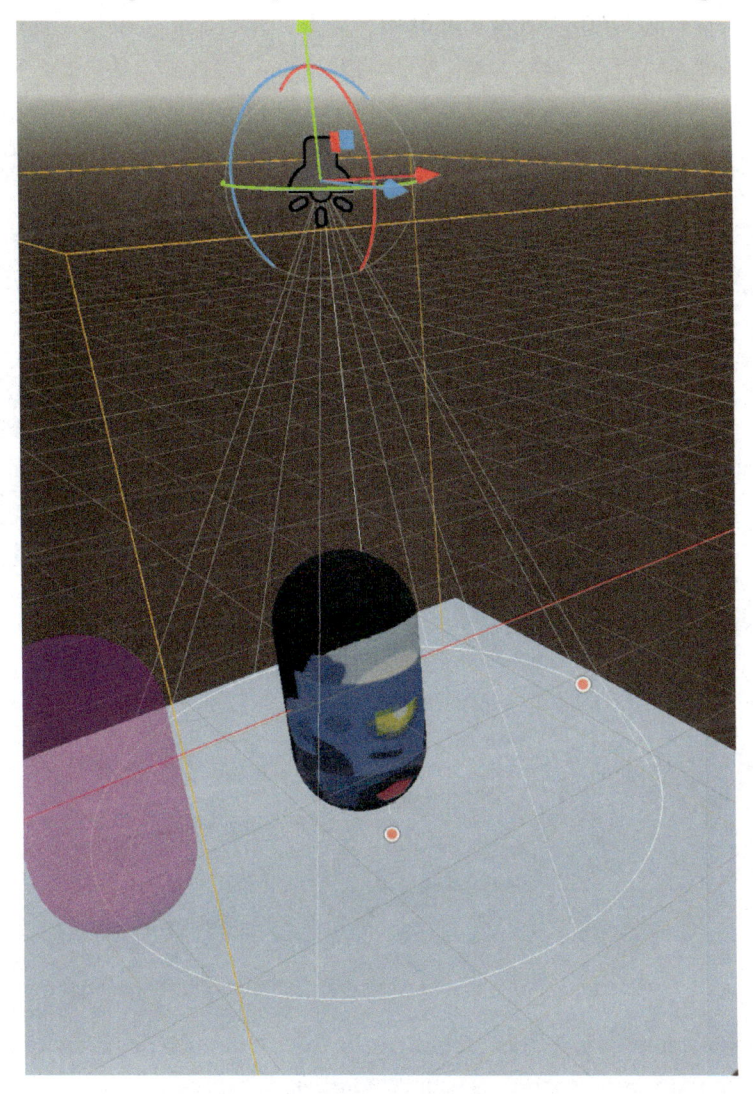

Figure 3.32 – Putting the SpotLight3D on our textured capsule mesh

Of course, we can also change the **Color** and **Energy** properties of the light, and we can enable shadows just as we did for **DirectionalLight3D**:

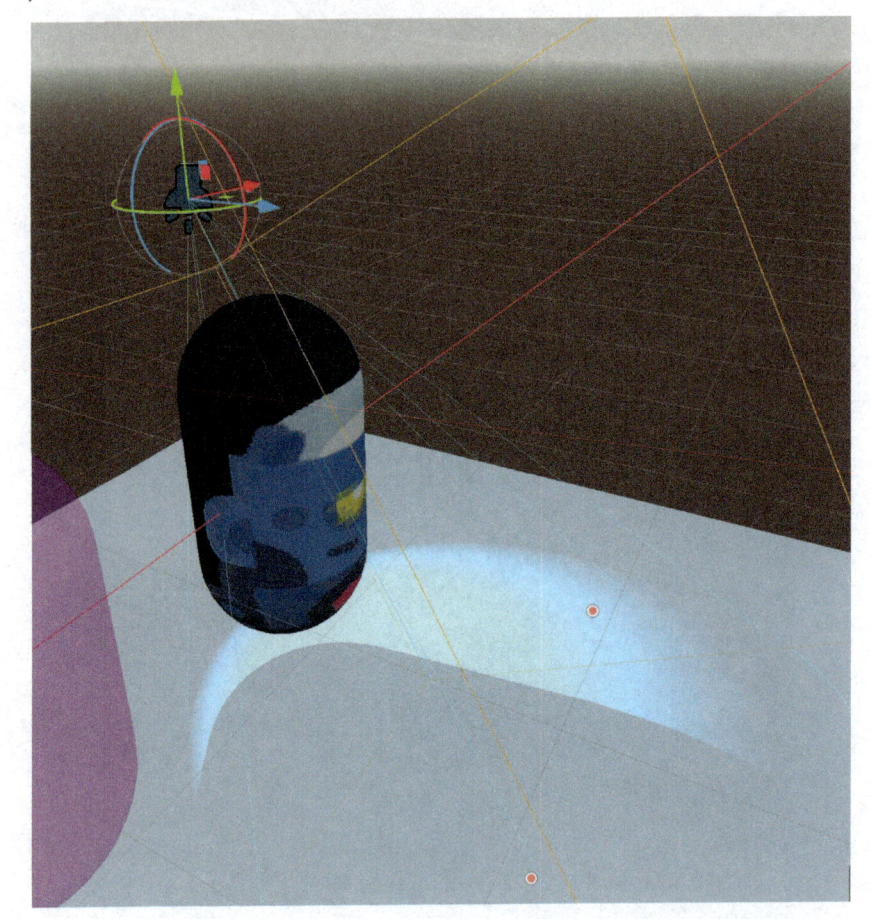

Figure 3.33 – Changing the color and angle of the spotlight and enabling shadows

Now that you know how to add and manipulate the three types of lights in Godot, you have the tools to create the right atmosphere for your 3D *Made in Godot* game.

Summary

In this chapter, you took your first steps into 3D game development with Godot. You learned how to create basic 3D objects using meshes, providing the building blocks for your scenes. We then explored how to enhance these objects by applying materials, adding color, texture, and depth to bring them to life. Finally, we introduced lighting, demonstrating how to use different types of lights to create an atmosphere, highlight important areas, and add realism to your scenes.

By mastering these skills, you now have the tools to design and illuminate simple 3D environments, setting the stage for more complex projects as you continue your journey in game development.

In the next chapter, we will be taking a detailed look at how to work with GDScript, the built-in programming language that was designed to work with Godot Engine.

Unlock this book's exclusive benefits now

Scan this QR code or go to `packtpub.com/unlock`, then search this book by name.

Note: Keep your purchase invoice ready before you start.

4

Scripting with GDScript

In this chapter, you'll begin your journey into GDScript, the scripting language at the heart of Godot. Scripting is a crucial part of game development, enabling you to control the behavior and interactions within your game world. By learning GDScript, you'll gain the ability to define game mechanics, create dynamic interactions, and build functionality that goes beyond static assets.

We'll start by showing you how to create, edit, and save scripts in Godot. Then, we'll introduce you to key programming concepts, such as variables and data types, and how they work together with Godot's order of execution. You'll explore mathematical and logical operators that allow you to perform calculations and comparisons, followed by an introduction to decision-making with `if`, `else if`, and `else` statements.

Finally, we'll delve into the use of functions, both built-in and custom, to structure your code efficiently.

In this chapter, we're going to cover the following main topics:

- Understanding GDScript
- Creating scripts
- Understanding functions
- Understanding variables
- Understanding operators
- Relational and comparison operators
- Using custom functions

By the end of this chapter, you'll have the foundational knowledge to script essential game mechanics and confidently control the logic and flow of your game.

Technical requirements

This chapter's code files are available here in the book's GitHub repository: `https://github.com/PacktPublishing/Godot-4-for-Beginners/tree/main/ch4/introtoscripting`

Visit this link to check out the video of the code being run: `https://packt.link/lmzgi`

Understanding GDScript

Godot has its own built-in scripting language, **GDScript**, a high-level, programming language that is like Python. Unlike Python, GDScript is optimized for Godot's scene-based design philosophy and can specify strict typing of variables.

Scripts are used to program custom behavior for our nodes. In the next few subheadings, we will look at how to create scripts, edit them, and save them.

Creating scripts

We've already worked with scripts, but repetition is a good teacher. So, let's remember scripts are usually attached to nodes.

Start by creating a new Godot project. I have named mine `IntroToScripting`. Now create a new 2D scene, which will give us **Node2D** as the root node in the scene tree.

Chapter 4

There are a few different ways to attach our script to this node. Select **Node2D** and, in **Inspector**, locate the **Script** property and choose **New Script...** from the **<empty>** dropdown.

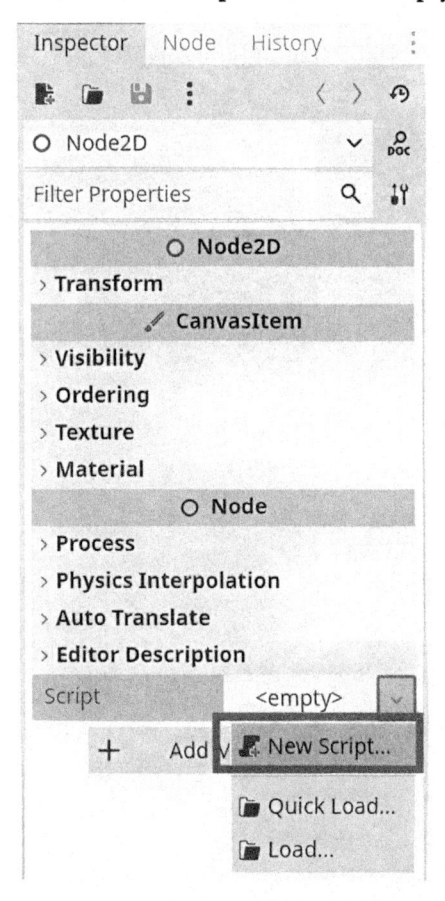

Figure 4.1 – Adding a new script via Inspector for Node

You could also *right-click* on the node you wish to attach the script to, and then click on **Attach Script...** on the pop-up menu or click on the script icon with the plus sign.

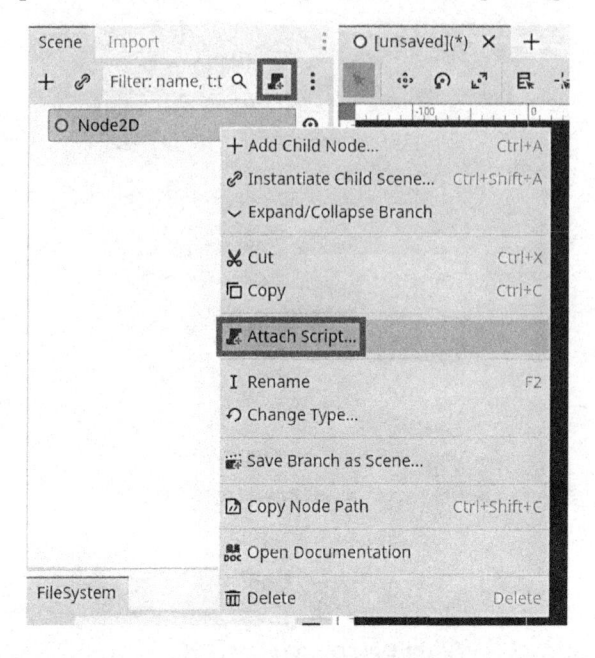

Figure 4.2 – Attaching a script by right-clicking the node

Give your script a name, such as `IntroToScripting`, and click **Create**.

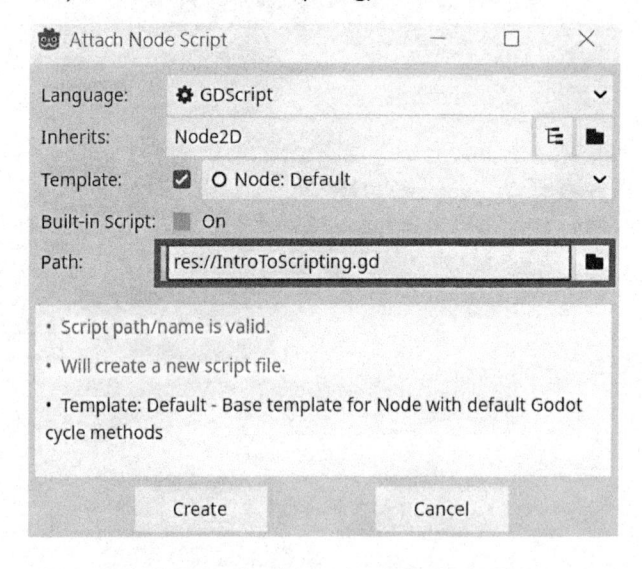

Figure 4.3 – Naming and creating the script

Chapter 4

We are now presented with the script editor. This is like a built-in **Integrated Development Environment (IDE)** for the GDScript programming language in Godot. This is a major benefit of Godot when comparing it to other engines, as you do not need to rely on a third-party program for your coding.

If you look at *Figure 4.3*, you will see we created the script with the checkbox next to **Template** *checked* to use the default node. This means that the script will be pre-populated with some code.

In *Figure 4.4*, we can see the generated code that is pre-populated in the script editor:

Figure 4.4 – The script editor

As *Figure 4.4* depicts, our script file has now appeared under **FileSystem**, with the .gd extension. Also, we can see two lists: **Filter Scripts**, which contains our new script, and **Filter Methods**, which contains the functions that exist in the script. Note that I also renamed **Node2D** to IntroToScripting to match the name of my script.

The script editor comes with code formatting. You can see the formatting because different parts of the code are different colors. This helps us understand and identify parts of the code quickly. You will notice that the func keyword is in *red*, and the function name is in *blue*. **Auto-complete** is also a feature and the editor will try to predict what you are typing and prompt you with options. This improves efficiency and helps you to find things when you are not sure what they are called.

Let's break down the code shown in *Figure 4.4* line by line:

1. **Line 1**: The extends keyword is in *red*, so we know it is a *keyword* and Node2D is in *dark green*, which means it is a *class reference*.

    GDScript is an object-oriented programming language, meaning it organizes code into *classes*. Think of a class as a blueprint for creating something. Node2D is a built-in class in Godot, already defined by the developers. By writing extends Node2D, we are telling Godot that we want to use everything Node2D can do, while also adding our own new features and behaviors.

2. **Line 4**: This line is *gray*, which means that it is a *comment*. This line is written by the programmer to explain what the code that follows it does. It helps make the code easier to understand. The hash symbol (#) tells the computer to ignore this line when running the program; it's just for humans to read.

3. **Line 5**: The func keyword is in *red*, which shows it's a special keyword in GDScript. _ready() is in light green, meaning it's a *built-in* function already created by the developers for us. The round brackets, (), tell us this is a method, and the colon, :, means that everything indented after that is part of the method.

4. **Line 6**: The pass keyword tells the computer to skip the line. You can't have an empty function, so pass stops the program from giving an error. There's also an inline comment, which is a note reminding you to replace this line with your own code to do things in this function.

5. **Line 9**: The comment here explains that the _process function runs once every frame of the game. Think of a frame as a single picture in a fast-moving animation. The game shows lots of frames per second to create smooth motion. The delta variable is the time difference between the current frame and the last one, and we use it to make sure the game's movement and animations stay smooth and consistent, no matter how fast or slow the computer running the game is.

6. **Line 10**: Once again, we see the func keyword, which tells us we are defining a function. _process is shown in green, meaning it's a built-in function provided by Godot. Inside the brackets, we see the word delta. This is a *parameter*, which is like a small piece of information that gets passed into the function to help it perform its task. In this case, delta is used to represent the time between frames, ensuring the game runs smoothly.

7. **Line 11**: The pass keyword appears again. The pass keyword tells the computer to skip this line. You can't have an empty function, so pass stops the program from giving an error.

Now that you've learned the basics of scripting, the next section will explore one of the most essential tools in GDScript: functions. We'll dive into how functions work, starting with built-in functions such as _ready and _process, which help control your game's flow and behavior.

Understanding functions

A **function** is like a set of instructions that tell the computer to do something specific. Think of it as a mini program inside your code. You give it a name, and when you *call* that name, the function runs and does its job. For example, if you had a function called player_jump(), every time you called it, the computer would follow the steps in that function to make the player jump. Functions help organize your code, so you don't have to write the same instructions repeatedly.

Some functions are built in because the people who made the programming language or engine (like Godot) have already created them to handle common or essential tasks.

For example, there's a built-in function that tells the game to update the screen every frame. You don't have to write that yourself because it's something almost every game needs, and it saves you time.

But we also need to write our own functions because every game or program is different. You might want to make a function that moves a character in a special way or checks whether a player has won a level. Since only you know exactly what your game needs to do, you can create custom functions to handle those specific tasks.

In Godot, built-in functions such as _ready and _process play a vital role in controlling how your game behaves and updates over time. Here's what each of these functions does:

- _ready: The _ready function is like the *starting point* for a node. Think of it as the moment when everything is set up and ready to go, like when the curtains rise at the start of a play. The _ready function is the first function that runs once the node is in the scene tree along with all its children. Nodes are loaded from the bottom to the top and child nodes are loaded before their parent. You can put any code inside this function that you want to run right when the object is ready, such as showing a character on the screen or starting an animation.

- **_process**: The _process function is like the *heartbeat* of your game object. It runs repeatedly, once for every frame (like every snapshot of your game). You use it to update things continuously, such as moving a character or keeping track of the time. The delta inside the function is a small value that tells you how much time has passed since the last frame, so you can make sure everything happens smoothly, no matter how fast or slow the computer runs the game.

Now that you understand how functions work, you can take on board the concept of the game loop.

Understanding the game loop

Most games run inside a loop that keeps updating what's happening in the game—such as moving characters, checking for collisions, and drawing graphics to the screen. This is called the **game loop**. It runs many times per second (often 60 times per second or more), and every time it runs, it updates and redraws the game.

In Godot, you don't usually write the loop yourself. Instead, Godot handles it for you and gives you special functions you can use to plug into the game loop. The three most common ones are discussed in the subsequent sections.

_ready()

This function is called once when the node and its children are added to the scene tree and are ready to go. It's like setting up your LEGO model before the game starts.

Use _ready() to do the following:

- Set initial values
- Connect signals
- Hide or show things at the start
- Prepare anything that only needs to happen once

_process(delta)

This function runs every frame. It's used for things that should happen constantly such as checking input, changing animations, or moving something smoothly.

Use _process(delta) for the following:

- Player input
- Animations

- UI updates
- Non-physics-related updates

Note that `delta` is the amount of time (in seconds) since the last frame. This helps you keep movement smooth even if the frame rate changes.

_physics_process(delta)

This is like `_process`, but it runs at a fixed rate (by default, 60 times per second). This makes it perfect for anything involving physics, such as moving a character with collision.

Use `_physics_process(delta)` for the following:

- Physics calculations
- Movement with `move_and_slide()` or `move_and_collide()`
- Gravity and jumping

To demonstrate how the `physics_process` function works, follow these steps:

1. Create a new scene with **Sprite2D** as the root node, as shown in *Figure 4.5*:

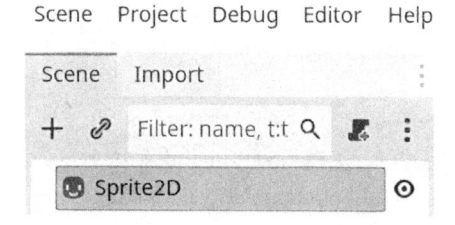

Figure 4.5 – A Sprite2D node as the root of the scene

2. Use the Godot `icon.svg` file as the texture for the sprite.
3. Attach a script to the node by right-clicking on it and choosing **Attach Script...** or clicking on the script icon with the + symbol. Add the following code to the script:

```
extends Sprite2D
var speed = 100
var velocity = Vector2.ZERO

func _ready():
    print("Sprite is ready to move!")

func _process(delta):
```

```
    # Check input and set direction
    velocity = Vector2.ZERO
    if Input.is_action_pressed("ui_right"):
        velocity.x += 1
    if Input.is_action_pressed("ui_left"):
        velocity.x -= 1

func _physics_process(delta):
    # Move the sprite using physics
    position += velocity * speed * delta
```

> **Quick tip**: Enhance your coding experience with the **AI Code Explainer** and **Quick Copy** features. Open this book in the next-gen Packt Reader. Click the **Copy** button (1) to quickly copy code into your coding environment, or click the **Explain** button (2) to get the AI assistant to explain a block of code to you.

```
function calculate(a, b) {
  return {sum: a + b};
};
```

The next-gen Packt Reader is included for free with the purchase of this book. Scan the QR code OR go to packtpub.com/unlock, then use the search bar to find this book by name. Double-check the edition shown to make sure you get the right one.

When you run the scene, you will see the message appear in the **Output** window once the scene loads, then you can move the sprite to the left and the right using the arrow keys and the game loop constantly updates the screen.

In the next section, we'll explore one of the most fundamental aspects of programming—**variables**. You'll learn what variables are, how they store data, and how they are used to manage game information such as player stats, scores, and more.

Understanding variables

Think of a variable like a labeled box where you can store information. Just like how you can put something inside a box and come back to use it later, a variable holds a piece of information, such as a number or a word, that you can use and change while your program runs.

For example, if you're making a game and want to keep track of the player's health, you would create a variable called health. Every time the player finds a heart or gets injured, you can add to or subtract from the health variable. It helps your program remember and work with data, just like a box holds your stuff until you need it.

We can store different types of data in our variables, but the most common ones are as follows:

- Integers (whole numbers) such as 1, 2, 3
- Real numbers (floating point or decimal numbers) such as 0.1, 0.2, 0.3
- Strings of text (collections of characters) such as Hello World, ABC, "@:!3"
- Boolean values (true and false values) such as True, False, 0, 1

In the next section, we'll explore variables, a fundamental concept in programming. You'll learn how to define variables in Godot and follow best practices for organizing them in your scripts.

Creating a variable

It is good practice in programming to put our variables at the top of our script under the class definition or extension of that class. We will put ours under the extends Node2D line.

Variables need to be defined by giving them a name and a value to store. We write the var keyword to tell the compiler that this is a variable. Now we identify our variable by giving it a name (we will use the name health). To assign it a value, we use the equals sign. This is called the **assignment operator** in programming, and it is not the same as *equality* in mathematics. Its role is to assign the value on its right to the variable on its left.

Finally, we must assign a starting or default value – in this case, we will set health to 100:

```
extends Node2D
var health = 100
```

Creating the variable and assigning a value only serves to store the value in the computer's memory. We can access this value by using the name of the variable. We can then do something with the value such as outputting it to the screen.

To do that, we need to call the built-in print function and give it the name of our variable to print. We can only display this value once the node is ready. The best place to call the print function is from the _ready function:

```
extends Node2D
var health = 100

#Called when the node enters the scene tree for the first time.
func _ready():
    print(health)
```

Next, run the program. Choose to use the current scene as the main scene if prompted. Note that you will not see any output in the game window. Instead, the value will be displayed in the console of the **Output** window.

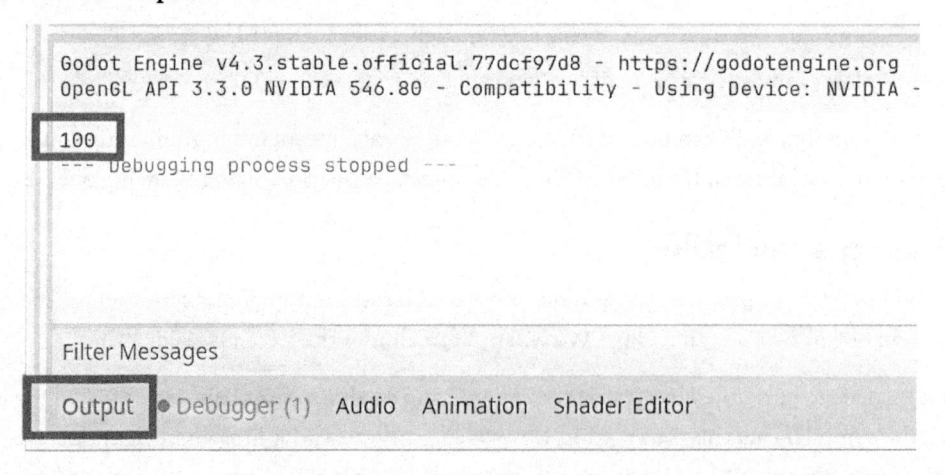

Figure 4.6 – The value of the health variable is displayed in the Output console

With variables established, it's important to understand the different types of data they can hold. In the next section, we'll explore data types, which define the kind of information your variables store, from numbers to text and beyond.

Data types

I touched on the different types of data that we can store in variables at the start of the chapter. It might help to think of data types like different kinds of containers for holding specific kinds of information. Just like you wouldn't store water in a paper box or keep food in a bottle, in programming, you use different *types* of variables depending on the kind of data you're working with.

Here are some examples:

- Numbers go in a container called int (for whole numbers) or float (for numbers with decimals)
- Text goes into a container called string, representing characters grouped together like individual beads on a string (letters, numbers, or symbols)
- Boolean holds only true or false—like a simple yes or no answer

Using the right type helps the program know what to expect and how to handle the information.

Since GDScript, like Python, is a dynamic programming language, we *do not* have to specify the type of variable we want to store. This makes programming much faster. However, as a program gets larger, and more team members are working on the project, it is easier to find errors and bugs by specifying the data type of the variable.

This will prevent people from trying to store the wrong type of data in the wrong variable.

We could change our health variable as follows:

```
extends Node2D
var health : int = 100
```

This will not affect the program output.

When we want to make fine adjustments to a value, for example, to have more granular control over the player's jump height, we can use float. This is a decimal number, and it can be created as follows:

```
extends Node2D
var health : int = 100
var jump_strength : float = 220.5
```

In this code, we're declaring a variable called `jump_strength` and specifying that its data type is `float`, which allows it to store decimal numbers. By setting it to 220.5, we're giving more precise control over how high a character can jump, as decimal values offer finer adjustments than whole numbers. This is especially useful for game mechanics such as jump height, where small tweaks can have a big impact on gameplay.

In the next section, we'll explore naming conventions in programming, which are important guidelines for how to name your variables, functions, and other elements. Following these conventions not only makes your code easier to read and understand but also helps avoid errors and confusion as your project grows.

Naming conventions

The way that we name our nodes, scenes, variables, and functions is important too. Naming conventions are like guidelines for how we name things in programming, such as variables, functions, or classes. They help make your code easier to read and understand, not only for you but also for others who might work on your project.

Good naming conventions make it clear what something does. Imagine if you named everything randomly, such as calling your player's score x and your enemy's health y. It would be confusing and hard to follow, especially in big projects.

By following naming conventions, you keep your code organized and readable, making it easier to maintain and share with others.

The naming conventions used by GDScript and Godot developers are as follows:

- **snake_case**: This is used for scenes, variables, and functions. It is called `snake_case` because each new word is connected with an underscore, making the combination look like a little snake.
- **SCREAMING_SNAKE_CASE**: This is used for constants. All alphabetic characters are uppercase.
- **PascalCase**: This is used for classes and nodes in the scene. Each new word begins with a capital letter.

The most important element when naming things is that the name should be meaningful and descriptive so that the program becomes self-documenting.

Often, for cooldowns and testing the state of things in play, we will use a Boolean value. An example could be to check if the player is currently dashing:

```
extends Node2D
var health : int = 100
var jump_strength : float = 220.5
var is_dashing : bool = true
```

In the preceding code, a Boolean variable called `is_dashing` is being declared and initialized with the value true. This means that the player is currently in a dashing state. Boolean variables like this one are often used to track whether a certain condition is true or false in the game.

The last variable we will look at here is String. A **String** is used to store combinations of characters and, most often, we use this for storing text. Note that when we define String, we write it with a capital letter. This is because String is a class and is different from the other data types as it is not primitive. Additionally, String has many methods associated with it. We could use String to store the name of the player.

In the next example, we declare and initialize a String variable. Strings are used to store text, such as a player's name. The following line of code creates a variable called `player_name` and assigns it a default value of `"Unknown Player"`. This allows us to store and display a player's name in the game.

If you look at the following code, you will notice that strings are assigned their own unique golden color so that they are easily spotted in your code.

```
extends Node2D
var health : int = 100
var jump_strength : float = 220.5
var is_dashing : bool = true
var player_name : String = "Unknown Player"
```

In the upcoming section, we'll explore the concept of order of operations in programming. Understanding how operations are executed in a specific sequence is crucial for writing accurate and efficient code. This ensures that calculations and logic are performed in the correct order to achieve the desired outcomes.

Understanding operators

Operators are the symbols used to carry out operations in programming.

These operators are essential tools that allow you to perform different operations such as mathematical calculations, comparisons, and logical evaluations, helping you control how your code behaves and interacts with data.

First, let's look at the **mathematical operators**:

- **Addition**: The + sign is used to increase the value of a variable by an amount
- **Subtraction**: The – sign is used to decrease the value of a variable by an amount
- **Multiplication**: The * sign is used to multiply the value of a variable by another value
- **Division**: The / sign is used to divide the value of a variable by another value

We can experiment with using these operators with the `player_level` variable in our program.

In our code, the player's level is 23. If we add 7, it will be 30. Look at the _ready function here to see this in action:

```
func _ready():
    print(player_name)
    print(player_level)
    print(player_exp)
    print(has_key)
    
    player_level = player+level + 7
    print(player_level)
```

You will notice now that the output is first 23, and then, when it prints again, it changes to 30.

It's important to note that assignment operations work from right to left. In this case, we are taking the value 7, adding it to the current value of `player_level`, and then using the assignment operator (=) to store the result back into the `player_level` variable on the left side. This means the existing value of `player_level` is updated with the new result.

When programming, we always want to focus on efficiency, and this means avoiding repetition. As you can see, we repeated the variable name. To avoid this in the future, we can use a new operator called the **shortcut operator**, and we can refactor our code more efficiently as follows:

```
#player_level = player_level + 7
player_level += 7
print(player_level)
```

If we wanted to reduce the level to 0, we could subtract 30:

```
player_level -= 30
print(player_level)
```

We can do the same for multiplication and division:

```
25  >|   player_level *= 2
26  >|   print (player_level)
27  >|
28  >|   player_level /= 2
29  >|   print (player_level)
```

Figure 4.7 – Multiplication and division

You can also add variables together. If we create a variable called spike_damage, then every time the player hits some spikes, we can reduce their health by that value:

```
30  >|   var spike_damage : int = 10
31  >|   print(health)
32  >|   health -= spike_damage
33  >|   print(health)
```

Figure 4.8 – Using the spike_damage variable

Before we start solving more complex expressions, it's important to understand the order in which operations are carried out in maths.

Order of operations

Although the computer runs one line at a time from the top of the program to the bottom, just like in cooking, where you need to do things in a certain order (like mixing ingredients before baking), in math and programming, there's a specific order in which calculations are done.

The order of operations tells the computer which parts of a calculation to do first. Here's a simple way to remember it using **PEMDAS**:

- **Parentheses**: Do the calculations inside parentheses first
- **Exponents**: Then, calculate powers or roots (such as squaring a number)
- **Multiplication and Division**: Next, do multiplication and division from left to right
- **Addition and Subtraction**: Finally, do addition and subtraction from left to right

For example, in the expression *3 + 5 * 2*, the computer will first do the multiplication (*5 * 2 = 10*), and then the addition (*3 + 10 = 13*), because multiplication comes before addition in the order of operations.

Understanding this is important because it ensures that your calculations are done correctly!

Practice exercise

To practice using variables, try creating four variables that could be used to store information about a player. Each of these variables should use a different data type.

This exercise also introduces an important concept: variable scope – watch out for it in the explanation below.

The four variables are as follows:

- Player name
- Player level
- Player experience points
- Does the player have the key or not?

The solution to the exercise is as follows:

- `var player_name : String = "Riptide"`
- `var player_level : int = 23`
- `var player_exp : float = 123.45`
- `var has_key : bool = false`

We can print all of them, each on a new line in the _ready function:

```
func _ready():
    print(player_name)
    print(player_level)
    print(player_exp)
    print(has_key)
```

Executing the preceding code will print the values to the console.

> Variable scope
>
> In the preceding solution, a variable was declared and initialized within the _ready function. This limits the variable's scope to local, meaning it is only accessible within the _ready function where it was declared. Unlike class variables (which are defined at the top of the program and accessible throughout the class), local variables can only be used in the specific function or block of code where they are defined. This is known as **variable scope**.

In the next section, we'll explore relational and comparison operators in Godot. These operators allow you to compare values, helping your code make decisions by checking conditions such as whether one value is greater than, less than, or equal to another.

Relational and comparison operators

Often, we need to compare values to determine whether they meet a specific condition—true or false. This allows our code to branch and perform different actions based on the result of the comparison. To evaluate these conditions, we use relational operators, which help us compare values.

The different operators available for comparison are as follows:

- **Equality**: Two equals signs (==) are used to test if two values are the same
- **Greater than**: Using angle brackets (>), we can compare if one value is bigger
- **Greater than or equal to**: Using (>=), we can test if the value is bigger than or the same as another value
- **Less than**: Using angle brackets (<), we can compare if one value is smaller

- **Less than or equal to**: Using angle brackets (<=) with an equals sign, we can test if the value is smaller or the same as another value
- **Not equals**: Using an exclamation mark and an equals sign (!-), we can test if one value is not the same as another value

We use these operators with `if` statements, which are fundamental in programming. These `if` statements allow us to check if a condition is true, and only when it is true does the block of code inside the statement run. This makes our game more flexible, enabling it to perform different actions depending on the result of the tested conditions.

All of this is demonstrated in the following code:

```
var player_lives : int = 3
if health == 0:
    player_lives -= 1

if player_lives < 1:
    print("GAME OVER!")

if player_lives <= 0:
    print("GAME OVER!")

if spike_damage > health:
    print("GAME OVER!")

if player_exp >= 1000:
    player_level += 1
    print("LEVEL UP")

if has_key != true:
    print("DOOR LOCKED")
```

In the preceding code, our game produces different output based on the value of the variables being compared.

To make our game respond differently based on certain conditions, we can use the `if`, `elif`, and `else` keywords. The `if` statement checks if a condition is *true* and runs the code inside it. If the condition is `false`, we can use `elif` (short for `else if`) to check another condition. Finally, `else` is used as a *default* that runs if none of the previous conditions are true.

For example, let's say we want to check the number of lives a player has and respond accordingly, as shown in the following code:

```
if player_lives > 0:
    print("Keep playing!")
elif player_lives == 0:
    print("Game Over!")
else:
    print("Invalid number of lives!")
```

The preceding code allows the player to continue playing if they have lives remaining; if they do not, it prints the game over and, for abnormal values, it shows an error.

Practice exercise

To get some experience with the concept, write a script that checks the player's health using the health variable we created. Display different messages based on their health status.

- If health is 80 or more, print "You're in great shape!"
- If health is between 50 and 79, print "You're doing okay, but be careful!"
- If health is below 50, print "Warning! Your health is low!"
- If health is 0 or less, print "Game over! You've run out of health."

Use if, elif, and else statements to complete this task.

The solution is given here:

```
# Check the player's health and print the appropriate message
if health >= 80:
    print("You're in great shape!")
elif health >= 50:
    print("You're doing okay, but be careful!")
elif health > 0:
    print("Warning! Your health is low!")
else:
    print("Game over! You've run out of health.")
```

The preceding code displays the correct message depending on the value of the player's health variable.

In the next section, we'll dive into creating custom functions in Godot. You'll learn how to define your own functions to organize your code, make it reusable, and add unique functionality to your game projects.

Using custom functions

Part of keeping our code clean and organized involves creating our own custom functions. Custom functions allow us to break down our code into smaller, reusable pieces, making it easier to understand and maintain. We aren't limited to only using functions that come with Godot—we can define our own to perform specific tasks in our game.

To create a custom function, we use the `func` keyword, followed by the function name (this is how we will identify the function in the code). After the name, we add two round brackets `()` that can hold any information (parameters) we want to pass to the function. Finally, we end the function header with a colon (:), and on the next line, we define what the function will do (this is called the function body).

We already have a variable that stores how much damage a spike does. What if we wrote a custom function that could be called every time we are hit by a spike:

```
# Custom function to handle spike damage and return remaining #health
func take_spike_damage():
    health -= damage_amount
    if health <= 0:
        print("Game Over")
        return 0 # Return 0 if health is depleted
    else:
        print("Player's current health: ", health)
```

The preceding code can be called (asked to run) whenever the player takes damage from a spike.

For the preceding code to work, we need to move `spike_damage` to the top to make it a class (script) variable. This is demonstrated here:

```
extends Node2D
var health : int = 100
var jump_strength : float = 220.5
var is_dashing : bool = true
var player_name : String = "Riptide"
var player_level : int = 23
```

```
var player_exp : float = 123.45
var has_key : bool = false
var spike_damage : int = 10
```

In the preceding code, the spike_damage variable has been moved to the top of the program to change its scope to include the entire script (class).

To run the code in our take_spike_damage function, we need to call it. This will depend on the context of the game but, for our example, we will call it from the _ready function:

```
# Called when the node enters the scene tree for the first time.
func _ready():
    take_spike_damage()
```

In the preceding code, we call the take_spike_damage() function (ask it to run), and all the code inside the function runs, and the game is updated with the result.

In the upcoming section, we'll explore arguments and parameters in functions. You'll learn how to pass information into your custom functions to make them more flexible and dynamic, allowing you to control their behavior based on the values you provide.

Arguments and parameters or function inputs

Functions can accept input values and produce output, allowing us to write adaptable, reusable code. These inputs, referred to as parameters in GDScript, let us pass information to a function when it's called. The data we send to the function is known as an **argument**, and the **parameter** works like a placeholder variable that holds this value within the function.

For example, in Godot's built-in _process(delta) function, the delta parameter is passed in, representing the time elapsed since the previous frame. Parameters make it possible for functions to behave differently depending on the data they receive, giving us flexibility in our code.

We can update the `take_spike_damage()` function to accept a parameter that defines how much damage a spike causes. This way, the function can handle different damage values whenever it's called:

```
# Custom function to handle spike damage with a parameter
func take_spike_damage(damage_amount):
    health -= damage_amount
    if health <= 0:
        print("Game Over")
    else:
        print("Player's current health: ", health)
```

In the preceding code, we have added a parameter to our function so that we can change the amount of damage each spike does.

Remember, we must change the call to the function too since we must provide a value for the damage amount:

```
# Called when the node enters the scene tree for the first time.
func _ready():
    #Calling the function with different damage values
    take_spike_damage(10) #Spike causes 10 damage
    take_spike_damage(5) #Spike causes 5 damage
```

In the preceding code, we have to remember to provide the amount of damage the spike does to our function.

In the next section, we'll look at how functions can return output in Godot by using the `return` keyword. This allows a function to send back a result or value after performing its task, which can then be used elsewhere in your game.

Functions can return output

Functions don't just accept inputs; they can also produce outputs. In programming, this is achieved through **return values**. A return value is the result that a function provides after performing its task. By using the `return` keyword, you can send a value back to the place where the function was called. This allows functions to perform calculations or data processing and then give back the result for further use.

We can modify our previous example to include a function that calculates and returns the player's remaining health after taking damage. This will demonstrate how functions can provide useful results.

```
# Custom function to handle spike damage and return remaining health
func take_spike_damage(damage_amount) -> int:
    health -= damage_amount
    if health <= 0:
        print("Game Over")
        return 0 # Return 0 if health is depleted
    else:
        print("Player's current health: ", health)
        return health # Return the remaining health
```

In the preceding code, we have changed our function to return the value of the player's health variable.

We also need to modify our call to the function and store and use the result:

```
# Called when the node enters the scene tree for the first time.
func _ready():
    #Example of using the function and storing the returned value
    var remaining_health = take_spike_damage(10)
    #Assume damage_amount is 10
    print("Remaining Health: ", remaining_health)
```

In the preceding code, we now store the result returned by the function in a new variable, which we then print out.

It is time to practice what was learned.

Create a function to manage player health based on damage taken. To do that, follow these steps:

1. Create a function called `calculate_health_after_damage`.
2. This function should have two parameters: `current_health` and `damage`.
3. Inside the function, subtract `damage` from `current_health` and return the new health value.

This is an example of the use of the function when calling it:

```
#Called when the node enters the scene tree for the first time.
func _ready():
    var player_health = 100
    var spike_damage = 20
    var new_health = calculate_health_after_damage(player_health, spike_damage)
    print("Player's new health:", new_health)
```

In the preceding code, we store the result of calculating the player's health after taking damage in a new variable and we then print out that result.

The solution to the exercise is shown here:

```
# Define the function to calculate the player's health after taking damage
func calculate_health_after_damage(current_health: int, damage: int) -> int:
    var new_health = current_health - damage
    return new_health
```

In the preceding code, the solution shows that we have to declare a function that accepts two arguments, subtracts them, and returns the result as an integer.

Summary

In this chapter, we explored essential GDScript concepts, from creating, editing, and saving scripts to understanding variables, data types, and the order of execution. We also delved into mathematical and logical operators, control flow using `if`, `elif`, and `else` statements, and the importance of built-in and custom functions such as `ready` and `process`. These skills are crucial for scripting fundamental game mechanics, giving you the tools to start building dynamic, interactive game worlds.

In the next chapter, we'll take a deep dive into vectors—a vital concept for game development that underpins movement, direction, and positioning in your game. Understanding vectors is the next logical step, as they play a key role in controlling the flow and interaction of objects in 2D or 3D space.

Join our community on Discord

Join our community's Discord space for discussions with the author and other readers:

`https://packt.link/godot-4-game-dev`

Part 2

Working with the Godot Engine

In this part of the book, you'll deepen your practical knowledge of how to work effectively with the Godot engine. We'll begin by demystifying vectors, one of the most essential tools in any game developer's toolkit, through clear explanations and real-world examples. Then, you'll put your skills into action by building a complete 2D mini-game over two chapters. This hands-on project will guide you through the full game creation process, from scripting player mechanics to designing levels and handling game logic. By the end of this part, you'll have the experience and confidence to start building your own 2D games in Godot.

This part of the book includes the following chapters:

- *Chapter 5, Understanding Vectors*
- *Chapter 6, Creating a 2D Mini-Game in Godot – Part 1*
- *Chapter 7, Creating a 2D Mini-Game in Godot – Part 2*

5
Understanding Vectors

Vectors are one of the most fundamental concepts in game development, helping developers represent direction, movement, and positioning in both 2D and 3D space. In this chapter, you'll dive into the basics of what vectors are and why they play a vital role in game mechanics. You'll learn how to use vectors effectively within the Godot engine—both through the visual interface and in code—to control and influence your game objects.

In this chapter, we're going to cover the following main topics:

- What are vectors?
- Using vectors in Godot

By the end of this chapter, you will have gained a practical understanding of how to manipulate vectors, apply them to movement, and solve game development problems that involve direction and position. Whether you're developing a platformer, an RPG, or a 3D adventure game, mastering vectors will provide you with powerful tools to control player movement, enemy AI, and environmental interactions.

Technical requirements

This chapter's code files are available here in the book's GitHub repository: `https://github.com/PacktPublishing/Godot-4-for-Beginners/tree/main/ch5/vectors`

Visit this link to check out the video of the code being run: `https://packt.link/6sNsX`

What are vectors?

If you're familiar with the idea of a point, think of a **vector** as similar but with a key difference: a vector not only represents a *position* in space but also includes information about *direction* and *magnitude* (how far and in what direction it moves from its starting point, or origin). A **point**, on the other hand, is just a location and doesn't include any information about direction or movement. This is shown in *Figure 5.1*:

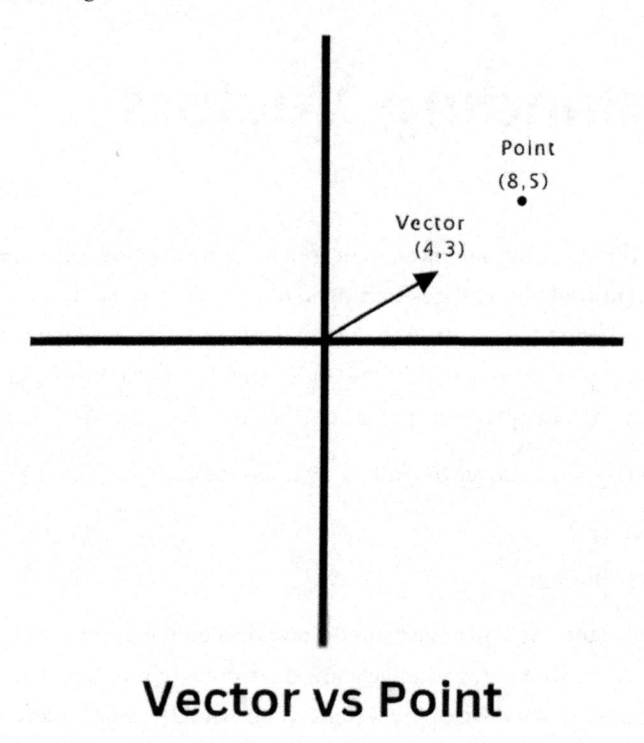

Vector vs Point

Figure 5.1 – Demonstration of a vector versus a point in 2D space

In *Figure 5.1*, the vector is shown as an arrow. The arrowhead indicates the *direction* in which the vector is pointing, while the length of the arrow (from the tail to the head) represents its *magnitude*, or how far it extends from its starting point. The point at position **(8,5)** is a static location and has no direction or magnitude.

Chapter 5

If we draw an arrow from the origin to the point that we defined, we have created a vector. This is shown in *Figure 5.2*:

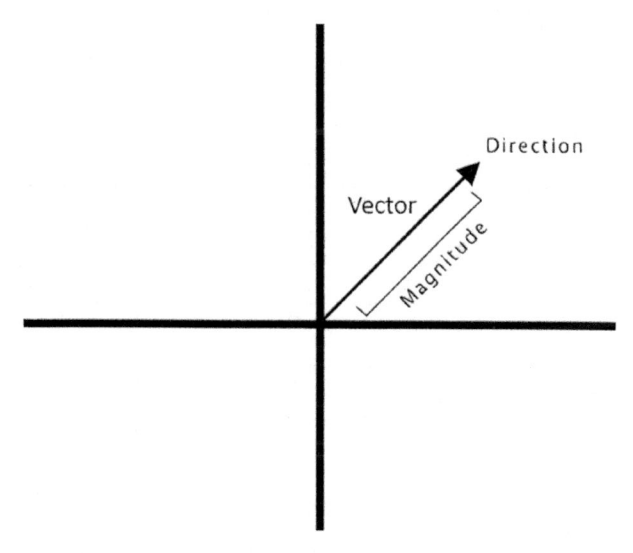

Figure 5.2 – A vector has a direction (angle) and a magnitude

In video games, vectors are used to represent a player's velocity, control their aiming direction, and determine their field of view (the direction they are facing)—all with a single vector. At the same time, we use a point to track the player's position continuously. This is shown in *Figure 5.3*:

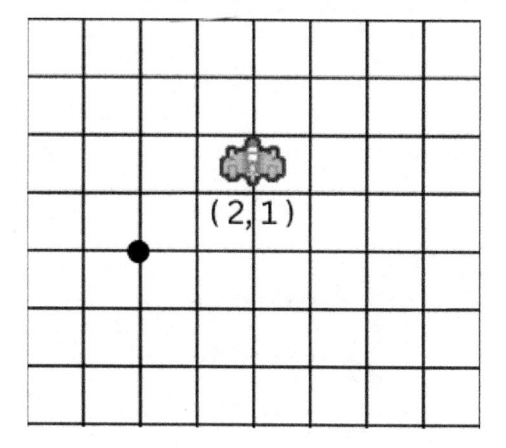

Figure 5.3 – A point representing the current position of the player

In *Figure 5.3*, we can see that the player is **2** units east of the origin and **1** unit north.

Velocity is the speed of something in a specific direction. In game development, it's used to describe how fast and in what direction an object, such as a player or enemy, is moving. Velocity is often represented by a vector, which shows both the *speed* (magnitude) and *direction* of movement.

If we wanted our player to move up and to the left, we could use a velocity vector of **(-2,3)** to do so. This is represented in *Figure 5.4*:

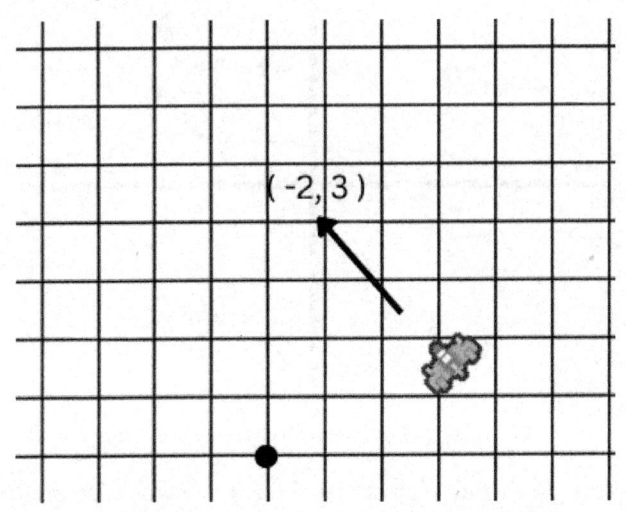

Figure 5.4 – A vector depicting the velocity of the player

In *Figure 5.4*, the *velocity vector* indicates that the player will move **2** units left and **3** units up. Note that the *x* coordinate is always given before the *y* coordinate.

Vectors can also tell us which direction the player is facing. *Figure 5.5* shows how a vector can be used to indicate the direction the player is facing in the game.

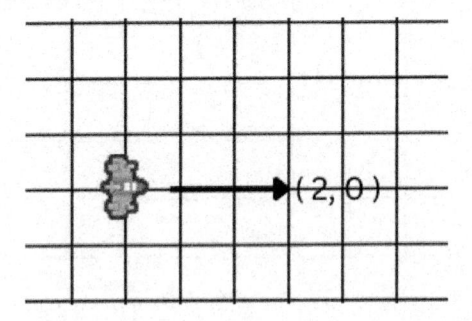

Figure 5.5 – A vector to indicate direction

In *Figure 5.5*, the *direction vector* tells us that the player is pointing to the right (rotated 90 degrees).

On their own, vectors are just numbers—they don't have much meaning without context. For example, the vector (1, 0) could represent direction, position, or velocity depending on how it's used. To make these vectors meaningful, we need to assign units. In Godot, 2D units are measured in *pixels*, while 3D units are measured in *meters*.

For instance, if we have a player character in a 2D game, the vector (1, 0) represents a movement to the right. In this case, the following applies:

- The "1" means the player moves one unit (or pixel) in the horizontal direction (*x* axis)
- The "0" means the player doesn't move up or down (*y* axis)

If the player moves according to this vector in every frame, the character will steadily move to the right by 1 pixel each frame.

When we only want direction without caring about the distance or speed, we can *normalize* the vector. A **normalized vector** has a length (or magnitude) of 1 and still points in the same direction. This is especially useful when combining direction with other values, such as when multiplying a direction vector by a speed to get velocity.

For example, if we normalize the vector (2, 0), we get (1, 0). It still points right, but now has a standard length of 1, making it easy to scale consistently in game logic.

Coordinates in Godot

An important quirk of screens is that the origin **(0, 0)** is in the top-left corner of the screen. This means that **y** is negative as we move upward and positive as we go downward. This is shown by the vector **(4, 3)** in *Figure 5.6*:

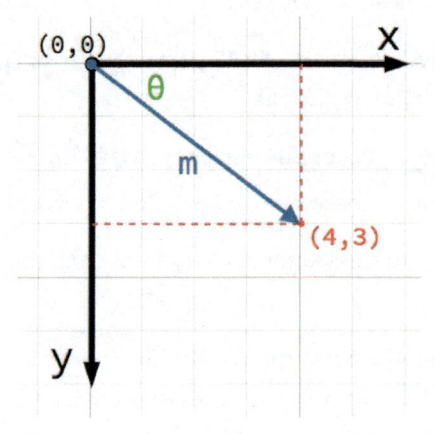

Figure 5.6 – Computers render the screen downward from the top left (This image is by Godot Engine contributors and is licensed under CC BY 3.0)

In *Figure 5.6*, the vector **(4, 3)** has a direction or rotation of angle **theta** and a length or magnitude of **m**. In this case, the *arrow* is a position vector indicating a point in space relative to the origin.

One important thing to remember about vectors is that they usually show direction and size (how far or fast something moves), but not the starting position. Think of a vector like an arrow: it shows you which way to go and how fast, but not where you are on the map. To know the actual position of an object, you need to combine the vector with a starting point or reference.

However, there's a special case that's worth mentioning: **position vectors**. In mathematics and game development (including Godot), a vector such as Vector2(2, 3) can also represent a position in 2D space. This type of vector is understood to start at the origin (0, 0) and point to the coordinates (2, 3). In this case, the vector tells you where something is located relative to the origin.

So, depending on the context, vectors can do either of the following:

- Show how far and in what direction something is moving (velocity or force)
- Indicate a position relative to the origin (like coordinates in space)

Chapter 5

Understanding this difference helps avoid confusion, especially when working with movement systems, physics, or spatial reasoning in your games. If you invert a position vector; you effectively point back from the position to the origin—another helpful way to understand how vectors work in different contexts.

For example, in a game, a vector can tell you which way a player is moving and how fast, but the player's starting position is given separately as a point. This is demonstrated in *Figure 5.7*:

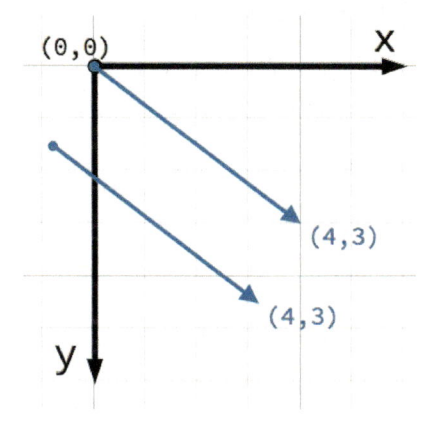

Figure 5.7 – Two identical vectors (This image is by Godot Engine contributors and is licensed under CC BY 3.0)

In *Figure 5.7*, both vectors represent a point of **4** units to the right and **3** units below the starting point.

We now have a conceptual understanding of vectors. In the next section, we can look at how to implement them in Godot.

Using vectors in Godot

In Godot, there are two classes to represent vectors. 2D vectors use **Vector2** and 3D vectors use **Vector3**. Vector2 accepts an *x* and a *y* parameter, and Vector3 accepts *x*, *y*, and *z* parameters. Let's take a look at Vector2 in more detail.

Vector2 is a **class**, which means it's not just a simple data type like a number—it's a more advanced structure that includes built-in functions (or methods) to work with 2D coordinates. While it behaves like a data type because it holds two numbers (*x* and *y*), it also allows you to perform operations such as adding, scaling, or rotating vectors.

It's worth noting that Godot handles many values that might seem like simple types as classes. For example, as mentioned in *Chapter 4*, even *text* in Godot is managed by the `String` class. This is a bit different from some other engines or languages, where strings are considered basic types without methods.

So, when you're working with something such as `Vector2`, you're really working with a powerful tool that's designed to help you easily manage 2D positions, directions, and movements in your game, with lots of useful functions built right in.

If we wanted the player to move one unit (or pixel) in the horizontal direction (*x* axis) and not up or down at all, and ensure the player moves every frame, we could use the code that follows:

```
var movement_vector = Vector2(1, 0)

func _process(delta):
    position += movement_vector
```

The effect of this in Godot is shown by the **Sprite2D** moving across the screen, as shown in *Figure 5.8*:

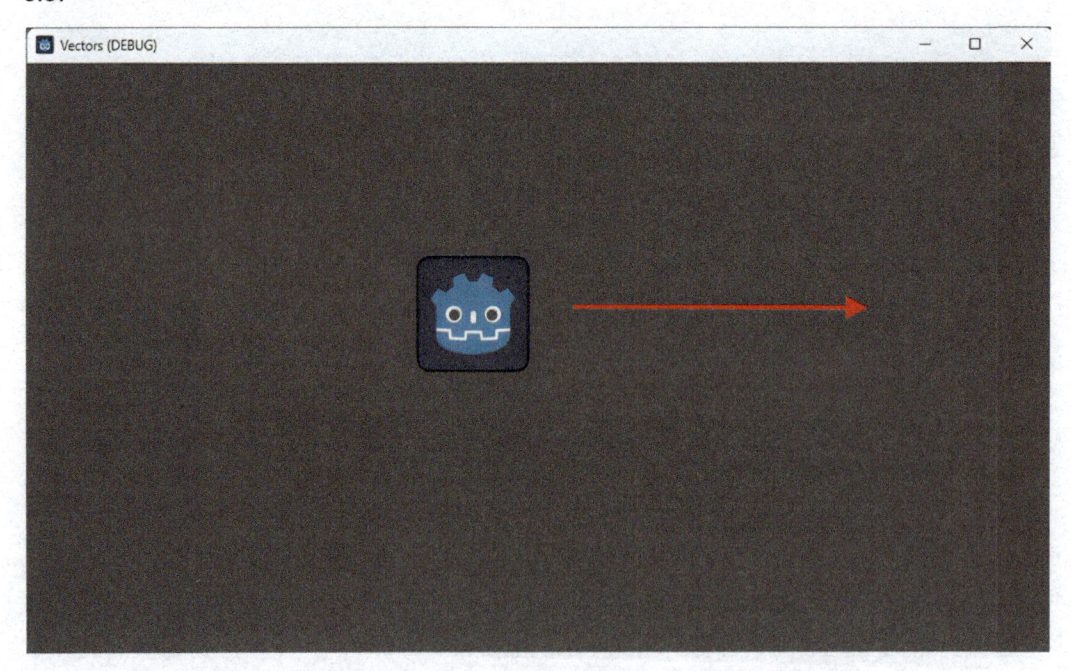

Figure 5.8 – The Godot sprite moves across the screen to the right

Figure 5.8 shows the sprite moving across the screen with the *x* value changing by 1 each frame and the *y* value not changing at all.

It is important to note that we can access the x and y variables of the vector individually using **dot notation**, as shown in the following code:

```
# Access the individual x and y components of the position
var x_position = position.x
var y_position = position.y

# Display the x and y components in the output console
print("Sprite Position - X: ", x_position, " Y: ", y_position)
```

In this code, we store the current x and y positions of the sprite in separate variables and then print them out to see how they change as the sprite moves across the screen.

The effect of this in Godot is shown in the output console as the **Sprite2D** is moving across the screen in *Figure 5.9*:

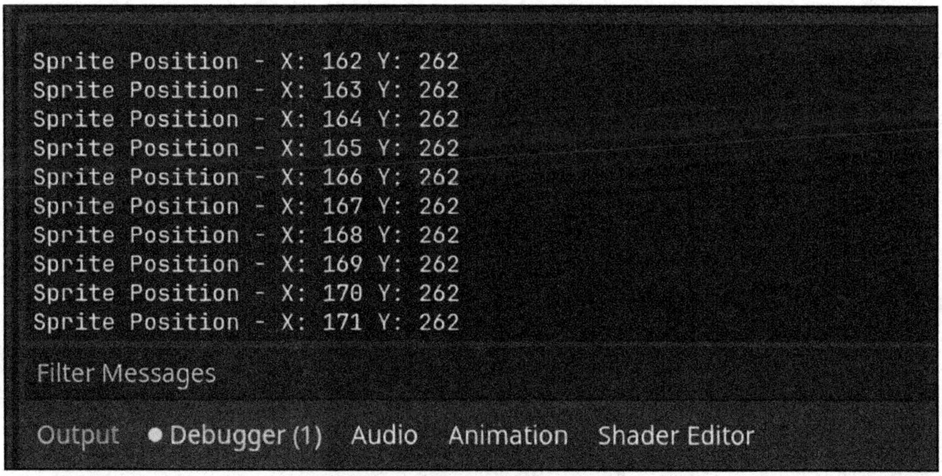

```
Sprite Position - X: 162 Y: 262
Sprite Position - X: 163 Y: 262
Sprite Position - X: 164 Y: 262
Sprite Position - X: 165 Y: 262
Sprite Position - X: 166 Y: 262
Sprite Position - X: 167 Y: 262
Sprite Position - X: 168 Y: 262
Sprite Position - X: 169 Y: 262
Sprite Position - X: 170 Y: 262
Sprite Position - X: 171 Y: 262
```

Figure 5.9 – The console displays the x and y parameters of the vector as the sprite moves

Figure 5.9 demonstrates how we always have access to the parameters of the vector. We can use this information to detect when we are near the edges of the Viewport and then reverse the `movement_vector`. This will make the sprite *bounce* off the sides of the screen. Implement this behavior using the following code:

```
# Store the x and y positions of the edges of the screen
var horizontal_edge = get_viewport_rect().size.x
var vertical_edge = get_viewport_rect().size.y

# Check for screen boundaries to reverse direction
if x_position < 0 or x_position > horizontal_edge:
    # Reverse the x direction
    movement_vector.x *= -1
if y_position < 0 or y_position > vertical_edge:
    # Reverse the y direction
    movement_vector.y *= -1
```

This code successfully restricts or clamps the movement of the sprite so that it remains within the screen boundary.

We can also perform mathematical operations on vectors such as addition, subtraction, and multiplication. This is essential because it allows us to manipulate objects' positions, movements, and directions in a more dynamic and flexible way. Thankfully, the game engine will perform all these calculations for you, but it is good to understand what it is doing.

Movement and positioning

In game development, movement and positioning are at the core of creating dynamic and engaging gameplay. In Godot, vectors are essential tools for defining positions, directions, and velocities in both 2D and 3D spaces. By understanding how to use vectors, you can move characters, projectiles, and objects smoothly and accurately within your game world.

This section will introduce you to working with vectors in Godot, showing you how to calculate directions, handle player movement, and position objects effectively. These concepts form the foundation for creating responsive and realistic game mechanics.

Vector addition

We use **addition** to update an object's position by adding a movement vector to its current position. For example, when you move a character across the screen, you add a direction vector to the character's position vector in each frame.

Vector addition is shown in *Figure 5.10*. The corresponding **x** and **y** values are added together (Vector A**(2,5)** in *blue* added to Vector B**(3,1)** in *green*, which results in Vector C**(5,6)** in *red*).

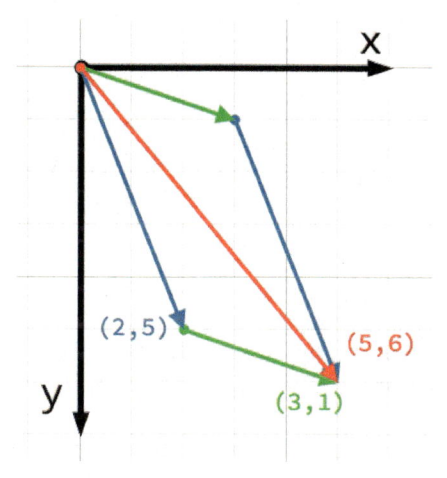

Figure 5.10 – Adding Vector (2,5) to Vector (3,1), resulting in Vector (5,6)

Figure 5.10 also shows that the order in which you add the vectors doesn't matter, as the resulting vector will always be the same.

To understand how this works in a game, we can consider the example of a character jumping. This is shown in *Figure 5.11*:

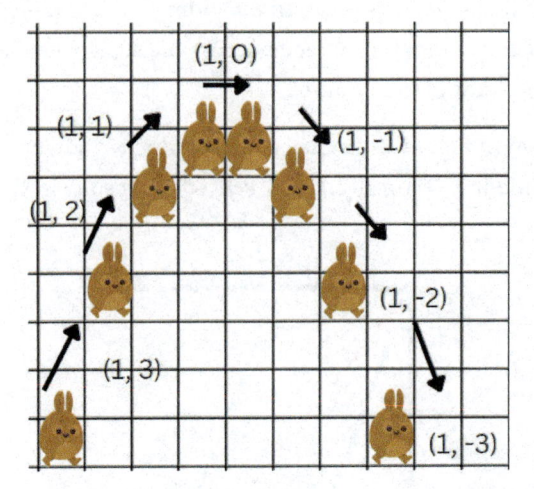

Figure 5.11 – Jumping using vector addition

To understand the jump mechanic, we can look at it frame by frame. Gravity is always pulling the character downward; therefore, the acceleration vector is always (0, -1).

The starting position is (0,0). When the jump button is pressed, the velocity vector is set to **(1,3)** and the character moves up and to the right. If we add the velocity to the position vector, we get a new velocity vector of **(1,3)**. However, we must add the acceleration vector, and the new result is velocity of **(1,2)**. If we continue in this manner, we can move through the entire jump cycle.

Vector subtraction

Subtraction helps calculate the distance or difference between two points, such as the distance between a player and an enemy, which can be used for collision detection or AI behaviors.

Vector Subtraction works in a similar way—subtracting each component individually, vector subtraction helps determine a vector that points from one position to another.

For example, imagine a ball is positioned at **(1,2)** and a hole is at **(4,3)**. To find the direction the ball needs to roll to reach the hole, you can find the difference by subtracting the ball's position from the hole's position.

This is illustrated in *Figure 5.12*:

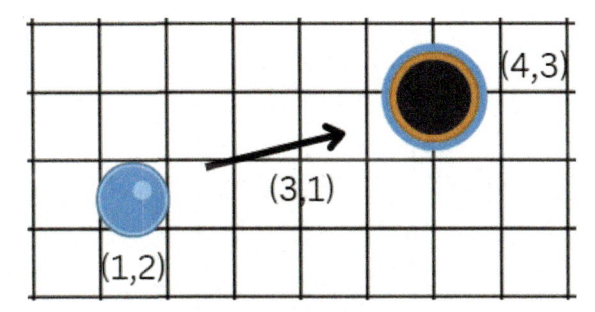

Figure 5.12 – Vector subtraction

Figure 5.12 demonstrates how vector subtraction can be used to calculate the length and direction needed to reach a certain point.

The next fundamental operation we perform with vectors is multiplication.

Vector multiplication

Vectors have values for both direction and magnitude, but a value that only represents magnitude is called a **scalar**.

When we talk about vectors, each number inside the vector is called a *component*, and a single number itself is called a *scalar*. For example, (3, 4) is a vector, while 5 is a scalar. In games, multiplying a vector by a scalar can be useful for changing its size (magnitude) without changing its direction.

A normalized vector is a special kind of vector that has a length (or magnitude) of exactly 1. It still points in the same direction, but its size has been reduced to 1 unit. This is often used to represent direction without affecting distance or speed.

For example, if a player is facing right, we might use a normalized direction vector such as (1, 0). If we then multiply this by a scalar value, such as 100, we get (100, 0), which can represent a position of 100 pixels to the right. This is useful for calculating a target or arrival position:

```
var direction = Vector2(1, 0).normalized()
var distance = 100
var arrival_position = player.position + direction * distance
```

We can also see how vector multiplication can be used to scale an image. Imagine the player gets a power-up that makes them grow. The player's size is represented as a vector, say (1, 2), meaning they have a width of 1 and a height of 2. If the power-up makes the player grow to twice their size, we multiply the size vector by a scalar of 2.

This is illustrated in *Figure 5.13*:

Figure 5.13 – The effect of scaling (scalar multiplication)

In *Figure 5.13*, multiplying the size vector by a scalar makes the player twice as large in both width and height, but their overall shape and proportions stay the same.

Multiplying a vector by a scalar effectively lengthens the vector without changing direction. This can also be demonstrated with arrows, as shown in *Figure 5.14*:

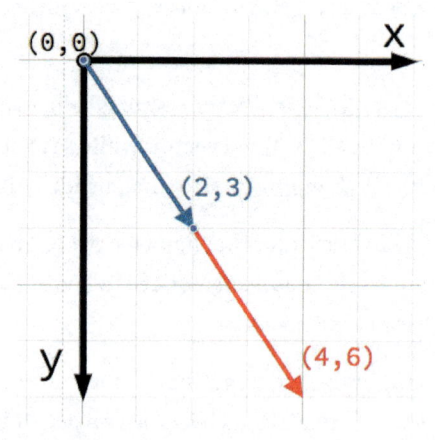

Figure 5.14 – Illustrating scalar multiplication (This image is by Godot Engine contributors and is licensed under CC BY 3.0)

Figure 5.14 shows that multiplying a vector by a scalar will result in a longer vector. It is also important to note that multiplying a negative scalar will reverse the direction.

Vector length

The distance from the origin to the *x* and *y* positions of the vector is known as the **length of the vector**. This is also known as the **magnitude of the vector**. To find this length, Godot has a built-in length() function:

```
var vector_length: float = vector.length()
```

To understand how the length() function works, think of this example. If a character is moving in a 2D platformer with a velocity vector v(4, 3), we might want to determine how fast the character is moving to adjust animations or implement effects such as dust clouds when they land.

To find the character's speed, we calculate the length (or magnitude) of the velocity vector v. We can visualize this vector as forming a right triangle, where one side is 3 (the *x* component) and the other side is 4 (the *y* component). Using the Pythagorean theorem, we can find the hypotenuse, which represents the speed of the character. The formula for the magnitude of a vector with components (*x*, *y*) and the resulting speed is shown in *Figure 5.15*:

$$\text{Speed} = \sqrt{4^2 + 3^2} = \sqrt{16 + 9} = \sqrt{25} = 5$$

Figure 5.15 – Using the Pythagorean theorem to determine vector magnitude

Figure 5.15 demonstrates how the length() function works to calculate the magnitude of a vector. This means the character is moving at a speed of **5** units per second in the game world. This is visualized in *Figure 5.16*:

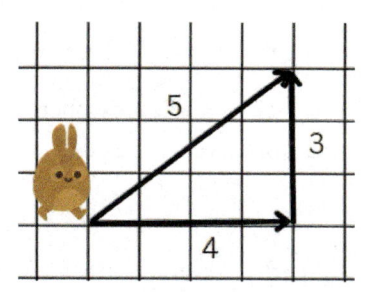

Figure 5.16 – Visual representation of the length

Figure 5.16 demonstrates how the length of a vector is calculated. Note that this also applies to 3D vectors.

Distance

Often, we want to find the **distance** between two objects, such as the player and a motion sensor, to determine whether the player is close enough to trigger an alarm. We can do this using the `distance_to()` function in Godot. For instance, if the player is at position (3,3) and the motion sensor is at position (1,2), we can calculate the distance between them to check whether the player is within range of the sensor, which could activate the alarm.

The math behind the `distance_to()` function combines vector subtraction and vector length. To calculate the distance [D], we subtract the player vector [P] from the motion sensor vector [M] and then calculate the length of the resulting vector:

$$D = (P - M).length()$$

$$D = \sqrt{[(3-1)^2 + (3-2)^2]} = \sqrt{[4+1]} = \sqrt{5} \approx 2.24$$

This equation is demonstrated in *Figure 5.17*:

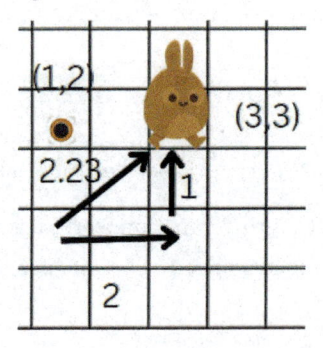

Figure 5.17 – Calculating the distance to an object

Figure 5.17 shows how the distance to another object is calculated. It doesn't matter if you subtract the player vector from the motion sensor vector or the other way around; the result is the same.

Normalization

When working with directions (rather than positions or velocities), it's essential that they have a unit length, meaning a length of 1. This simplifies our calculations.

For example, imagine a robot that needs to move in the direction of (1,0) to deliver a package at a constant speed of 20 m/s. What would the velocity of the robot be? Because the direction vector has a length of 1, we can easily multiply it by the robot's speed to calculate its velocity: (20,0). If the direction vector had any other length, the robot would move either too fast or too slow.

A vector with a length of 1 is called **normalized**. So, how do we normalize a vector (set its length to 1)?

It's simple: we just divide each component by the vector's length.

Since this is such a common operation, Godot has a built-in function to do it for us. The function is called `normalized()` and can be used in our example as follows:

```
extends Node2D

# Called when the node enters the scene tree for the first time.
func _ready():
    # Normalize direction vector so it has a length of 1
    direction = direction.normalized()
    
    # Calculate velocity by multiplying direction by speed
    velocity = direction * speed
```

There is still a lot to learn about vectors, and there are other operations such as the **dot product** and the **cross product**. All of this is part of the field of mathematics called **linear algebra**. However, you now have enough of an understanding to make great Godot games, and the engine will do all the mathematics for us!

Summary

In this chapter, we explored the fundamental concept of vectors and their crucial role in game development. You learned how to manipulate vectors within the Godot engine, applying vector addition, subtraction, and multiplication to control movement and positioning. We also covered important topics such as calculating vector length, determining distances between objects, and normalizing vectors for consistent directionality.

By mastering these concepts, you are now equipped to use vectors effectively in your game projects, enhancing gameplay mechanics and interactions.

In the next chapter, we are going to turn from theory to practice as we create our first 2D mini game in Godot!

Unlock this book's exclusive benefits now

Scan this QR code or go to packtpub.com/unlock, then search this book by name.

Note: Keep your purchase invoice ready before you start.

6
Creating a 2D Mini-Game in Godot – Part 1

In this chapter, you'll take a major step by building your very first 2D platformer level in Godot. You'll learn how to design and construct a level using a tilemap, and then populate it with key gameplay elements: a player character that moves and jumps, a patrolling enemy to avoid, and collectible items to reward exploration. You'll also set up a checkpoint system to allow players to progress through the level.

This experience will give you the hands-on practice needed to take your game development skills to the next level, as you'll learn how to manipulate key elements of level design and gameplay mechanics in Godot. With this knowledge, you'll be able to design more complex levels and gameplay features in future projects.

In this chapter, we're going to cover the following main topics:

- Building the level with a TileMap
- Creating and controlling the player
- Adding the **CharacterBody2D** template for the `Player` script
- Cleaning the code

By the end of this chapter, you'll be able to create an interactive, fully playable platformer level and understand how these components work together to form the foundation of many platformer games.

Technical requirements

To start with the chapter, you should know how to do the following:

- Create a new Godot project
- Create nodes
- Create scenes

You should also know about variables and functions for use in GDScript (see *Chapter 4*).

This chapter's code files are available here in the book's GitHub repository: https://github.com/PacktPublishing/Godot-4-for-Beginners/tree/main/ch6

Visit this link to check out the video of the code being run: https://packt.link/DcrOS

The game assets used in this project are released under a **Creative Commons Zero** (**CC0**) license by Pixel Frog. Pixel Frog has allowed us to distribute, remix, adapt, and build upon the material in any medium or format, even for commercial purposes.

They can be found here:

- **Pixel Adventure**: https://pixelfrog-assets.itch.io/pixel-adventure-1
- **Pixel Adventure 2**: https://pixelfrog-assets.itch.io/pixel-adventure-2

Building the level with a TileMap

Building 2D levels with **TileMaps** is an efficient and organized way to create game environments by reusing small, pre-designed tiles. This approach not only saves time and resources but also allows for easy adjustments and consistent visuals across your level design.

In this section, we'll build the foundation of our 2D platformer by creating a level with a TileMap, allowing us to efficiently design and organize the game environment. TileMaps are essential because they make it easy to create detailed, grid-based levels while optimizing performance, keeping game worlds manageable and visually consistent.

Let's begin the process of building our level by creating a new scene and adding essential nodes. Follow these steps to set up a functional, well-organized level using a **TileMapLayer**:

1. Create a new Godot Project and give it a name – I have called it PixelAdventure.
2. We need a scene to represent the first level of the game. To do this, we create a new 2D scene, which will have **Node2D** as the root. Rename **Node2D** to Level1.

Chapter 6

3. We are now ready to add a **TileMapLayer** node to the **Level1** scene. A **TileMapLayer** node uses a **TileSet**, which contains a list of tiles that are used to create grid-based maps. TileMaps are used in 2D game development to efficiently create large, consistent levels by reusing small, predefined tiles. This improves the performance of the game and also makes it easy to edit and customize levels.

4. Add a new **TileMapLayer** node as a child of **Level1**. Your scene tree will resemble. *Figure 6.1* shows this as follows:

Figure 6.1 – Scene tree after adding the TileMapLayer node

5. Every **TileMapLayer** node needs a TileSet so that we can place individual tiles in the scene to create the level. To create the TileSet, select the **TileMapLayer** node, then, in the **Inspector**, find the **Tile Set** property and click on **New TileSet**, as shown in *Figure 6.2*:

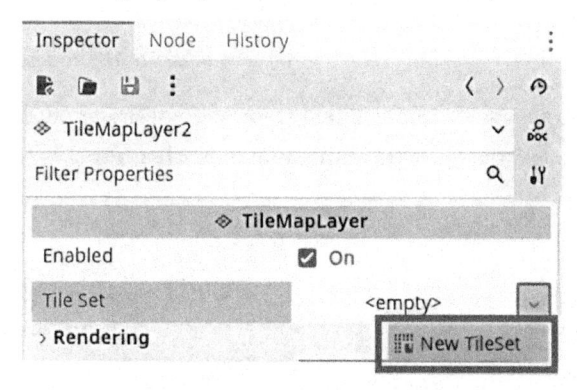

Figure 6.2 – Creating a new Tile Set

6. Then click on **TileSet**, which will make the **TileMap** and **TileSet** tabs at the bottom center of the screen visible, as shown in *Figure 6.3*:

Figure 6.3 – The TileSet and TileMap tabs

7. In the `Terrain` folder of the `Pixel Adventure` assets, there is an image file called `Terrain (16 x 16).png`. Create a folder in your Godot file system called `Assets`, then create a subfolder called `TileMap`. Drag and drop the `Terrain` image file into the `TileMap` folder, as shown in *Figure 6.4*:

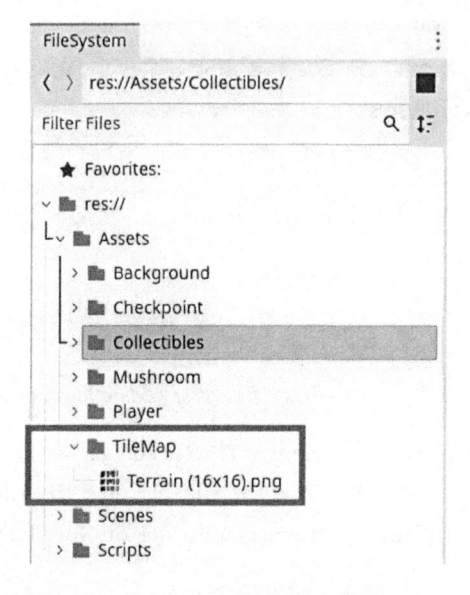

Figure 6.4 – Terrain.png added to TileMap folder

8. Now that the image is in our **FileSystem**, we can drag and drop it into the **TileSet** tab, which will allow us to use the individual tiles. This is shown in *Figure 6.5*:

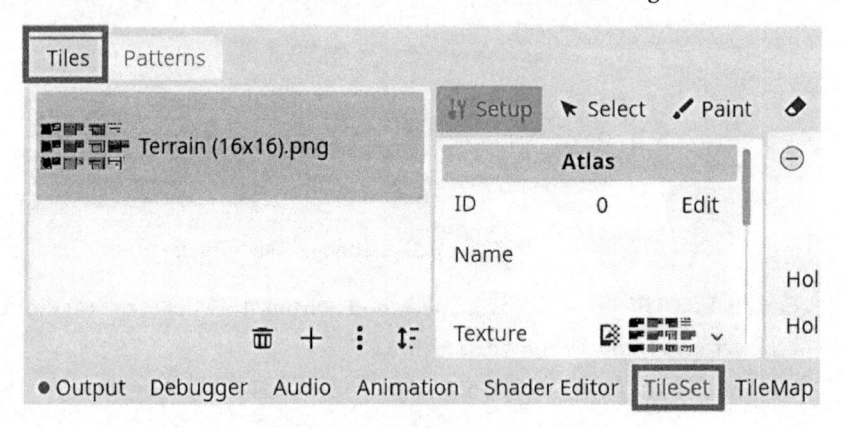

Figure 6.5 – The TileSet is now loaded

Chapter 6

9. We will not change anything on the TileSet at the moment. Our goal is to paint the level. To do this, switch over to the **TileMap** tab and press *D* or click on the **Paint** button. Now select tiles in the map and draw them in the Viewport onscreen, as shown in *Figure 6.6*:

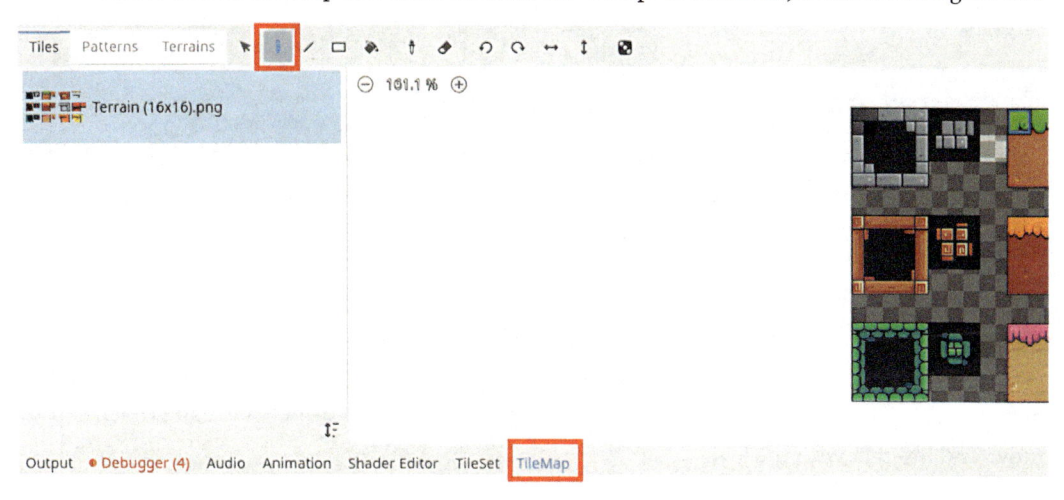

Figure 6.6 – Painting tiles by selecting tiles and using the Paint tool

Figure 6.6 shows how you can use the **Paint** tool to select tiles and then paint them into the scene by clicking. You can also hold *shift + click* to paint multiple tiles at the same time. Go ahead and paint a level. You can do anything you like, and you are welcome to copy my level, which is shown in *Figure 6.7*:

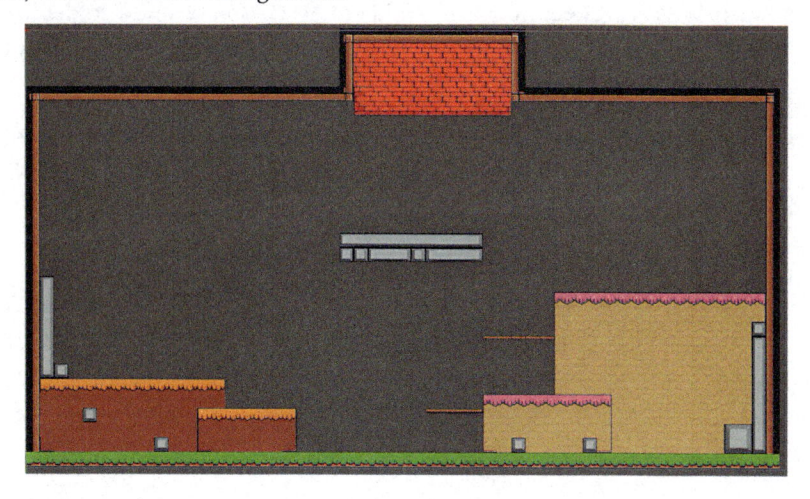

Figure 6.7 – An example of a contained level

As *Figure 6.7* shows, we now have a level for players to explore. It is important to understand that this level is currently purely decorative – we cannot even detect collisions as this world has no physics! In the next section, we will add the player and then return to our TileSet to implement physics.

Creating and controlling the player

Now that we have a world, we need a player to explore it! In this section, we'll focus on building the foundation for a fully interactive 2D level. Each step will help us create a playable environment while introducing essential Godot tools and techniques.

First, we'll add a background to provide visual context for the level. Then, we'll create and configure a **CharacterBody2D** node as our player, complete with an **AnimatedSprite2D** node to bring it to life and **CollisionShape2D** node to enable physics interactions. After setting up the player's animations, we'll conclude by scripting the character controller, allowing the player to move and interact with the level.

By the end of this section, you'll have a functional and visually appealing player character ready to explore the 2D world you've created.

Adding the background

We will follow the given steps to add the background to the level:

1. Add a new **TextureRect** node as a child of **Level1**. Create a new folder in the file system called Background and add the images from the Background folder of your downloaded assets to it.

2. In **Inspector**, use the Brown.png background image for **Texture**. Set the **Expand Mode** property to **Keep Size** and the **Stretch Mode** property to **Tile**.

Chapter 6

3. Now, drag **TextureRect** to fill the entire Viewport and more if you wish. We have just created a tiled background.

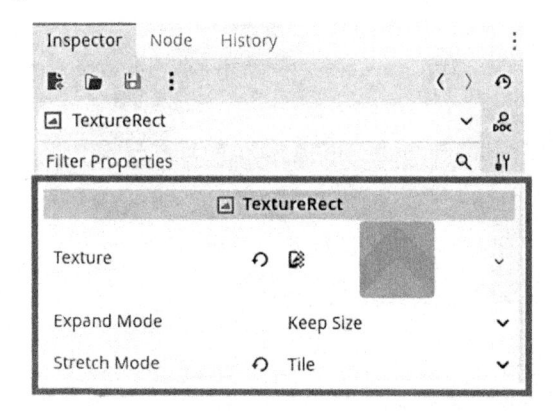

Figure 6.8 – Changing the properties of TextureRect

4. To ensure that the background appears behind every other node in the scene, position the **TextureRect** node at the top of the scene tree as shown in *Figure 6.9*:

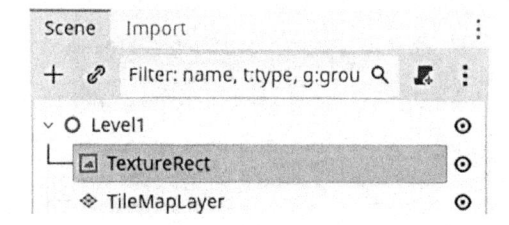

Figure 6.9 – Lower nodes appear in front of higher nodes

Figure 6.9 demonstrates the order in which nodes are handled in the tree. It is in a top-down fashion, starting at the root and going down each branch in turn. The level now has a background and looks more polished.

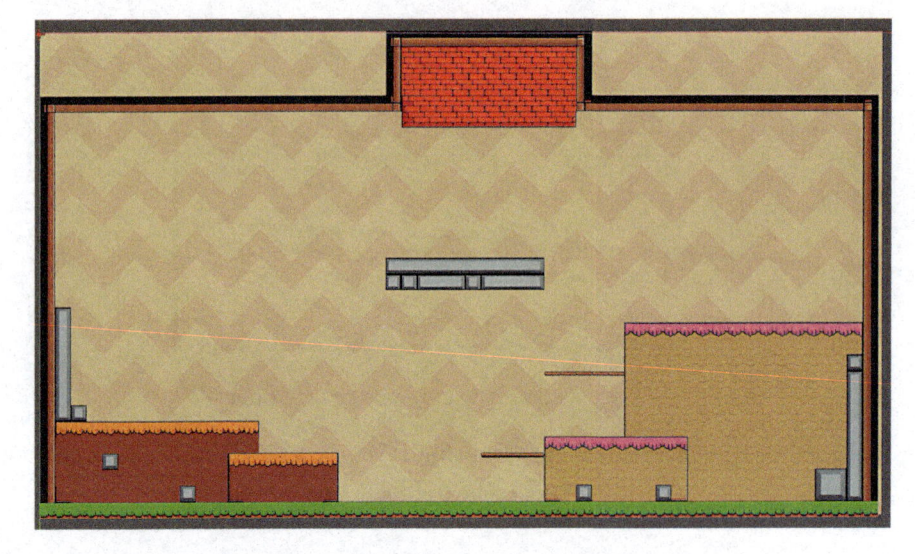

Figure 6.10 – A background helps to round off a level

The player character is now ready to make an appearance. Create a new scene and add a **CharacterBody2D** node as the root, then rename it to `Player`. Add an **AnimatedSprite2D** node as a child as shown in *Figure 6.11*:

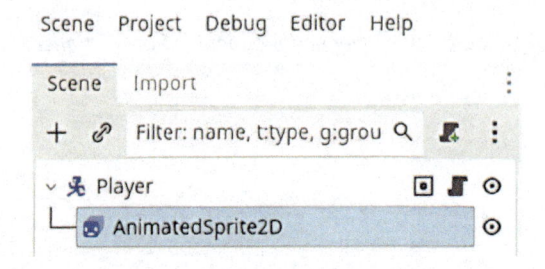

Figure 6.11 – Adding an AnimatedSprite2D node to the player

Figure 6.11 shows the **AnimatedSprite2D** node. This is a sprite node that contains multiple textures as frames to play for animation. In the next section, we will set up various animations for the player's actions.

Setting up the player animations

To animate a sprite, we use multiple frames that depict the sprite at various stages of motion. These frames are often grouped together in a single image known as a **sprite sheet**. To animate the sprite, we first import the sprite sheet and then divide it into individual frames. To do this, select the **AnimatedSprite2D** node, and in **Inspector**, on the **Sprite Frames** property, click on **New SpriteFrames**. This is shown in *Figure 6.12*:

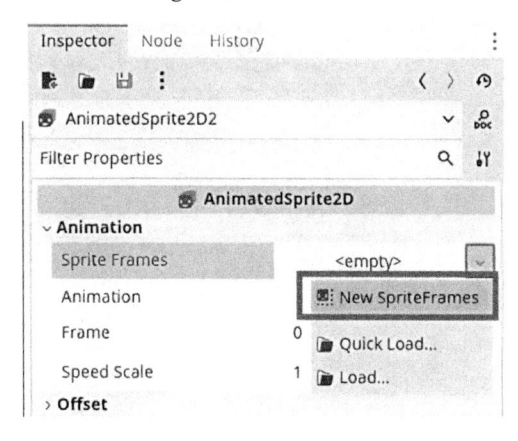

Figure 6.12 – New SpriteFrames

Clicking on **SpriteFrames** in **Inspector**, as in *Figure 6.12*, will open the **SpriteFrames** area at the bottom of the screen (see *Figure 6.13*). This is the space where we can import frames and create new animations.

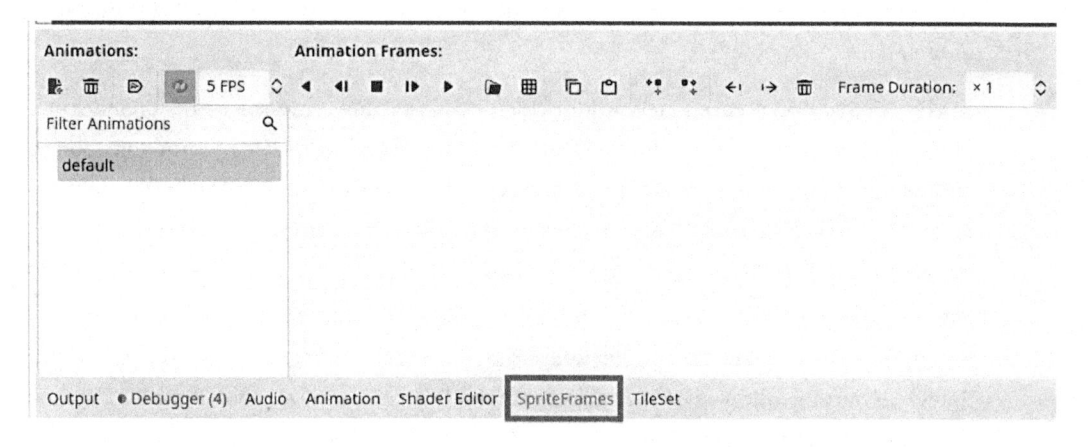

Figure 6.13 – The SpriteFrames area

As shown in *Figure 6.13*, we currently have only the default animation, and no images or frames associated with it. We will now create animations for all the players' actions and then import the sprites associated with each action from their sprite sheet. To do this, follow these steps:

1. Start by renaming the default animation to `idle`. Then click on the **Add Animation** button or press *Ctrl + N*. Rename that animation to `run`.
2. Create the following list of animations: `double_jump`, `fall`, `jump`, and `wall_slide`. These are shown in *Figure 6.14*:

Figure 6.14 – All the animations for the player actions

Now that we have the animation names ready, as in *Figure 6.14*, we can bring in the images associated with each one.

3. In the **FileSystem**, create a new folder called `Player`. Now, find the `Main Characters` folder in the assets you downloaded from Pixel Frog and drag the images for your player character into the `Player` folder in the file system. I chose to use the ninja frog character. Select the `idle` animation and then click on the **Add frames from sprite sheet** button or press *Ctrl + Shift + O*.
4. Now select the `idle` image file in your `Assets` folder. You must count the player images and update the **Horizontal** and **Vertical** frame properties as required. Then click on the **Select All** button, followed by the **Add x Frame(s)** button. This is shown for the idle frames of the ninja frog in *Figure 6.15*:

Chapter 6   141

Figure 6.15 – Setting the Horizontal and Vertical Frames and adding them to the animation

5. After cutting the individual frames from the image (sprite sheet) as in *Figure 6.15*, your **SpriteFrames** window will update with the images to be used for the `idle` animation. This is shown in *Figure 6.16*:

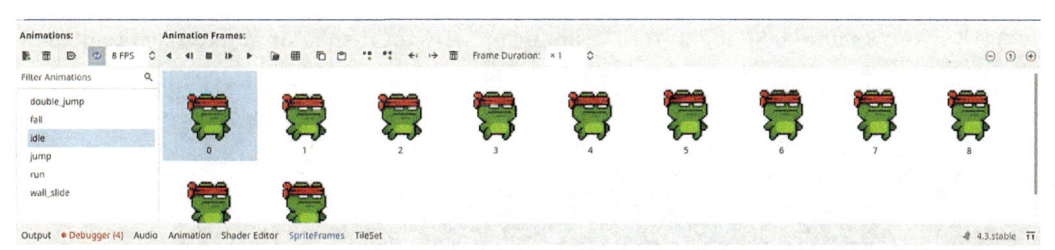

Figure 6.16 – The frames for the idle animation

As you can see in *Figure 6.16*, there are controls for the animations in the bar at the top. I have set the `idle` frame rate to **8 FPS**, and looping is on. You can play with these settings to find the ones that you like. You can see this in *Figure 6.17*.

Figure 6.17 – Animation controls with looping and FPS highlighted

To set up the rest of the player animations, follow and repeat the same steps as you have done for the `idle` animation. Our next task will be to ensure that the player can collide with objects by assigning them a hitbox.

> **Important note**
>
> You may have noticed that the player appears blurry in the scene. This is because of the default texture filter. Click on **Project** | **Project Settings** | **Rendering** | **Textures** and change **Default Texture Filter** to **Nearest**. This is the best setting for pixel art.

Detecting collisions

Detecting when and where objects collide in a game, as well as identifying which objects are involved, is a key aspect of game development. In Godot, we handle this by assigning each object to a **CollisionShape2D** node. This node allows us to define and adjust the shape that surrounds the object, ensuring accurate collision detection.

The following are the steps for assigning a **CollisionShape2D** node:

1. Add **CollisionShape2D** node as a child of **Player**.
2. Choose **RectangleShape2D** for the **Shape** property in **Inspector** and resize it to fit your player. This rectangle forms the bounding box for collisions on the player and is shown in *Figure 6.18*:

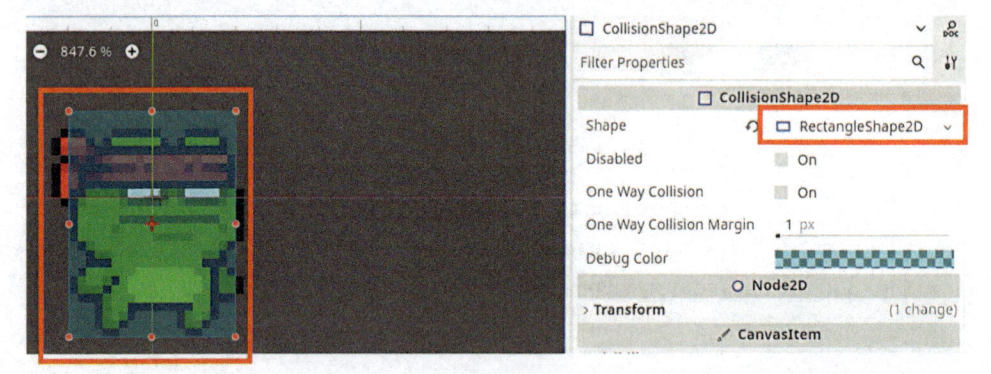

Figure 6.18 – Assigning RectangleShape2D to the CollisionShape2D node and resulting bounding box

As shown in *Figure 6.18*, anything entering the rectangular collision shape will register a collision. The shape is not visible during gameplay.

3. Save the **Player** scene as `player.tscn`, and then drag and drop the file from **FileSystem** into the **Level1** scene.

You now have a player in your level! However, if you play the game, the player is stationary because no movement has been implemented yet. We will implement this later.

TileMap collisions

As stated before, our current level is just a painting; none of the tiles have collision detection, and our player cannot move. To set up collisions on our tiles, we need to add an element to our physics layers. To do this, follow these steps:

1. Select the **TileMapLayer** node in **Inspector** and click on **Tile Set**.
2. In the **Physics Layers** property, click **Add Element**. This is shown in *Figure 6.19*:

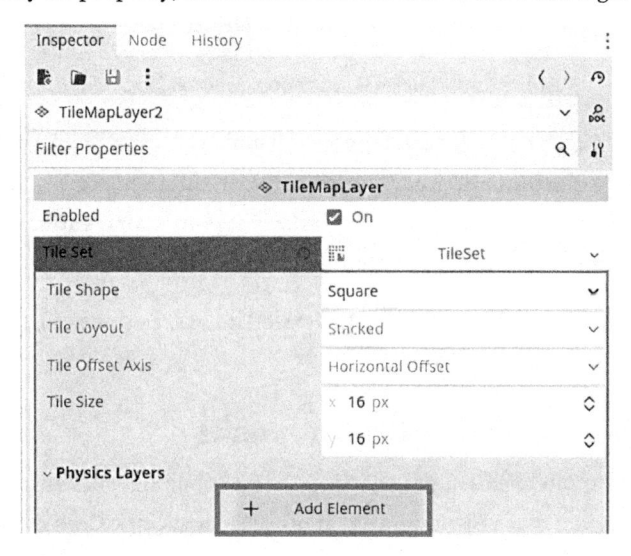

Figure 6.19 - Adding an element to Physics Layers of a TileSet

Once you have added an element to **Physics Layers** of the TileSet, as shown in *Figure 6.19*, your TileSet will have two new properties in **Physics Layers** – **Collision Layer** and **Collision Mask**. This is shown in *Figure 6.20*:

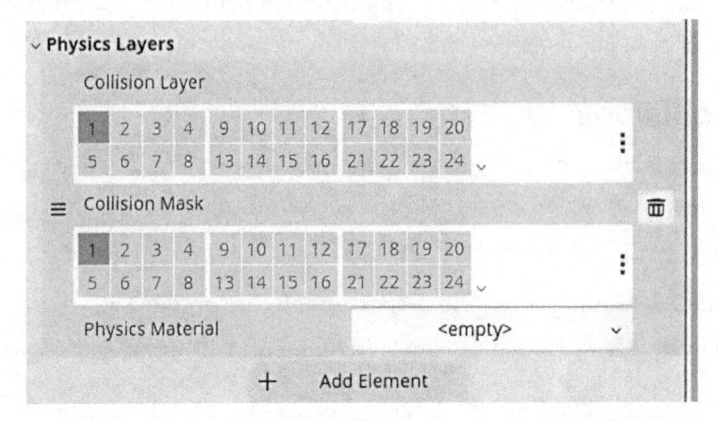

Figure 6.20 – Collision Layer and Collision Mask of the TileSet

As can be seen in *Figure 6.20*, the concept of collision layers and masks in Godot 4 plays a crucial role in managing collisions and interactions between different elements in the game world. Understanding how to work with layers and masks is essential for creating complex and interactive game environments. These will be explained in more detail in the next section.

Make sure you have added *two* **Physics Layers** elements, as one set is for ground tiles and the other will be used for passthrough tiles.

Collision layers and collision masks

Collision layers are categories or groups that an object belongs to, which determine which other objects it can interact with. By assigning an object to a specific **Collision Layer**, we place it in a group that defines its potential interactions. For example, if object X is assigned to layer 1, it's treated as part of layer 1. Other objects can then be set up to detect and respond to objects in that layer, depending on their own collision settings.

Collision masks, on the other hand, define which layers an object can detect and interact with. For instance, if object X is on layer **1** but has a **Collision Mask** set to layer **2**, object X will only collide with objects that are on layer **2**. This separation between layers and masks allows us to control which objects interact, making it easy to ensure, for example, that enemies only collide with players and not each other.

Chapter 6   145

In *Figure 6.20*, **Collision Layer 1** is *on*, and **Collision Mask 1** is *on*. This means that the objects on layer 1 will collide with objects on mask 1. This is not very useful as it means that the objects will collide with themselves (which is impossible), so we will change this soon.

Keeping track of which numbers collide with which can be very difficult and even more so as your game becomes bigger and more complex. It is therefore recommended that you rename your layers to represent the things that exist on them.

In our level, most tiles will act as solid objects that the player can stand on and collide with. However, to make the level more dynamic, some tiles will function as "jump-through" or "pass-through" platforms. These allow the player to jump up from below and land on the platform. If the player presses down while on the platform, they will fall back through to the ground below, adding an extra layer of interaction to the gameplay. This is shown in *Figure 6.21*.

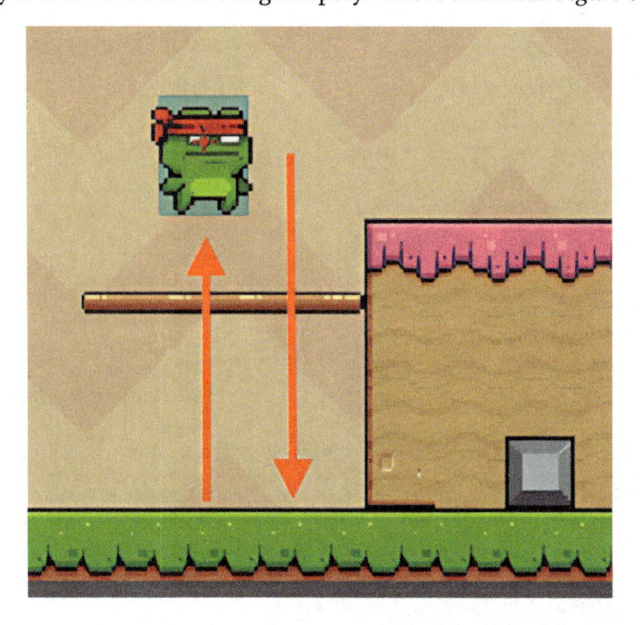

Figure 6.21 – A jump-through platform

Because some of our tiles need to be solid and some need to be pass-through, we will add a second element to **Physics Layers** of the TileSet, then name the layers so that we can keep track of the interactions. Do this by clicking on the three vertical dots to the right of the layer numbers and clicking on **Edit Layer Names**. I have named **Layer 1**: player, **Layer 2**: ground, and **Layer 3**: pass_through. This is shown in *Figure 6.22*:

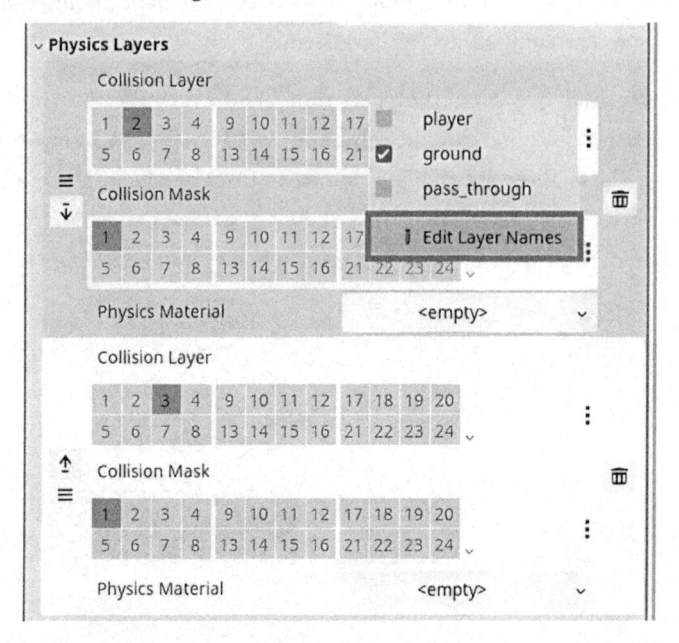

Figure 6.22 – Two sets of physics layers and the Edit Layer Names button

As shown in *Figure 6.22*, clicking on **Edit Layer Names** will allow you to name each layer. You can see how I have named my layers in *Figure 6.23*:

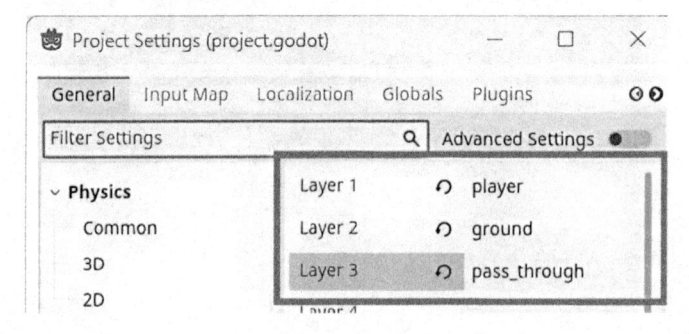

Figure 6.23 – Naming the collision layers

Chapter 6

If you have a look at *Figure 6.22*, in the first physics layer, **Collision Layer 2** (ground) is *on* and **Collision Mask 1** (player) is *on*. This means that the ground will collide with the player.

In the second physics layer, **Collision Layer 3** (pass_through) is *on*, and **Collision Mask 1** is *on*. This means that the pass-through will collide with the player.

We must also remember to turn on the corresponding layers in the **Player** node, as shown in *Figure 6.24*. This is so that the player looks for collisions on the ground and pass_through layers; otherwise, they would fall through the level.

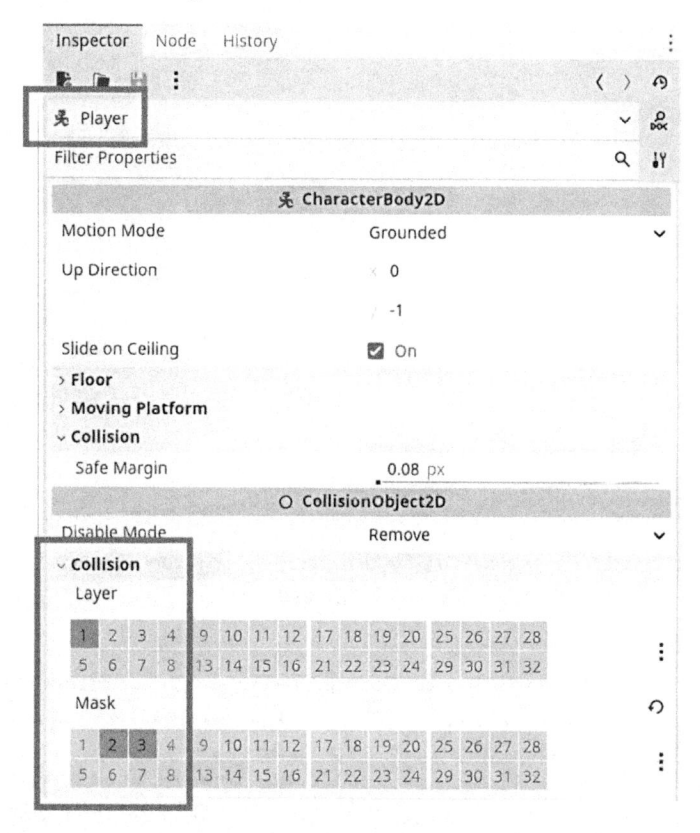

Figure 6.24 – Setting the collision layers in Player

In *Figure 6.24*, we are in the **Player** node, and we have turned **Collision Layer 1** (player) *on* and **Collision Mask 2** (ground) and **Collision Mask 3** (pass_through) *on*. This means that we have enabled collisions in the opposite direction so that the player will now collide with the ground and the pass-through.

The final step of making our level interactive is to paint the tiles in the TileSet as collision tiles.

Painting the tiles

To paint the tiles in the TileSet as collision tiles, follow these steps:

1. First, we need to select our **TileMapLayer** node, open **TileSet** at the bottom of the screen, and then click on **Paint**.
2. In **Paint Properties**, select **Physics Layer 0**. This is the ground layer. Now, paint over all the tiles that you want to be ground tiles. I have chosen to leave the far-right tiles as pass_through tiles and have *not* painted them as colliders. This is shown in *Figure 6.25*:

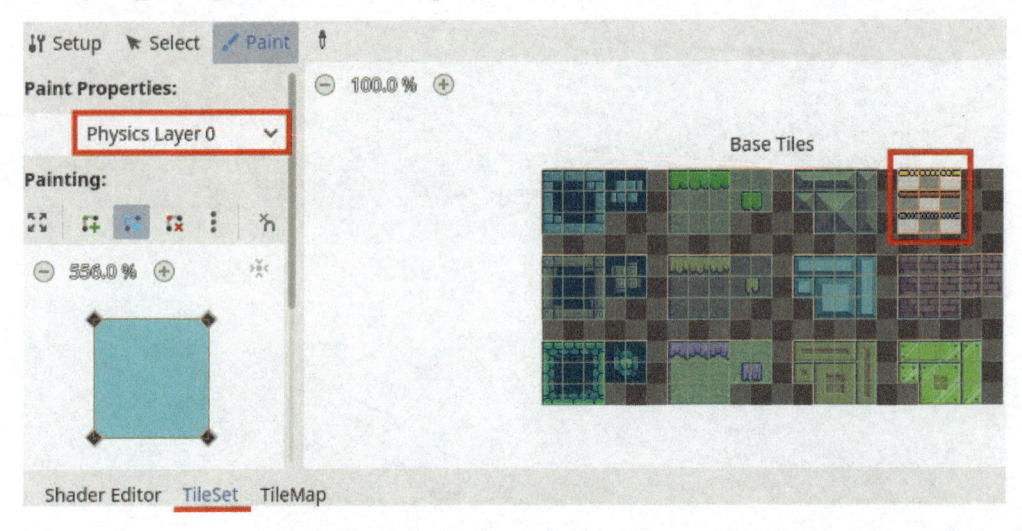

Figure 6.25 – Ground tiles are shaded – note the unshaded tiles reserved for pass-through

🔍 **Quick tip**: Need to see a high-resolution version of this image? Open this book in the next-gen Packt Reader or view it in the PDF/ePub copy.

🔒 **The next-gen Packt Reader** and a **free PDF/ePub copy** of this book are included with your purchase. Scan the QR code OR visit packtpub.com/unlock, then use the search bar to find this book by name. Double-check the edition shown to make sure you get the right one.

Chapter 6 149

3. Now switch to **Physics Layer 1**. This is the layer for the `pass_through` tiles. Now we will paint the tiles we saved. You can adjust the collision polygon for each individual tile. Make sure that you also set **polygon_0_one_way** to checked. This will allow the player to jump through the tile from below. Now paint all the `pass_through` tiles with this brush. This is shown in *Figure 6.26*:

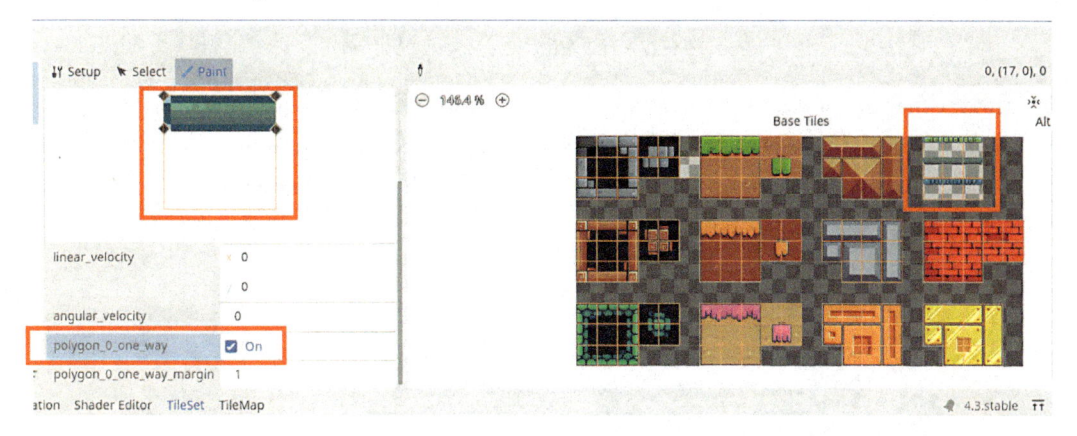

Figure 6.26 – Adjusting the collision polygon, one-way collision, and painting the pass-through tiles

4. After adjusting the tiles as shown in *Figure 6.25* and *Figure 6.26*, you can run and test the game. Although the player can collide with the tiles, there are no forces (such as gravity) acting on the player, and it does not respond to input – you are basically stuck wherever you are placed.

In the next section, we will work on scripting the player to control movement, animations, and interactions, and to apply forces such as gravity.

Adding the CharacterBody2D template for the Player script

Godot provides pre-written code templates for basic player movement. This saves us from having to reinvent the wheel and allows us to make games faster.

In the **Player** scene, select your **Player** node and click on the **Attach New Script** icon as shown in *Figure 6.27*:

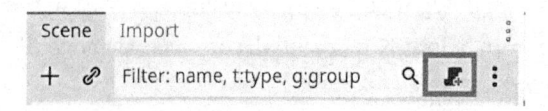

Figure 6.27 – The Attach New Script button

As can be seen in *Figure 6.27*, you can attach a script to any node in Godot to customize its behavior by selecting it and clicking on the **Attach New Script** button. When you click the button, you will be presented with some options for creating the script, as shown in *Figure 6.28*:

Figure 6.28 – Note the Basic Movement template being used

As *Figure 6.28* shows, the script will be created using a template, which means that there will be pre-generated code for basic movement and also gravity. The script for this is as follows:

```
extends CharacterBody2D
const SPEED = 300.0
const JUMP_VELOCITY = -400.0

func _physics_process(delta):
    # Add the gravity
    if not is_on_floor():
```

Chapter 6

```
            velocity += get_gravity() * delta

    # Handle jump
    if Input.is_action_just_pressed("ui_accept") and is_on_floor():
        velocity.y = JUMP_VELOCITY

    # Get the movement direction and handle deceleration
    var direction = Input.get_axis("ui_left", "ui_right")
    if direction:
        velocity.x = direction * SPEED
    else:
        velocity.x = move_toward(velocity.x, 0, SPEED)

    move_and_slide()
```

💡 **Quick tip**: Enhance your coding experience with the **AI Code Explainer** and **Quick Copy** features. Open this book in the next-gen Packt Reader. Click the **Copy** button **(1)** to quickly copy code into your coding environment, or click the **Explain** button **(2)** to get the AI assistant to explain a block of code to you.

```
function calculate(a, b) {
   return {sum: a + b};
};
```

🔒 **The next-gen Packt Reader** is included for free with the purchase of this book. Scan the QR code OR go to packtpub.com/unlock, then use the search bar to find this book by name. Double-check the edition shown to make sure you get the right one.

To make our project more manageable and to give it more structure, we will move a lot of this code into new functions. Before we do that, we should understand the code line by line:

- `extends CharacterBody2D`: This line tells Godot that this script is extending (or using) the functionality of a built-in node called **CharacterBody2D**. This node is specifically designed for 2D characters that move, such as a player.
- `const SPEED = 300.0` and `const JUMP_VELOCITY = -400.0`: These two lines define **constants**. A constant is a value that won't change during the game.
- `SPEED`: This controls how fast the character can move left or right.
- `JUMP_VELOCITY`: This defines how fast and high the character will jump. A negative value means the character will move upward when they jump.
- `func _physics_process(delta)`: This function is called every time the game processes physics and is fixed at 60 frames per second. The `delta` parameter represents the time that has passed since the last frame, ensuring smooth movement.
- Next, let's look at the following block:

  ```
  # Add the gravity
  if not is_on_floor():
      velocity += get_gravity() * delta
  ```

  This block adds gravity to the character if they are not on the floor (in the air):

  - `is_on_floor()` checks if the character is touching the ground.
  - `get_gravity()` fetches the current gravity value and, multiplying it by `delta`, ensures that gravity affects the character at a consistent rate.
  - The `velocity` variable is a built-in variable representing how fast the character is moving in both the x (horizontal) and y (vertical) directions. Adding the gravity value affects the y velocity (making the character fall).

- Let's look at the next block:

  ```
  #Handle jump
  if Input.is_action_just_pressed("ui_accept") and is_on_floor():
      velocity.y = JUMP_VELOCITY
  ```

Chapter 6

This block handles jumping. It is explained as follows:

- `Input.is_action_just_pressed("ui_accept")` checks if the player pressed the jump button (which is mapped to "ui_accept" by default). This is the *spacebar*.
- `is_on_floor()` ensures the player can only jump if they're standing on the ground.
- When both conditions are true, the character's y velocity is set to JUMP_VELOCITY, which makes them jump upward.

- Now, we move on to the following block:

```
#Get the movement direction and handle deceleration
var direction = Input.get_axis("ui_left", "ui_right")
```

This line gets the player's input for left and right movement:

- `Input.get_axis("ui_left", "ui_right")` returns -1 if the player is holding the *left* key, +1 if they're holding the *right* key, and 0 if neither is pressed.

- Moving on to the next block:

```
if direction:
    velocity.x = direction * SPEED
else:
    velocity.x = move_toward(velocity.x, 0, SPEED)
```

If there's input (the player presses the *left* or *right* key), the character's x-axis velocity is set to move in that direction at the speed defined by SPEED.

If there's no input, the character gradually slows down using `move_toward()`, which makes the x velocity smoothly approach 0, simulating deceleration.

- `move_and_slide()`: This moves the character based on the velocity. It also handles sliding along surfaces, such as the floor or walls, making movement smooth.

Now that we understand how the basic movement code works, it's time to focus on improving its structure. Writing clean, organized code is crucial for making our projects easier to read, maintain, and expand as they grow in complexity. To achieve this, we'll refactor the movement code by breaking it down into individual functions, which will enhance both readability and reusability.

Cleaning the code

Breaking your code into *separate functions* is part of the **clean code** concept, which helps maintain organization and clarity as your project grows. By structuring your code this way, it becomes easier to read, test, and debug. Each function focuses on a specific task, reducing redundancy and making it simpler to spot and fix issues when they arise. This approach also makes your project more scalable, as adding new features or changes becomes smoother without cluttering up your core code.

Adding gravity, handling the jump, and getting the direction can all be placed in their own functions. Change your code to match what you see in the following code block:

```
extends CharacterBody2D

# Constants for how fast the player moves and how high they can jump
const SPEED = 300.0
const JUMP_VELOCITY = -400.0

# This function runs every physics frame (ideal for movement and collision)
func _physics_process(delta):
	# Apply gravity if the player is not on the floor
	apply_gravity(delta)
	# Check for jump input and apply jump force
	handle_jump()
	# Handle left/right movement input
	handle_movement(delta)
	# Move the character and handle collisions with the environment
	move_and_slide()

# This function adds gravity to the player's velocity
func apply_gravity(delta):
	# Only apply gravity if the player is in the air
	if not is_on_floor():
		velocity += get_gravity() * delta

# This function makes the player jump when the jump key is pressed
func handle_jump():
```

```
    # Only allow jumping if the player is currently on the ground
    if Input.is_action_just_pressed("ui_accept") and is_on_floor():
        velocity.y = JUMP_VELOCITY

# This function handles horizontal movement input
func handle_movement(delta):
    # Get the left/right movement input as a value between -1 and 1
    var direction = Input.get_axis("ui_left", "ui_right")
    
    # If there is movement input, update the velocity in that direction
    if direction:
        velocity.x = direction * SPEED
    else:
        # If no input, gradually slow the player down to a stop
        velocity.x = move_toward(velocity.x, 0, SPEED)
```

The code functions in the same way as before, but now specific actions reside in their own functions, so it is easier to find errors and make improvements.

The code is now clean and broken down into smaller and more maintainable parts. In the next chapter, we will be customizing more of the players' behaviors and playing the animations. We will also add a collectible, an enemy, and a checkpoint to complete the level.

Summary

In this chapter, we covered essential steps in building your first 2D platformer level in Godot. We started by setting up a TileSet within the **TileMapLayer** node with collision layers and painting the level using the TileMap system. From there, we created the player character, importing the necessary animated sprite frames for different animations. With the character in place, we implemented a default script using Godot's **CharacterBody2D** template. Finally, we took the time to clean and organize the code by splitting it into individual functions, a key part of following the clean code principles.

In the next chapter, we will animate the player and code special abilities such as double-jump and wall sliding. We will also set up collectible items, an enemy to defeat, and a checkpoint to reach to finish the level.

Join our community on Discord

Join our community's Discord space for discussions with the author and other readers:

https://packt.link/godot-4-game-dev

7

Creating a 2D Mini-Game in Godot – Part 2

In the previous chapter, we guided you through the process of creating your first complete 2D platformer level in Godot. We built the level using a **TileMap**, set up the player character with animations, and cleaned up the default basic movement script. Now, it's time to take things further by adding more complex mechanics and refining how the player interacts with the game world.

In this chapter, you'll learn how to trigger player animations directly through code. We'll also dive into custom behaviors such as wall-sliding, double-jumping, and falling through platforms—common mechanics in many platform games. We will also add collectible items and a patrolling enemy. Finally, we'll script a checkpoint system for completing levels, allowing players to progress through the game.

In this chapter, we're going to cover the following main topics:

- Controlling player animations with code
- Wall-sliding and double-jumping mechanics
- Falling through platforms
- Adding collectible items
- Adding a patrolling enemy
- Implementing level completion

By the end of this chapter, you'll have a deeper understanding of how to bring your game mechanics to life with code and create a more dynamic and engaging platformer experience.

Technical requirements

By this point in the book, you should know how to do the following:

- Create nodes
- Create scenes

You should also know about variables and functions for use in GDScript (see *Chapter 4*).

This chapter's code files are available here in the book's GitHub repository: https://github.com/PacktPublishing/Godot-4-for-Beginners/tree/main/ch7

Visit this link to check out the video of the code being run: https://packt.link/goVK2

The game assets used in this project are released under a **Creative Commons Zero** (**CC0**) license by Pixel Frog. Pixel Frog has allowed us to distribute, remix, adapt, and build upon the material in any medium or format, even for commercial purposes.

They can be found here:

- **Pixel Adventure 1**: https://pixelfrog-assets.itch.io/pixel-adventure-1
- **Pixel Adventure 2**: https://pixelfrog-assets.itch.io/pixel-adventure-2

Controlling player animations with code

Animations play a crucial role in bringing your game to life, making player actions feel smooth and responsive. In this section, we'll explore how to trigger different player animations in code. By learning how to control animations programmatically, you'll gain the ability to seamlessly transition between movement states such as idle, running, and jumping, enhancing the overall feel and polish of your game.

Take a moment to consider the conditions that will trigger each animation that we created in the previous chapter. We should try to imagine what will cause the animation to play so that we can implement it in the code:

- The *idle* animation is triggered when the player is stationary (both x and y velocities are 0).
- The *run* animation is triggered when the player moves left or right. To ensure the sprite faces the correct direction, we'll flip it based on movement direction.
- The *fall* animation is triggered when the player is moving downward (the y velocity is increasing) and is not wall-sliding.
- The *jump* animation plays when the player is moving upward (the y velocity is decreasing) during their first jump (to prevent the player from spamming *jump* to *float* or *fly*).

- The *double-jump* animation occurs when the player is already airborne, jumps again, and is not wall-sliding.
- The *wall-slide* animation triggers when the player is sliding down a wall and pressing toward the wall. The sprite will flip to face away from the wall they are sliding on.

In the previous chapter, we imported and named all the animations, and we now have a clear understanding of the conditions under which each animation should be triggered. However, to implement these animations effectively, there are some missing pieces:

- We have no way of knowing whether the player is currently wall-sliding
- We have no way of knowing whether this is the player's first jump
- We have no way of knowing whether this is a double jump

These checks are crucial because our animations need to accurately represent the player's actions and state. For instance, triggering the wall-slide animation requires us to detect when the player is sliding against a wall. Similarly, distinguishing between the first jump and a double jump ensures that the correct animation plays for each action.

Helper variables

By addressing these gaps with **helper variables**, we can create a more dynamic and responsive player character, where the animations align seamlessly with the gameplay mechanics established in the previous chapter.

To ensure our character animations reflect the player's actions, we need to track certain states, such as whether the player is wall-sliding or how many jumps they've performed. To do this, we'll introduce two new variables.

Add the following variables at the top of your `Player` script, just after the constants:

```
var jump_count = 0
var is_wall_sliding = false
```

These variables will help us manage and detect the conditions needed to trigger the correct animations.

The preceding variables will solve our problems; we just need to use them in the correct place. Starting with the `jump_count` variable. When the player jumps or double jumps, we increase `jump_count` by 1. When the player is on the floor again, we reset `jump_count` to 0.

In the `handle_jump()` function, increment `jump_count` as follows:

```
func handle_jump():
    # Reset jump count if the player is on the floor
    if is_on_floor():
        jump_count = 0
    # Jump from the floor (first jump)
    if Input.is_action_just_pressed("ui_accept") and is_on_floor():
        velocity.y = JUMP_VELOCITY
        jump_count += 1

    # Double jump in the air
    elif Input.is_action_just_pressed("ui_accept") and jump_count < 2:
        velocity.y = JUMP_VELOCITY
        jump_count += 1
```

In the preceding code, when the player jumps, `jump_count` is increased by 1, and when the player lands on the floor, `jump_count` resets to `0`.

Now that we've added the necessary variables to track the player's state, we can start implementing mechanics that use them in the next section.

Wall-sliding and double-jumping mechanics

In this section, we will create dedicated functions to handle *wall-sliding* and *double-jumping*, ensuring smooth and responsive movement for the player. These mechanics will not only enhance gameplay but also tie directly into triggering the appropriate animations. We will also create an *animate* function that calls all the specific animations.

Wall-sliding and double-jumping are unique player movements that require additional logic to function correctly. By separating these actions into their own functions, we can keep the code organized and easier to maintain while ensuring that each mechanic behaves as intended. Let's start by creating these dedicated functions.

Double-jump function

The **double jump** is a classic mechanic in platformer games, giving players an extra boost and greater control over their movement. To implement this feature, we need to track when the player is in the air and determine whether a second jump is allowed.

This section will walk you through creating a function to handle the double-jump logic, ensuring a smooth and responsive experience for the player.

Let's look at the following code:

```
func double_jump():
    # Handle double jump
    if Input.is_action_just_pressed("ui_accept") and !is_on_floor() and jump_count < 2:
        velocity.y = JUMP_VELOCITY
        jump_count += 1
```

In the preceding double-jump function, first, check whether the player has pressed the *jump* key and whether they are currently in the air (not on the floor) and the jump count is less than 2 (to prevent flying). If all these conditions are true, then the player can jump a second time.

Wall-slide function

Wall-sliding depends on another value to work: **friction**. This is so that we can slide down the wall at a slower rate than if we fall. To see that in action, add a new constant at the top of the program as follows:

```
const SPEED = 150.0
const JUMP_VELOCITY = -400.0
const FRICTION = 100
```

The preceding constant called `friction` will be the speed at which we slide down the wall. The value of `100` is chosen because it delivers the best effect; however, you could choose any number you feel looks best to you when testing.

Now, implement the `wall_slide` function:

```
func wall_slide(delta):
    if is_on_wall() and !is_on_floor():
        if Input.is_action_pressed("ui_left") or Input.is_action_pressed("ui_right"):
            is_wall_sliding = true
        else:
            is_wall_sliding = false
    else:
        is_wall_sliding = false
```

```
    if is_wall_sliding:
        velocity.y = min(velocity.y, FRICTION)
```

The `wall_slide` function enables the wall-sliding mechanic for the player by checking specific conditions and modifying their movement. To better understand how this function works, let's break it down step by step in the following sections.

Checking conditions

The first `if` condition checks whether the player is touching a wall (`is_on_wall()`) and is not grounded (`!is_on_floor()`).

This verifies two things:

- Whether the player is touching a wall using the `is_on_wall()` function
- Whether the player is not grounded, as determined by the `!is_on_floor()` condition

Detecting input

Inside the wall detection block, the following line checks for player input:

```
if Input.is_action_pressed("ui_left") or Input.is_action_pressed("ui_right")
```

This condition determines whether the player is pressing either the *left* (`ui_left`) or *right* (`ui_right`) movement keys. This leads to two scenarios:

- If either key is pressed, the code sets `is_wall_sliding = true`, enabling the wall slide
- If no key is pressed, the variable is set to `false`, stopping the wall slide

Resetting the wall slide

The `else` block ensures that if the player is not on a wall or is standing on the floor, `is_wall_sliding` is set to `false`. This prevents unintended sliding.

Limiting downward speed

The final check, `if is_wall_sliding:`, applies the line `velocity.y = min(velocity.y, FRICTION)` inside its block.

Here, the `min()` function compares the current downward velocity (`velocity.y`) with the pre-defined `FRICTION` value. If `velocity.y` is greater than `FRICTION` (meaning the player is falling too fast), `min()` returns the smaller of the two—the `FRICTION` value. This effectively caps the falling speed during a wall slide, ensuring the player descends at a controlled, slower rate.

This results in a smoother and more manageable wall-sliding experience, preventing rapid, uncontrolled drops down the wall.

By combining these checks and actions, the `wall_slide` function ensures the player can seamlessly transition into and out of a controlled wall slide based on their input and environment. This sets the foundation for intuitive gameplay mechanics.

Remember to call our new functions in the process function so that we can use them:

```
func _physics_process(delta):
    apply_gravity(delta)
    double_jump()
    wall_slide(delta)
    move_and_slide()
```

The `_physics_process(delta)` function is where all our custom movement and physics-related functions are called. By calling them, we are asking Godot to run these functions as part of the physics engine. `_physics_process()` is part of Godot's game loop and runs at a fixed interval, ensuring that the player's actions and interactions with the game world are updated consistently and in real time.

It's important to use `_physics_process()` for physics-based logic because it's synced with the physics engine. If we used `_process()` instead—which runs every rendered frame and can vary depending on frame rate—it could lead to jittery or inconsistent movement, especially on lower-performance machines. This is because `_process()` does not guarantee consistent timing, which is crucial for physics calculations.

Animate function

The next step is to rewrite the animation trigger conditions in the code. Each animation trigger is described with a comment.

The `AnimatedSprite2D` node will play the corresponding animation, but we need a reference to the node to call its functions. We can get the reference as the scene is ready (loaded), and so we give the variable the `@onready` annotation, as shown in the following code:

```
extends CharacterBody2D
@onready var animations = $AnimatedSprite2D
```

Next, we'll declare a new function and call it animate:

```
#Handle Animations
func animate():
    # Stationary player
    if velocity.x == 0 and velocity.y == 0:
        animations.play("idle")
    
    # Player moving horizontally (left or right)
    elif velocity.y == 0:
        animations.play("run")
    
    # Player is falling
    elif velocity.y > 0 and !is_wall_sliding:
        animations.play("fall")
    
    # Player is jumping (first jump)
    elif velocity.y < 0 and jumpCount == 0:
        animations.play("jump")
    
    # Player is double-jumping
    elif !is_on_floor() and jumpCount > 0 and !is_wall_sliding:
        animations.play("double_jump")
    
    # Player is sliding on wall
    elif is_wall_sliding:
        animations.play("wall_slide")
    
    # Flip the sprite based on movement direction
    animations.flip_h = velocity.x < 0
```

Remember to call the animate() function in the _physics_process() function:

```
func _physics_process(delta):
    apply_gravity(delta)
    standard_player_movement()
    double_jump()
    wall_slide(delta)
    animate()
    move_and_slide()
```

In the preceding code, we have again made sure to call all our custom functions to run repeatedly in the physics_process function.

Now, test the game and your player should animate! Our next step is to set up the *pass-through platforms* so that the player can jump up through a platform from below and press down to fall through the platform from above.

Falling through platforms

We created two different physics layers on the TileMap in *Chapter 6* so that the player can jump up and fall down through certain platforms. Because we made these tiles as *one-way tiles*, we can jump through them from below, with no need for coding.

Now, we need to set up the code that will allow our player to fall through these platforms when we are standing on them and pressing *down*. Our code should check whether the player is pressing *down* and then simply turn off **Collision Mask** number 3 (the pass-through layer). This means that the player will stop detecting collisions on the pass_through layer and will fall until it reaches a layer that it is detecting collisions for, which is the ground layer. This is demonstrated in the check_pass_through() function as shown here:

```
func check_pass_through():
    if Input.is_action_pressed("ui_down"):
        set_collision_mask_value(3, false)
    else:
        set_collision_mask_value(3, true)
```

As can be seen in the preceding code, a new function has been created named check_pass_through(). It then checks whether the user is pressing the *down* key and, if so, it sets the value of **Collision Mask** layer number 3 to false (disabled). If the player is not pressing the *down* key, the value will be reset to true (enabled).

Remember to add `check_pass_through()` to your list of function calls in the `_physics_process()`; otherwise, the function will not run!

```
func _physics_process(delta):
    apply_gravity(delta)
    standard_player_movement()
    double_jump()
    wall_slide(delta)
    animate()
    check_pass_through()
    move_and_slide()
```

The player can now run, jump, double-jump, and wall-slide around the level as well as fall through special platforms. Our next step is to scatter some items around the level for the player to collect.

Adding collectible items

In many games, **collectible items** play a vital role in enhancing gameplay by providing rewards, power-ups, or essential resources to the player. These items can create a sense of progression, encourage exploration, and add layers of strategy to the game. In this section, we'll explore how to create a collectible item system in Godot.

You'll learn how to design a collectible item, detect when the player interacts with it, and implement logic to grant rewards or effects. By the end of this section, you'll have a reusable system that can be extended to include a variety of collectibles for your levels.

For the collectible item, we will use the Strawberry found in the `Items | Fruits` folder. However, you may use any item you wish as long as you adapt some of the steps that follow.

Strawberry scene (our collectible item)

For our game, the player will collect Strawberries. Once the player has collected all of the Strawberries on a level, a flag will appear which the player will touch to complete the level.

Follow these steps to create the collectible item scene:

1. Create a new scene and add **Area2D** as the root node. **Area2D** is an invisible node that defines a region of 2D space, which detects when objects have collided or stopped colliding with it.
2. Add an **AnimatedSprite2D** node as a child node.

Chapter 7 167

3. Recall that to animate a sprite, we use multiple frames that depict the sprite at various stages of motion. These frames are often grouped together in a single image known as a **sprite sheet**.

4. To animate the sprite, we first import the sprite sheet and then divide it into individual frames. To do this, select the **AnimatedSprite2D** node, and in the **Sprite Frames** property in **Inspector**, click on **New SpriteFrames**. This is shown in *Figure 7.1*:

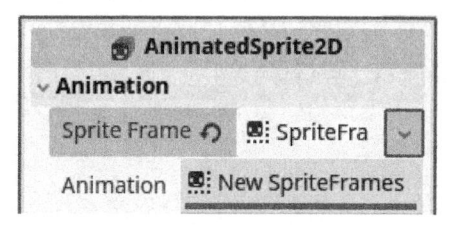

Figure 7.1 – Creating new SpriteFrames

5. Clicking on **New SpriteFrames** in **Inspector**, as shown in *Figure 7.1*, will open the **SpriteFrames** area at the bottom of the screen. This is the space where we can import frames and create and name new animations. This is shown in *Figure 7.2*:

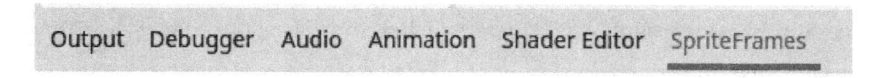

Figure 7.2 – The SpriteFrames area

As shown in *Figure 7.2*, we currently have only the default animation and no images or frames associated with it. We will now create animations for the `idle` animation and then import the sprites associated with it from the sprite sheet.

6. Start by renaming the default animation to `idle`.

7. In **FileSystem**, create a new folder called `Collectibles`.

8. Now, find the `Items | Fruits` folder in the assets you downloaded from Pixel Frog (see the *Technical requirements* section) and drag the images for your Strawberry into the **Collectibles** folder in **FileSystem**.

9. Select the **idle** animation and then click on **Add frames from a Sprite Sheet** button or press *Ctrl* + *Shift* + *O*. Now, select the `Idle` image file in your `Collectibles` folder.

10. Now, you must count the player images and update the **Horizontal** and **Vertical** frame properties (see *Figure 7.3*) as required.

11. Then, click on the **Select All** button followed by the **Add x Frame(s)** button. This is shown for the idle frames of the Strawberry in *Figure 7.3*:

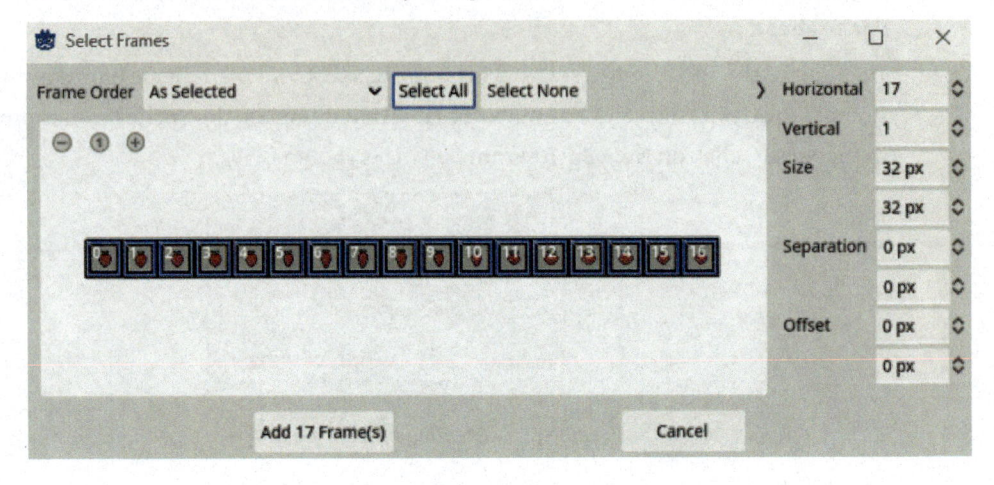

Figure 7.3 – Setting the Horizontal and Vertical frames and adding them to the animation

Now that you have cut the individual frames from the image (sprite sheet) as in *Figure 7.3*, your **SpriteFrames** window will update with the images to be used for the `idle` animation. This is shown in *Figure 7.4*:

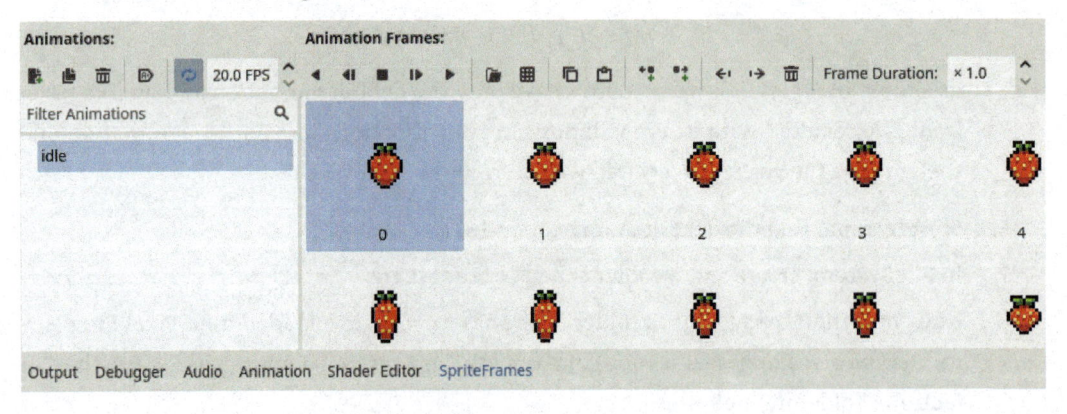

Figure 7.4 – The frames used for the idle animation

Chapter 7

> 🔍 **Quick tip**: Need to see a high-resolution version of this image? Open this book in the next-gen Packt Reader or view it in the PDF/ePub copy.
>
> 🔒 **The next-gen Packt Reader** and a **free PDF/ePub copy** of this book are included with your purchase. Scan the QR code OR visit packtpub.com/unlock, then use the search bar to find this book by name. Double-check the edition shown to make sure you get the right one.

12. As you can see in *Figure 7.4*, there are controls for the animations in the bar at the top. I have set the idle frame rate to **20 FPS**, and looping is on. You can play with these settings to find the ones you like. You can see this in *Figure 7.5*:

Figure 7.5 – Animation controls with looping and FPS highlighted

13. To complete the setup of the Strawberry collectible, we need to add a **CollisionShape2D** node as a child of the **Area2D** node. For the **Shape** property of the node, select **CapsuleShape2D** and adjust it in the Viewport to fit the Strawberry. This is shown in *Figure 7.6*:

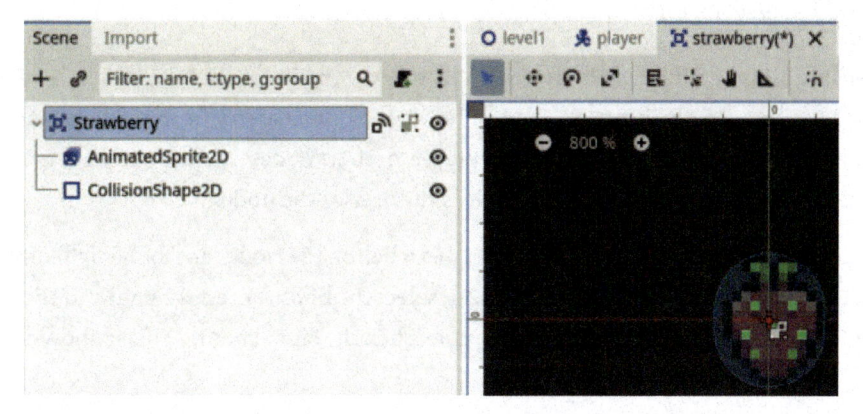

Figure 7.6 – Adjusting the collision to fit the Strawberry

The Strawberry can now collide with objects and detect when an object has collided with it. We will need to write code to animate the Strawberry and to do something when the player collides with it, such as removing the Strawberry and adding *1* to the player's Strawberry collection score.

Implementing the Strawberry script

The Strawberry only needs to do two things: animate and disappear when the player collects it. We will now program the Strawberry to do these two things.

In the **Strawberry** scene, select your **Strawberry** node and click on the **Attach New Script** button/icon, as shown in *Figure 7.7*:

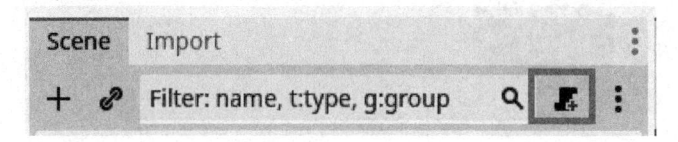

Figure 7.7 – The Attach New Script button/icon

The `idle` animation must play repeatedly; we have already set it to loop, so, in the `ready` function, we just need to start the animation. To make it easier to reference other nodes in a scene, Godot provides a built-in shortcut. By preceding a node's name with a dollar sign (**$**), we can quickly access that node and its functions directly.

This shortcut is particularly useful when frequently interacting with other nodes in a scene, such as controlling a character's animations or updating UI elements, as it keeps the code more readable and efficient. Use this shortcut to play the `idle` animation of the Strawberry, as shown in the following code:

```
func _ready():
    $AnimatedSprite2D.play("idle")
```

When our player collides with or overlaps a Strawberry, we want to *signal* the Strawberry to execute a function. In the function, we can remove the Strawberry from the level and add 1 to the number of Strawberries collected by the player. **Area2D** nodes can respond to a variety of built-in signals, one of which is when a body enters the area of the node.

To set this up, select the **Strawberry** node, then click on the **Node** tab (to the right of the **Inspector** tab). In the **Signals** category, under **Area2D**, select the **body_entered** signal and click on **Connect** in the bottom-right corner, or simply double-click the signal name. This is shown in *Figure 7.8*:

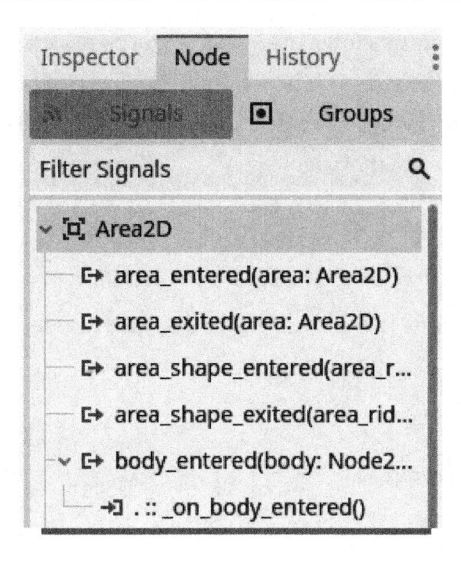

Figure 7.8 – The body_entered signal of Area2D

A new window will pop up, which is shown in *Figure 7.9*. You need not worry about the details now and simply click on the **Connect** button.

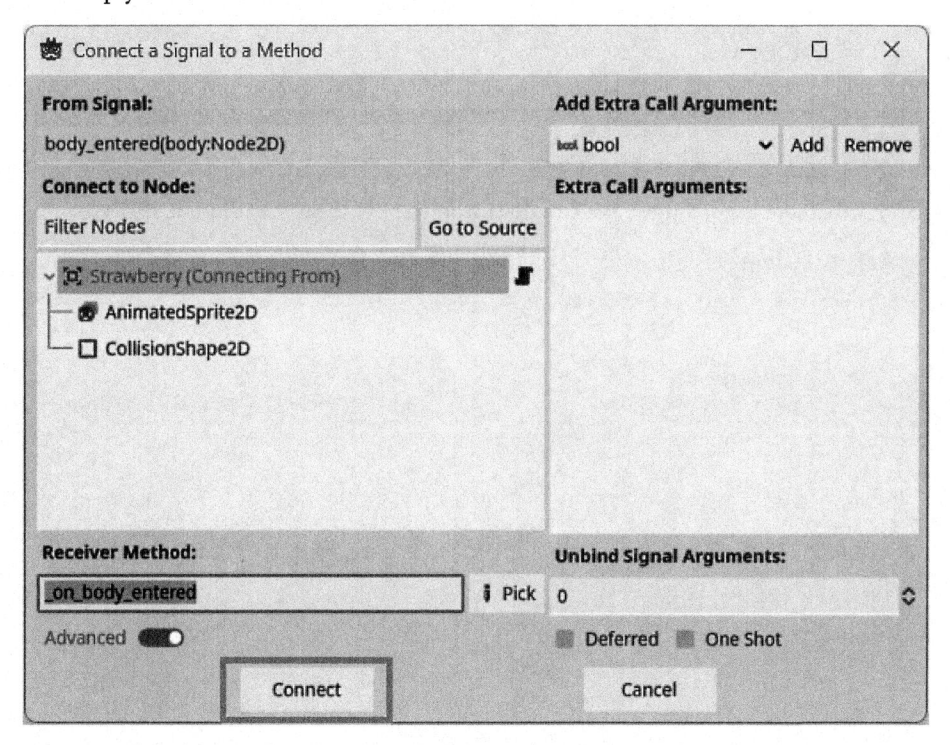

Figure 7.9 – Connecting a signal to a method (function)

Clicking on the **Connect** button, as shown in *Figure 7.9*, will create a new function in the Strawberry script called _on_body_entered(body). The parameter called body contains a reference to the object that collided with the Strawberry. To determine whether that *body* is the *player*, we can tag the player as part of a group called Player.

Here's how you do it:

1. Switch to your **Player** scene and select the **Player** node.
2. Again, click on the **Node** tab to the right of **Inspector**, then choose the **Groups** sub-tab.
3. Click on the + symbol to add a group.
4. Name the group Player.

These steps are shown in *Figure 7.10*.

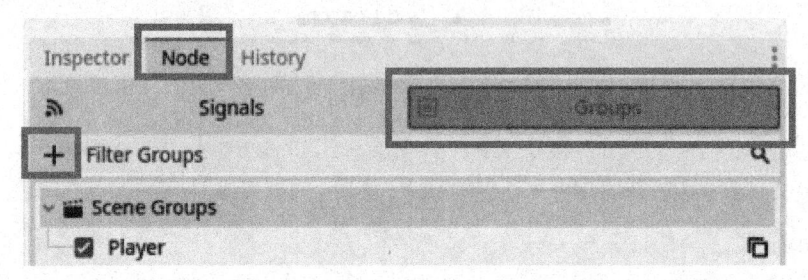

Figure 7.10 – The Node tab, Groups sub-tab, and the + symbol to add a new group

With the group ready, we can check whether the body that entered the Strawberry is in the **Player** group and if so, react accordingly. We can do this in the Strawberry script as shown:

```
func _on_body_entered(body):
    if body.is_in_group("Player"):
        #add to player score
        #remove the strawberry
```

Player will keep track of how many Strawberries it has collected. We need a variable in the Player script to keep count of the number of Strawberries the player has collected, and we need a function in the Player script to add one to the score each time a Strawberry is collected.

Return to the Player script and add the variable and function as shown in the code:

```
var jumpCount = 0
var is_wall_sliding = false
var strawberry_count = 0

func add_score(amount):
    strawberry_count += amount
```

The preceding code will increase the strawberry_count variable by an amount each time it is called. We will call it in the _on_body_entered(body) function of the Strawberry and remove the Strawberry from the scene once collected, as shown here:

```
func _on_body_entered(body):
    if body.is_in_group("Player"):
        body.add_score(1)
        queue_free() #remove strawberry
```

The built-in queue_free() function deletes a node from memory at the end of the current frame as soon as it is safe to do so. It is the recommended method for removing nodes from the scene.

With this code in place, when the Strawberry signals that another body has entered its space, a value of 1 will be added to the Strawberry count of the player, and the Strawberry will be removed from the scene.

Feel free to drag and drop the `strawberry.tscn` file into your level multiple times so that the player has something to collect, as shown in *Figure 7.11*:

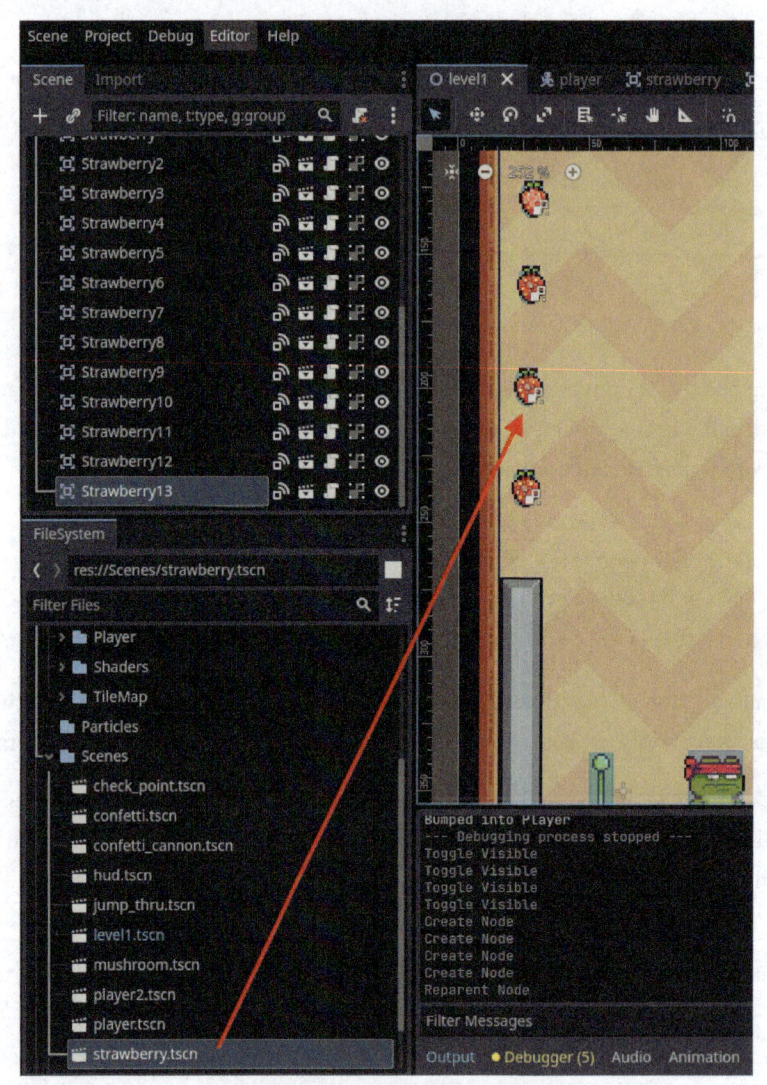

Figure 7.11 – Dragging and dropping Strawberries into the level

Chapter 7

The player can move through the level and collect Strawberries. To add a challenge, we need an enemy to patrol.

Adding a patrolling enemy

This is a reminder that the enemies can be found here: `https://pixelfrog-assets.itch.io/pixel-adventure-2`.

We will be using the **Mushroom** enemy. Create a new scene and set it up with **CharacterBody2D**, **AnimatedSprite2D**, and **CollisionShape2D** with **CapsuleShape2D** only covering part of the mushroom, as shown in *Figure 7.12*:

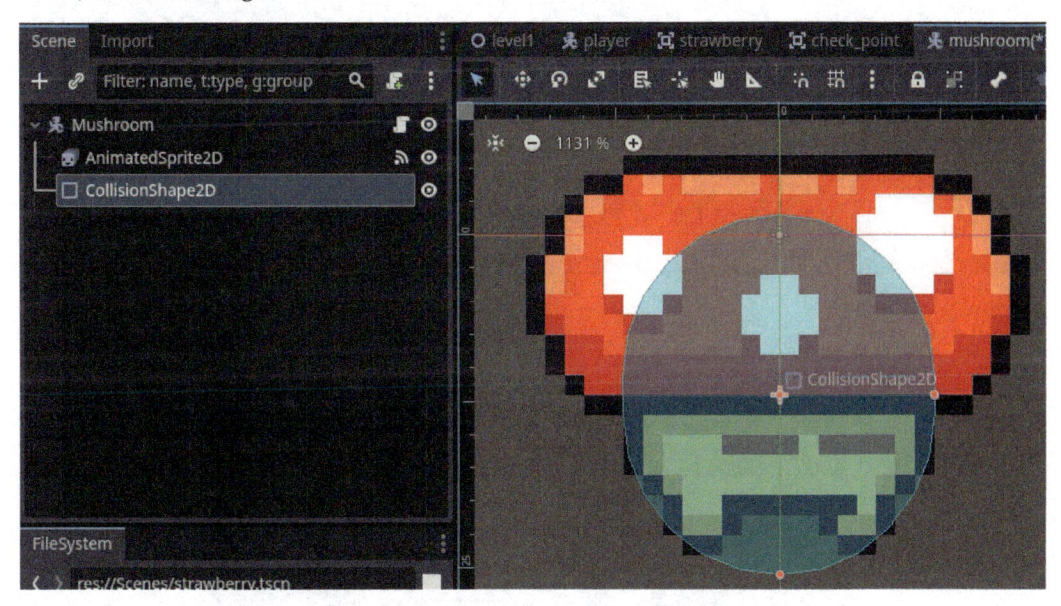

Figure 7.12 – Setting up the Mushroom scene

Use the sprite sheets provided in the `Mushroom` enemy folder and set up the SpriteFrames and animations for **idle** and **run** to be looped at **20 FPS**. I created my own **death** animation using one frame from **idle** and rotating it, as shown in *Figure 7.13*:

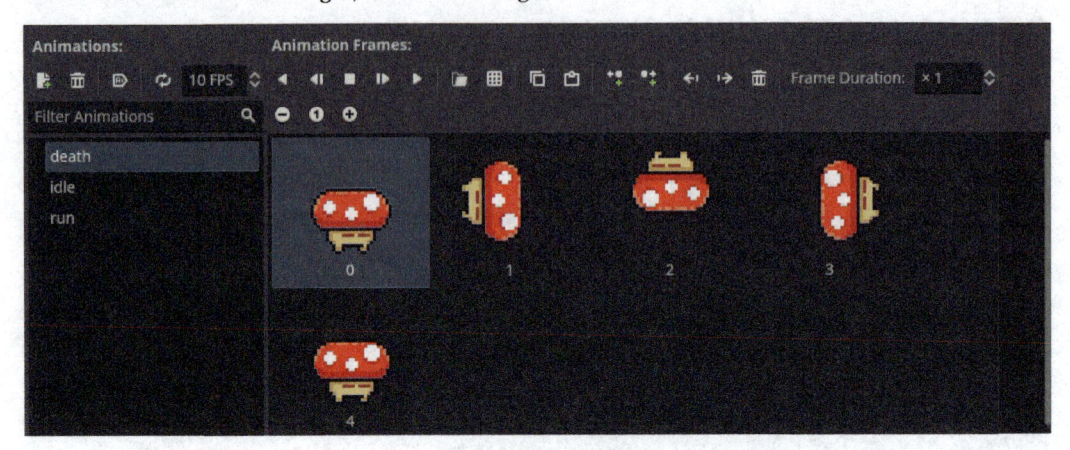

Figure 7.13 – Animations for the Mushroom enemy

Attach a new script to the **Mushroom** node and ensure that the template used is an empty object, as shown in *Figure 7.14*:

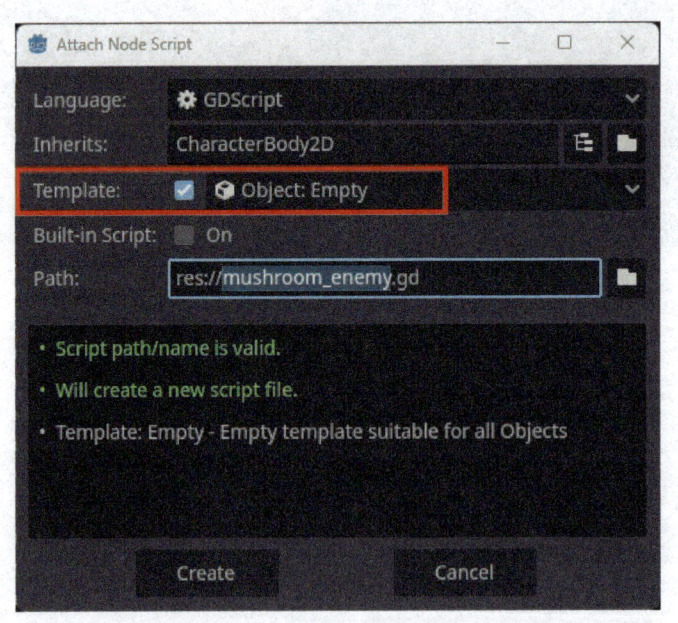

Figure 7.14 – Using the Object: Empty template for the Mushroom enemy

Using the **Empty** template will ensure that our script is created with no default or added code and is as simple as possible.

Add code to set values for the speed, direction, and health of the Mushroom, as shown in the code:

```
extends CharacterBody2D

const SPEED = 75
var direction = 1
var health = 1
```

Note that the `direction` variable will have values of `-1` or `1` to indicate left or right movement, respectively.

Now, we have variables to control the speed, direction, and health of the Mushroom enemy.

Also, add a function to apply gravity to the Mushroom, allowing it to fall and touch the ground, as shown in the following code:

```
func add_gravity(delta):
    # Add gravity.
    if not is_on_floor():
        velocity += get_gravity() * delta
```

If the Mushroom is not on the ground, gravity will pull it downward.

Now, create a function to make the Mushroom move. I have called mine `update_direction()` and all it does is make the enemy move to the right at a constant speed, as shown in the code:

```
func update_direction():
    # Move enemy at constant speed
    velocity.x = SPEED * direction
```

The velocity of the Mushroom in the horizontal plane is multiplied by speed and direction.

Both functions must also be called in the `_physics_process(delta)` function along with `move_and_slide()`, as shown in the code:

```
func _physics_process(delta):
    add_gravity(delta)
    update_direction()
    move_and_slide()
```

We must also set collisions on the Mushroom so that it can collide with the floor and the player. Do this by turning on **Collision Layer 1** and turning on **Collision Mask 1**, **2**, and **3**.

If you drop a Mushroom into the level now and run the game, the Mushroom will begin moving to the right until it collides with a wall.

We will detect when a Mushroom has collided with a wall using the built-in `is_on_wall()` function and reverse its direction, as shown in the code:

```
func reverse_direction():
    #Reverse direction when hitting a wall
    if is_on_wall():
        direction = -direction
```

Note that by inverting or negating the value of direction, we can determine whether the Mushroom moves to the left or the right.

Make sure to call `reverse_direction()` after you have called `move_and_slide()`, as shown in the following code, because otherwise, collisions will not be detected correctly:

```
func _physics_process(delta):
    add_gravity(delta)
    moveEnemy()
    move_and_slide()
    reverse_direction()
```

If you place your Mushroom on a floating platform, when it reaches the edge of the platform, it will fall off. To prevent this, use a **RayCast2D** node to detect when the Mushroom is near the edge and then reverse direction. Add a **RayCast2D** node as a child of **Mushroom**, as shown in *Figure 7.15*:

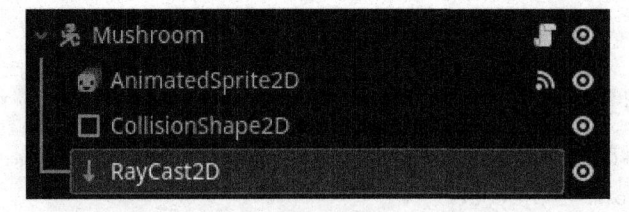

Figure 7.15 – Adding a RayCast node to our Mushroom node

Chapter 7

RayCast2D is simply an invisible ray cast by an object that looks for collisions in the direction in which it was sent. In this case, we are looking for collisions below us to determine when we are no longer on the floor. Our ray is cast a little to the right of our Mushroom (I used **Target Position x**: 0, **y**: 14 and **Transform Position x**: 15 and **y**: 7) so that we can see when we are approaching the *no floor zone* and reverse the direction before we fall off! Place your ray as shown in *Figure 7.16*:

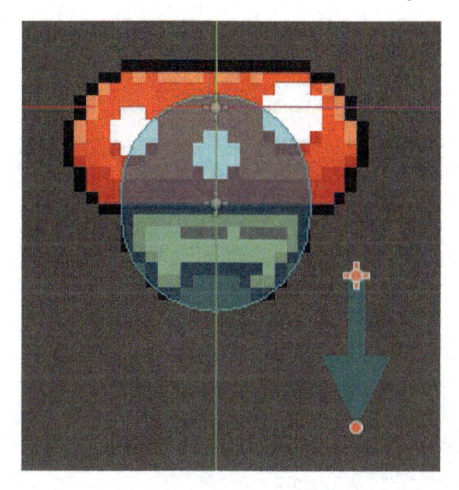

Figure 7.16 – Casting a ray downward from the right of the Mushroom

Now, we can write a function to reverse the direction of the Mushroom when the ray is not colliding with the floor and to move the ray to the opposite side so that it is always looking for no floor in the direction the Mushroom is moving, as shown:

```
func platform_edge():
    if not $RayCast2D.is_colliding():
        direction = -direction
        $RayCast2D.position.x *= -1
```

In the preceding code, as soon as the ray is no longer colliding with the ground, the Mushroom's movement direction is reversed and the ray is moved to the other side of the Mushroom to detect collisions in the direction that the Mushroom is moving. We must all turn on **Collision Mask 2** and **3** for the **RayCast2D** node so that it will detect the floor.

Remember to call this function after move_and_slide() in the _physics_process() function so that it runs after collisions have been detected. Finally, place a Mushroom on a platform to test that it patrols the platform and does not fall off.

Mushroom stomping

The player should be able to hurt the Mushroom only by attacking it from above. We will create a *hurt zone* or *death zone* for the Mushroom, which will consist of an **Area2D** and **CollisionShape2D** node with a **RectangleShape2D** node placed on top of the Mushroom.

The Mushroom will hurt the player if it attacks from the side. We will create a *hurt player* zone on either side of the Mushroom, again made up of **Area2D** and **CollisionShape2D** with **RectangleShape2D**. This is shown in *Figure 7.17*:

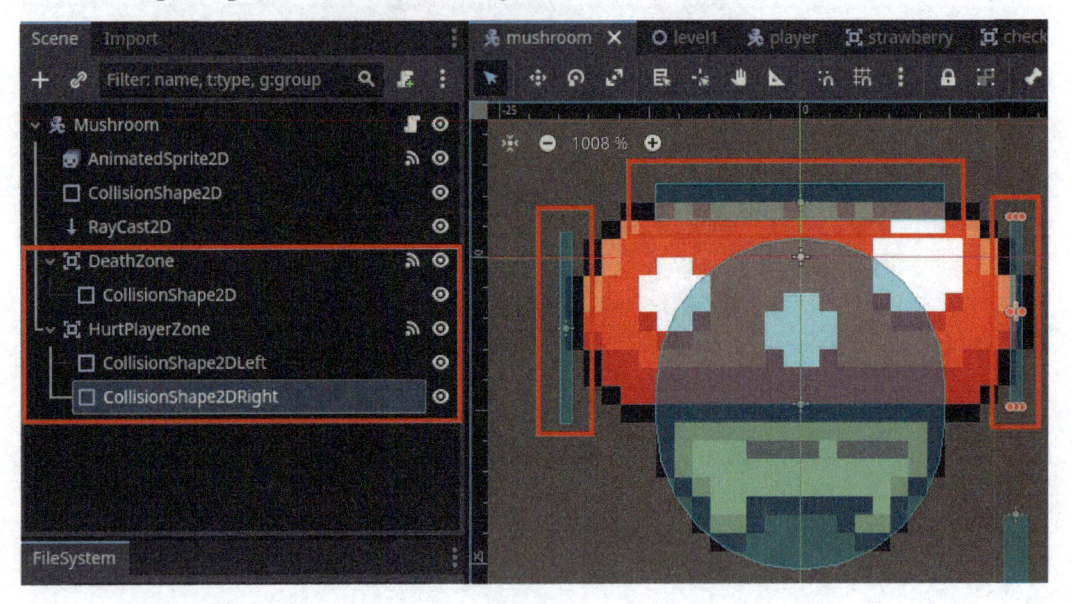

Figure 7.17 – Creating the death zone and hurt player zone

With these in place, we can make use of signals to detect when the player has entered one of the zones and then react accordingly.

Connect the _on_death_zone_body_entered() and _on_hurt_player_zone_body_entered() signals to the Mushroom script. Then, write code in the empty functions, as shown in the code:

```
func _on_death_zone_body_entered(body):
    if "Player" in body.name:
        body.velocity.y = -500
        health -= 1
```

```
func _on_hurt_player_zone_body_entered(body: Node2D):
    if "Player" in body.name:
        body.hurt()
```

There is no hurt() function in the Player script yet. We should create that now.

Open the Player script and add the following function so that the player can be hurt by the Mushroom enemies:

```
func hurt():
    print("Player hurt")
```

Take note that, for now, we just use a technique called **stub testing** in which we simply display a message to verify that the function was called correctly. Later, we will complete the full implementation of this function.

The _on_death_zone_body_entered(body) function runs whenever a body enters the *death zone* area (jumps onto the Mushroom from above). We check to see whether the body that entered the zone has the word Player in its name. This is an alternative and equivalent option to checking whether body.is_in_group("Player"). If the body does have the word Player in its name, we add 500 to the velocity of the player to make it appear to bounce off the Mushroom and we subtract 1 from the health of the Mushroom.

The _on_hurt_player_zone_body_entered() function runs when a body enters the Mushroom from the sides. Again, if this body is the player, we run the player's hurt() function, reducing the player's health.

When the Mushroom's health is 0, it should disable collisions, stop detecting collisions with the player, and play the death animation. This is achieved with the custom function shown as follows:

```
func mushroom_death():
    if health <= 0:
        $CollisionShape2D.disabled = true
        $HurtPlayerZone.monitoring = false
        $AnimatedSprite2D.play("death")
```

The `mushroom_death()` function should be called in the `_physics_process()` function, as shown in the code:

```
func _physics_process(delta):
    add_gravity(delta)
    moveEnemy()
    move_and_slide()
    reverse_direction()
    platform_edge()
    mushroom_death()
```

Connect the `_on_animated_sprite_2d_animation_finished()` signal of the `AnimatedSprite2D` node of the Mushroom. When the `death` animation is finished, it will trigger the function to remove the Mushroom from the scene, as shown in the code:

```
func _on_animated_sprite_2d_animation_finished():
    if $AnimatedSprite2D.animation == "death":
        queue_free()
```

Add some more Mushrooms and collectibles to your level. To prevent crowding the scene tree, add a new child node of the **Node** type. Rename it Enemies and drag all of the Mushrooms under it. You can do the same for **Collectibles**, as shown in *Figure 7.18*:

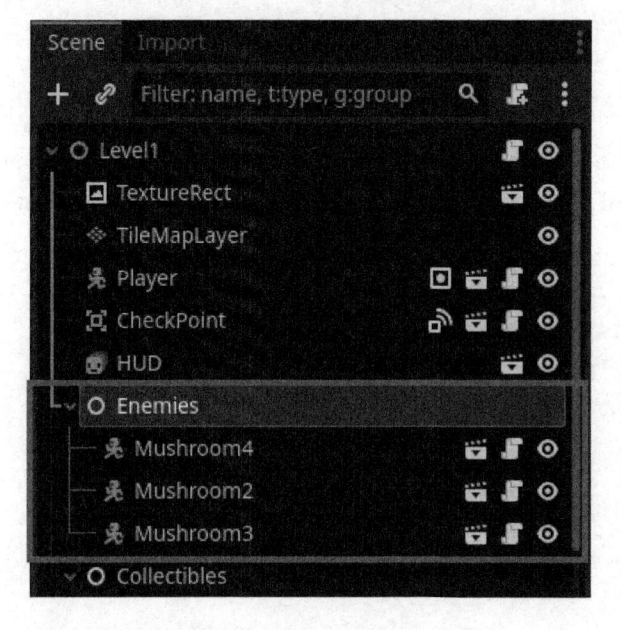

Figure 7.18 – Organizing the scene tree by grouping nodes

Now that the level has enemies and collectibles, we need a *win* condition. For our purposes, it will be that once the player has collected all of the Strawberries, a checkpoint flag will fly. Touching that flag will end the level. Let's learn more about level completion in the next section.

Implementing level completion

Level completion mechanics are a vital part of any game, providing players with a sense of accomplishment and closure. In this section, we'll create a system in which collecting all the Strawberries triggers a sequence of events: a checkpoint flag animates and flies out, signaling the completion of objectives. The player then moves to the flag, touching it to end the level.

This system not only adds visual and interactive flair but also reinforces the player's progress and goal achievement. By the end of this section, you'll have a polished and rewarding level completion sequence to enhance your game's overall experience.

Create a new scene with the following:

- **Area2D** as the root node (renamed to CheckPoint)
- **AnimatedSprite2D**
- **CollisionShape2D** with **RectangleShape2D**

The scene tree is shown in *Figure 7.19*:

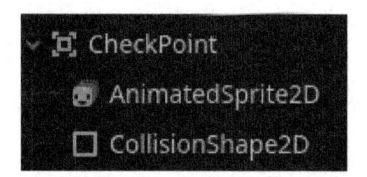

Figure 7.19 – Scene tree for the checkpoint scene

Create three animations for the flag, named flag_fly, idle, and trigger. In the assets folder from Pixel Frog, navigate to the Items | Checkpoints | Checkpoint folder.

- For the idle animation, use the single frame called Checkpoint (No Flag).png.
- For the trigger animation, use the Checkpoint (Flag Out).png sprite sheet. Do not loop the animation and run it at **20 FPS**.
- For the flag_fly animation, use the Checkpoint (Flag Idle).png sprite sheet. Loop the animation and run it at **20 FPS**.

An image of the `flag_fly` animation is shown as an example in *Figure 7.20*:

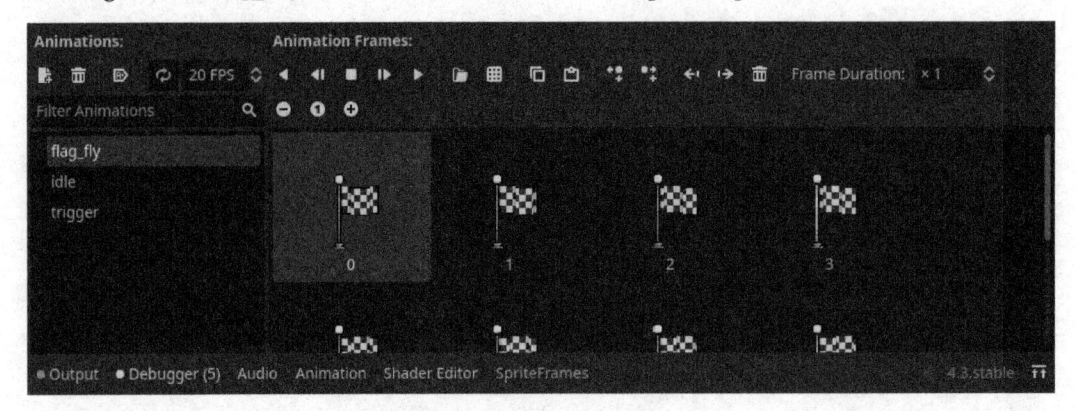

Figure 7.20 – Setting up the flag animations for the checkpoint

Attach a script to the **CheckPoint** node to customize its behavior. We will create our own signal to trigger the flag to fly out. Once the player has collected all of the Strawberries in the level, the player will emit the `trigger` signal. The `CheckPoint` code is shown and explained as follows:

```
extends Area2D
signal trigger
var level_complete = false

# signal that runs when the animation is finished playing
func _on_animated_sprite_2d_animation_finished():
    $AnimatedSprite2D.play("flag_fly")
    level_complete = true

# our own custom signal
func _on_trigger():
    $AnimatedSprite2D.play("trigger")

# A signal that runs when a body enters
func _on_body_entered(body):
    if level_complete:
        get_tree().quit()
```

As shown, we create our own signal and call it `trigger`. Then, in **Inspector**, we connect that signal to our script. We also have a Boolean variable called `level_complete` to determine when the level is complete. The `trigger` function linked to our signal plays the `trigger` animation and then signals that the animation is complete, which switches to the `flag_fly` animation and sets `level_complete` to true. For now, when the player touches the flag, the game will exit.

However, we need to emit the `trigger` signal from the `Player` script once they have collected all the Strawberries. Return to the `Player` script and add a new variable called `level_strawberries` to keep track of the number of Strawberries in the level, as shown:

```
var strawberry_count = 0
var level_strawberries
```

First, we should create a group called `checkpoint` and add the **CheckPoint** node to that group. To do this, select the **CheckPoint** node in **Inspector**, select the **Node** tab, then choose the **Groups** sub-tab and add a new group called `checkpoint`. This is shown in *Figure 7.21*:

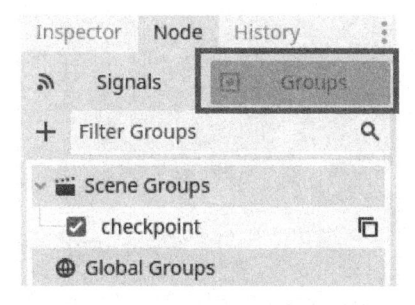

Figure 7.21 – Creating the checkpoint group

We also need a custom function that will check to see whether the level is complete and then emit the `trigger` signal. If `strawberry_count` (which is the number of Strawberries that the player has collected) matches `level_strawberries` (which is the total number of Strawberries in the level), then we get a reference to the checkpoint via its group name and emit the checkpoint's `trigger` signal. Finally, we reset the Strawberries to 0 so that the signal is only emitted once and not constantly. This is shown in the code as follows:

```
func complete_level():
    if strawberry_count == level_strawberries:
        var checkpoint =
        get_tree().get_first_node_in_group("checkpoint")
        checkpoint.emit_signal("trigger")
        strawberry_count = 0
```

Remember to call the new `complete_level()` function in the `_physics_process(delta)` function.

Since all the Strawberries are in the **Level1** scene, we need to attach a script to the **Level1** node so that it can count the Strawberries in the scene and update the `Player` variables. This is shown in *Figure 7.22*:

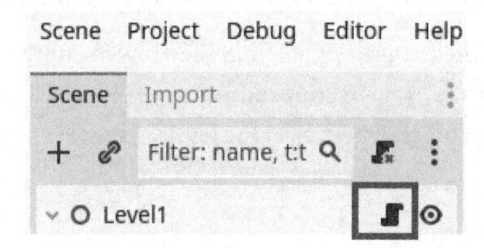

Figure 7.22 – Attaching a script to the level node

Counting the Strawberries in the level script is shown in the code as follows:

```
extends Node2D
@onready var player = $Player
@onready var strawberries = $Collectibles

func _ready() -> void:
    player.level_strawberries =
    strawberries.get_child_count()
```

In the preceding code, we get a reference to the `Player` scene as well as the `Collectibles` group of scenes (multiple Strawberries.) In the _ready function, we update the player's `level_strawberries` variable by setting it to the count of all the Strawberries in the level.

Now, add a **CheckPoint** scene to the level, and you have a way to complete it.

With that, the level is now playable!

Summary

In this chapter, we expanded our 2D platformer with essential gameplay mechanics and refined player interactions. We controlled player animations through code, ensuring smooth visual feedback for actions such as running, jumping, and wall-sliding. We also implemented wall-sliding and double-jumping, adding versatility to player movement, and introduced falling-through platforms for dynamic level navigation. Alongside these, we added collectible items to encourage exploration, a patrolling enemy to introduce a challenge, and a checkpoint for tracking level completion.

In the next chapter, we will transfer our 2D skills and make a 3D platformer!

> **Unlock this book's exclusive benefits now**
>
> Scan this QR code or go to packtpub.com/unlock, then search this book by name.
>
> *Note: Keep your purchase invoice ready before you start.*

Part 3

Building and Beyond – Your Game Development Journey

In this final part of the book, you'll take your skills to the next level by building a 3D mini-game from scratch across two detailed chapters. You'll then explore how to polish your game with visual and audio enhancements—often called "game juice"—to elevate the player experience. We'll also step back to examine core game design principles, helping you think critically about what makes games engaging and enjoyable. Finally, we'll wrap up with a carefully curated selection of resources to support your continued learning and growth as a game developer. By the end of this part, you'll be well-equipped to start creating your own complete games and refining your craft.

This part of the book includes the following chapters:

- *Chapter 8, Creating a 3D Mini-Game in Godot – Part 1*
- *Chapter 9, Creating a 3D Mini-Game in Godot – Part 2*
- *Chapter 10, Adding Game Juice*
- *Chapter 11, Understanding Game Design*
- *Chapter 12, Where to Next?*

8

Creating a 3D Mini-Game in Godot – Part 1

Creating a well-structured 3D game world requires understanding how to compose scenes, design levels, and implement functional controllers. In this chapter, we'll jump into the essential building blocks of 3D game creation in Godot. By learning how to compose and organize scenes, you'll develop a solid foundation for creating dynamic, interactive environments.

You'll start by building a 3D character scene and attaching a script to control its movement. Next, you'll learn how to design levels by combining static objects, collisions, and meshes. We'll also implement a camera controller that provides a smooth and responsive player view. Finally, we'll integrate everything into a complete level and test it to ensure functionality.

In this chapter, we're going to cover the following main topics:

- Working in 3D: a new dimension in Godot
- Building a 3D character
- Creating a level design
- Working with a `Character Controller` script
- Using variables
- Exploring functions
- Implementing a camera controller
- Running tests

By the end of this chapter, you'll be able to create reusable 3D scenes, control your player character, and design levels that are both visually appealing and functional. These skills are critical for building immersive 3D games and will set the stage for more advanced features in future chapters.

Technical requirements

This chapter's code files are available here in the book's GitHub repository: `https://github.com/PacktPublishing/Godot-4-for-Beginners/tree/main/ch8`

The game assets used in this project are released under a **Creative Commons Zero (CC0)** license by Essssam. Essssam has allowed us to distribute, remix, adapt, and build upon the material in any medium or format, even for commercial purposes.

They can be found here:

`https://essssam.itch.io/3d-leap-land`

Visit this link to check out the video of the code being run: `https://packt.link/6dr7h`

Working in 3D: a new dimension in Godot

Until now, we've been working exclusively in 2D – learning the fundamentals of Godot through flat scenes, sprites, and screen-space movement. In this chapter, we're stepping into 3D, where we'll be working with depth, perspective, lighting, and physics in a more complex environment.

While the transition from 2D to 3D can seem daunting at first, Godot's consistent node and scene-based design makes the leap much more manageable. The same principles of modularity and hierarchy still apply – only now we're dealing with 3D nodes such as **Node3D**, **MeshInstance3D**, and **Camera3D**, and building scenes in a three-dimensional space.

This chapter will walk you through the process of creating a basic 3D character. You'll learn how to assemble and organize the necessary components into a standalone scene, which can later be reused and integrated into a larger 3D world – just like we did in 2D.

Building a 3D character

Just because we are now working in *three dimensions* does not mean that the node and scene design philosophy of Godot has changed. We will continue to design different components of the game in their own scenes and then build a level or master scene using them.

Chapter 8

> **Important note**
>
> Note that you can fly around inside the 3D scene by holding down the *right mouse button* and using the *WASD* keys as in most games. If you use mouse scroll while holding the *right mouse button* down, you can set the movement speed.

We shall start with the `Player` scene. By following these steps, you'll create a fully functional 3D player character – one that can move around your 3D world using keyboard input and respond realistically to physics. This will lay the foundation for building a complete 3D game, starting with one of its most essential elements: the player.

1. Create a new Godot project and call it `Leap Land`.
2. Now, click on **Other Node** and add a **CharacterBody3D** node as the root, as shown in *Figure 8.1*:

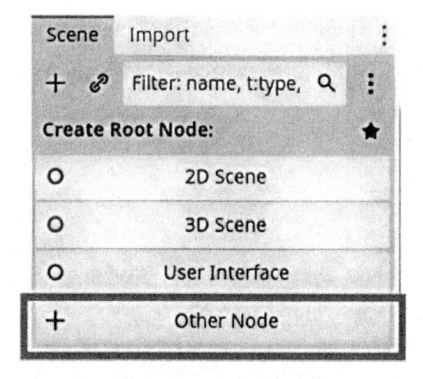

Figure 8.1 – Starting a new 3D scene

3. Rename the **CharacterBody3D** node to `Player`. This node is designed as a physics body, which is meant to be user-controlled.

4. Create a new folder in **FileSystem** and name it assets. Drag and drop the obj and tex folders from the 3D Leap Land asset pack into this folder. This is shown in *Figure 8.2*:

Figure 8.2 – Importing the obj and tex folders from 3D Leap Land

5. In 2D, we needed to attach a sprite to the **CharacterBody2D** node in order to display its texture. In 3D, we add a **MeshInstance3D** node as a child of **CharacterBody3D** node, as shown in *Figure 8.3*:

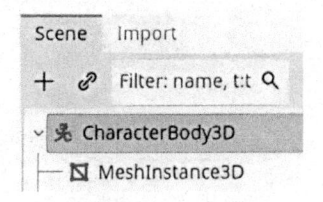

Figure 8.3 – Adding MeshInstance3D as a child

6. Select **MeshInstance3D node** and, in **Inspector,** find the **Mesh** property. It is currently <empty> but drag and drop slime.obj from **FileSystem** onto the **Mesh** property as shown in *Figure 8.4*:

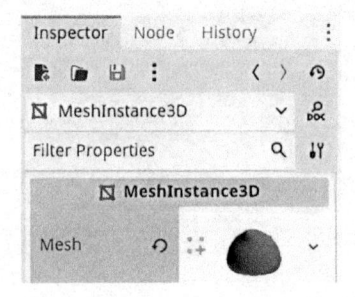

Figure 8.4 – Setting slime.obj as Mesh

Chapter 8   195

7. The slime in the scene is *gray*. To correct this, we must drag the texture file, `palette.png`, from the `tex` folder onto the slime in the Viewport. The slime will be textured as shown in *Figure 8.5*:

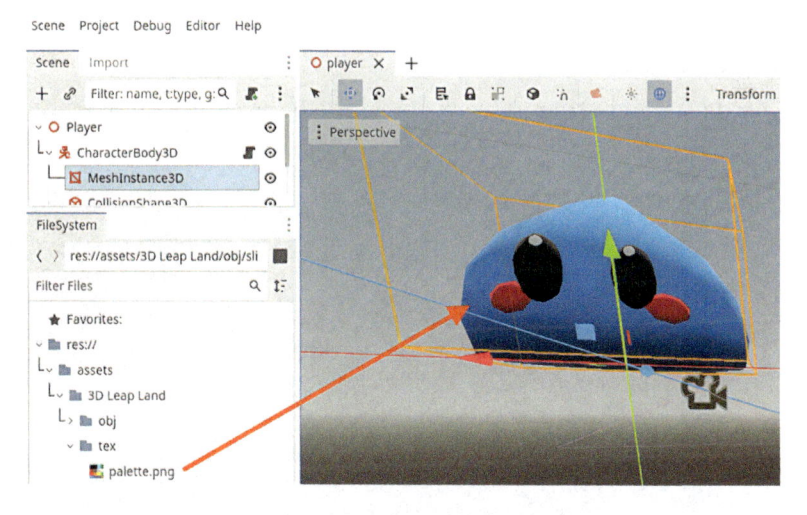

Figure 8.5 – Adding the texture to the slime

8. Now, give the player a hitbox by adding a **CollisionShape3D** node as a child. Then, in **Inspector**, find the **Shape** property, and select a new **SphereShape3D**. Use the *orange* handles to resize the hitbox to fit the slime. My **Position** values for the **CollisionShape3D** node were **x: 0.0, y: 0.15, z: 0.0**, but yours may vary.

9. To see anything, we need a camera in the scene. Add a **Camera3D** node as a child and move it so that it is in a position to see the entire slime. I placed mine at **x: 0, y: 1, z: -2.5** and set the rotation to **x: -15, y: -175, z: -1**. This is shown in *Figure 8.6*:

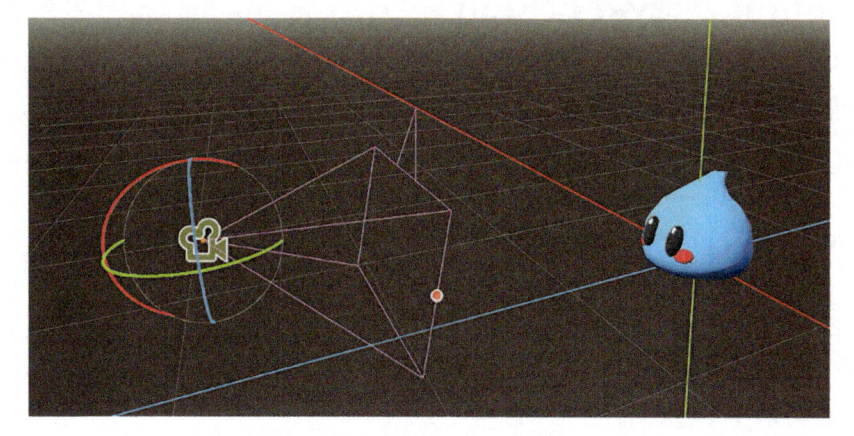

Figure 8.6 – Positioning the camera in the scene

10. Without light, we still won't see much. Add a **DirectionalLight3D** node as a child of the **CharacterBody3D** root node. This is light that goes out in all directions infinitely, like the sun. You can angle the light onto the player.
11. In the **Transform** property of **MeshInstance3D** node, rotate the mesh by 180 degrees around the *y*-axis.
12. Save the scene as `player.tscn` and preview it by pressing *F6*. It should look like *Figure 8.7*:

Figure 8.7 – The view of the slime in the game

The **Player** scene is now mostly complete and ready to be imported into more complex scenes, such as the level scene, and this is what we will work on next.

Creating a level design

Now that we've created our 3D player character, the next step is to build a level for them to exist and move around in.

Level design in Godot means creating the environment – the floors, walls, platforms, and scenery – that form the playable world of your game. In 3D, this involves placing and arranging 3D objects in space to define where the player can go, what they can interact with, and how the gameplay will unfold.

In this section, we'll create a basic 3D level using Godot's built-in nodes and tools. By the end, you'll have a space for your character to walk around and test movement.

Creating a level component

To build a level, we use various **level components**. These are the individual parts that make up the environment, such as floors, walls, ramps, or platforms. Level components are often made up of **StaticBody3D**, **MeshInstance3D**, and **CollisionShape3D** nodes.

Most parts of the level, such as the ground, walls, fences, bridges, and other non-moving structures, are created using the **StaticBody3D** node. These objects are not meant to move during gameplay and are unaffected by physics forces or collisions. Instead, they provide a stable and optimized foundation for the game's environment.

Using **StaticBody3D** node for stationary elements is important for several reasons:

- **Performance**: Godot optimizes **StaticBody3D** nodes by excluding them from costly physics calculations involving movement and collision resolution. This significantly reduces CPU usage, especially in complex scenes.
- **Physics stability**: Because these bodies are fixed in place, they provide reliable collision surfaces for moving objects such as players or enemies, ensuring consistent interactions.
- **Lighting and baking**: Static bodies also work well with light baking and global illumination systems. Since they don't move, lightmaps and shadows can be precomputed accurately, improving visual quality without runtime performance cost.

Although **StaticBody3D** nodes don't respond to physical forces, they can still be repositioned manually via code or animations, such as raising a drawbridge or lowering a platform when triggered. This gives you flexibility without sacrificing efficiency.

To visualize these components in 3D space, we use **MeshInstance3D** node, which displays the visible shape of an object. To make these objects interactable in the game world, such as allowing the player to walk on them or bump into them, we pair them with a **CollisionShape3D** node. Let's look at an example of creating a level component in the next section.

Example: creating a grass platform

The process of creating a level component is shown in the following steps and needs to be repeated for each component:

1. Create a new scene with **StaticBody3D** node as the root. Rename it `Grass`. Save it as `grass.tscn`.
2. Add a **MeshInstance3D** node and set the **Mesh** property to `ground_grass_4.obj`.
3. Drag `palette.png` onto the mesh to set the texture.

4. Add a **CollisionShape3D** node and select **New BoxShape3D**.
5. Use the handles to fit the hitbox around the ground model.

The scene should look as shown in *Figure 8.8*:

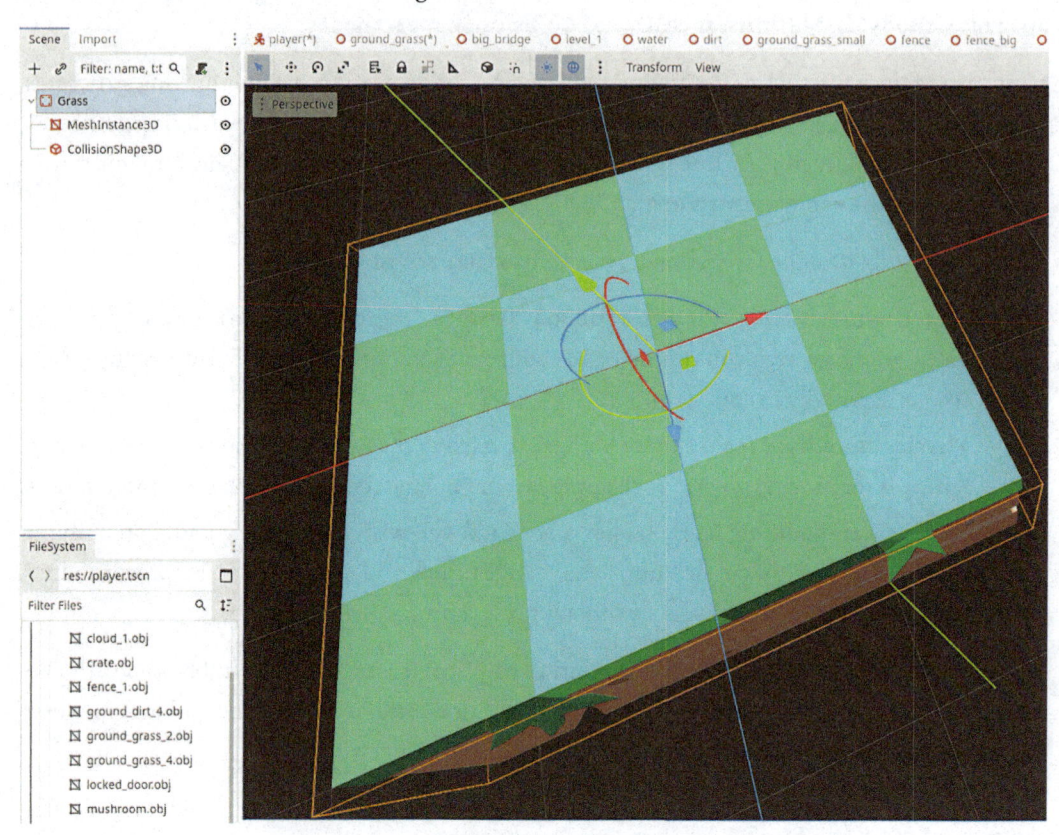

Figure 8.8 – The ground scene

> **Important note**
>
> Note that this process will need to be repeated for each component (piece of a level) you want to add to the level. This is annotated in *Figure 8.9*.

Chapter 8 199

Figure 8.9 – Arrows pointing to different level components (all individual scenes)

In the next section, we'll learn how to work with irregular collision shapes.

Handling irregular collision shapes

Some models do not conform to regular collision shapes such as boxes or spheres – for example, a curved or uneven structure, such as a bridge. Fortunately, Godot provides tools to help generate collision shapes for these more complex models automatically.

To see how this works in practice, we'll set up a **Bridge** scene using an irregular mesh and let Godot generate the collision structure for it:

1. Create a new scene with **StaticBody3D** as the root. Rename it to Bridge and save the scene as bridge.tscn.
2. Add a **MeshInstance3D** node and set the **Mesh** property to bridge_1.obj.
3. Drag palette.png onto the mesh to set the texture.
4. Select the **MeshInstance3D** node (the Bridge model).

5. Click on the **Mesh** menu at the top of the screen and click on **Create Collision Shape...** as shown in *Figure 8.10*:

Figure 8.10 – Autogenerating a collision shape for the Bridge scene

After clicking on **Create Collision Shape...**, a pop-up menu appears. For **Collision Shape placement**, choose **Sibling**, and for **Collision Shape Type**, choose **Trimesh**. This is shown in *Figure 8.11*:

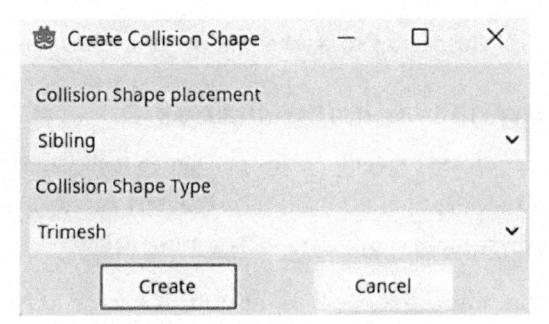

Figure 8.11 – Options for Godot to create the collision shape

- Choosing **Sibling** ensures that the generated collision shape is added as a separate node alongside the mesh, rather than as a child of it. This keeps the scene hierarchy clean and makes it easier to manage the mesh and its collision shape independently.
- Selecting **Trimesh** as the collision type is ideal for static 3D models (such as level geometry) that are not meant to move. A **Trimesh** collision creates a detailed shape that matches the mesh surface, which allows for accurate collision detection. However, it's best used only for static objects, as it is computationally expensive and not suitable for dynamic or moving objects.

6. Godot will generate a collision shape polygon for **Bridge**, and the resulting scene tree is shown in *Figure 8.12*:

Figure 8.12 – The scene tree for the Bridge scene

> **Important note**
>
> There is a drawback to allowing Godot to generate the collision shape for objects, and that is *performance*. Using simple or primitive shapes for collisions is preferable as it reduces the physics calculations required by a scene.

Creating the level layout

To begin creating the level, I started by exploring the models included in the asset pack. These models represent various environmental elements, such as terrain, structures, and props. I used the same process we followed earlier when setting up the grass and bridge: *importing the models into Godot and turning each into its own scene*.

By creating separate scenes for individual components, I was able to build a modular set of level elements. These scenes were then combined to form the complete level layout. You can follow the same approach—choose models from the downloaded asset pack (refer to the *Technical requirements* section), create scenes for each component, and then assemble them in a new scene to design your level.

Finally, make sure to add a **DirectionalLight3D** node to your level scene. This ensures the environment is properly lit, and that models appear with realistic shading and depth.

The level I have created is shown in *Figure 8.13*:

Figure 8.13 – An example level

Next, we'll learn more about organizing a level scene effectively.

Organizing the level scene

In *Figure 8.13*, each component in the level is a separate scene, making it easy to reuse and manage them independently. *Figure 8.14* shows the list of scene nodes I used to construct the level. Note that I have grouped similar or repeated objects – such as **Fences**, **Grass**, **Crates**, and **Rocks** – into their own parent nodes:

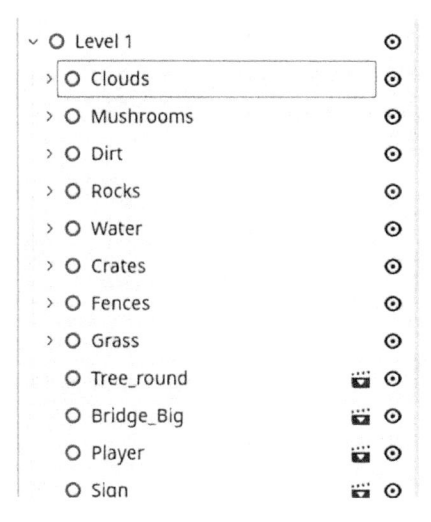

- Level 1
  - Clouds
  - Mushrooms
  - Dirt
  - Rocks
  - Water
  - Crates
  - Fences
  - Grass
  - Tree_round
  - Bridge_Big
  - Player
  - Sign

Figure 8.14 – The individual scenes making up the level

Grouping is important because it keeps the scene tree organized, especially for larger levels. It allows you to move or manipulate entire categories of objects together, which can save time and reduce errors. For example, if you want to disable all fences or apply a shader to all grass, having them grouped makes this much easier.

It's also worth noting that most of these objects, such as the ground, fences, rocks, and bridges, are static. They don't move during gameplay and should be implemented using **StaticBody3D** for better performance and accurate physics.

In contrast, dynamic objects such as the player are designed to move and react to the environment and are therefore implemented using physics-enabled nodes such as **CharacterBody3D**.

This kind of structure not only helps with level design but also ensures smooth performance and cleaner code management as your project grows.

As shown in *Figure 8.14*, we now have a complex **Level 1** scene that is made up of many smaller scenes. Although we have a player in the scene, there is no way to control it. In the next section, we will work on the Character Controller script.

Working with a Character Controller script

In this section, we will write a script that allows players to move the character around the 3D world. This script is essential because, without it, our character remains static – unable to walk, run, or jump through the level. By the end of this section, you'll have a fully controllable player character that can respond to input and interact with the game environment in a meaningful way.

Let's begin by adding a new script to the **CharacterBody3D** node of the **Player** scene. Make sure that **Template** is unchecked for **Empty** so that we do not get any pre-made code and can make a completely custom character controller as shown in *Figure 8.15*:

Figure 8.15 – Adding an empty script to the player

When the **Template** check box is not checked, as in *Figure 8.15*, we are presented with a script that only has one line:

```
extends CharacterBody3D
```

This line means that this script is adding to or customizing the built-in **CharacterBody3D** node in Godot. The **CharacterBody3D** node is used to create 3D characters, such as players or enemies, which can move, jump, or interact with the environment. By *extending* it, we can write our own code to make the character behave exactly how we want.

Although we added a camera to our **Player** scene, this won't be the only camera used during gameplay. Instead, we'll set up a second static camera in the level that we can rotate to view the player from different angles. In Godot, a scene can include multiple cameras, and you can choose which one is active by marking it as **Current** in **Inspector**.

Using variables

Before we dive into the code, let's take a moment to understand what it's doing. In this script, we'll define a few important properties that control how our player character moves, such as how fast they walk or how high they can jump. We'll use **exported variables**, which means these properties will not only be defined in code but will also be visible and editable directly in the Godot editor's **Inspector** panel.

This makes development more flexible and efficient. Designers and artists, for example, can fine-tune values such as movement speed, jump height, or gravity without needing to touch the code at all. Meanwhile, programmers can keep the logic organized in the script. This separation of concerns helps teams collaborate more effectively, allowing everyone to test and balance the gameplay quickly without risking breaking anything in the code.

Linking the Player script with the camera

We can now start preparing the character to interact with other components in the game world. One important element is the camera, which needs to follow the player smoothly as they move through the level. To make this possible, we'll set up a way for the `Player` script to communicate with a separate scene that controls the camera.

Later, we will create a **View** scene that will act as the camera controller. We'll give our camera a target to follow (which will be the *player*). We will also add a reference to this **View** so that we can control the camera's behavior, such as rotation or zoom, directly from the `Player` script.

Begin by adding these two lines to the `Player` script:

```
@export_subgroup("Components")
@export var view: Node3D
```

Here, the @export annotation makes a variable visible in **Inspector**. In this case, it also organizes the variable under a new category or subgroup called **Components** within the properties of the **CharacterBody3D** node. The variable view will now appear in that subgroup, and it is designed to reference a **Node3D** node, which we will create later to serve as the camera controller. This is shown in *Figure 8.16*:

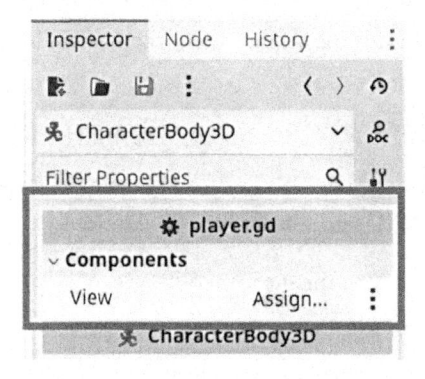

Figure 8.16 – Exporting a group called Components and a variable called View

As can be seen in *Figure 8.16*, adding the `@export` annotation makes a variable editable directly in the Godot editor, allowing you to change its value without modifying the code. This is especially useful for testing, as you can adjust values in real time while the game is running.

Next, export another group for the movement properties of the player with a variable for movement speed and jump strength:

```
@export_subgroup("Properties")
@export var movement_speed = 250
@export var jump_strength = 7
```

Because these variables are available in **Inspector**, we can find the right *feel* for the movement of our player by adjusting the values as we test the game.

Now let's add some general-purpose variables for the player:

- `movement_velocity`: To store how the player moves through 3D space
- `rotation_direction`: To keep track of the direction the player is turning in
- `gravity`: To simulate the effect of gravity on the player

So, let's add the following lines to the `Player` script:

```
var movement_velocity: Vector3
var rotation_direction: float
var vertical_velocity = 0
```

Let's understand the important elements in this code snippet:

- `movement_velocity` stores the velocity vector based on player input for movement
- `rotation_direction` holds the angle the character should rotate toward based on movement direction
- `vertical_velocity` keeps track of the vertical force acting on the character

In addition to movement, we need variables to manage the player's jumping abilities and track collectibles. Specifically, we'll add variables to do the following:

- Detect when the player is on the ground
- Control single and double jumps
- Count how many Gems the player has collected

Chapter 8

Let's define these variables in the script:

```
var previously_floored = false
var jump_single = true
var jump_double = true
var gems = 0
var smoothing_factor = 10

const GRAVITY = 25
```

In this code snippet, `previously_floored` tracks whether the character was on the ground during the last frame and is useful for detecting landings. This will become clearer when it is used in code further on.

Finally, we need a reference variable for the 3D mesh that visually represents the character. We'll use this reference to adjust the model's scale during jumping and landing – an easy way to add visual appeal known in animation as *squash and stretch*.

```
@onready var model = $MeshInstance3D
```

This line tells Godot to assign the **MeshInstance3D** node (a child of the current node) to the variable model, but only after the scene is fully loaded and ready. The `@onready` keyword ensures that the node exists when this reference is made.

Alternative method for adding reference variables

There is a shortcut for adding reference variables such as the preceding one used for the player model. You drag the node that you want to reference into the script, and, as you are about to release the mouse button, hold *Ctrl* on the keyboard. Godot will automatically type out the reference for you, and you can rename it if you wish. This is shown in *Figure 8.17*:

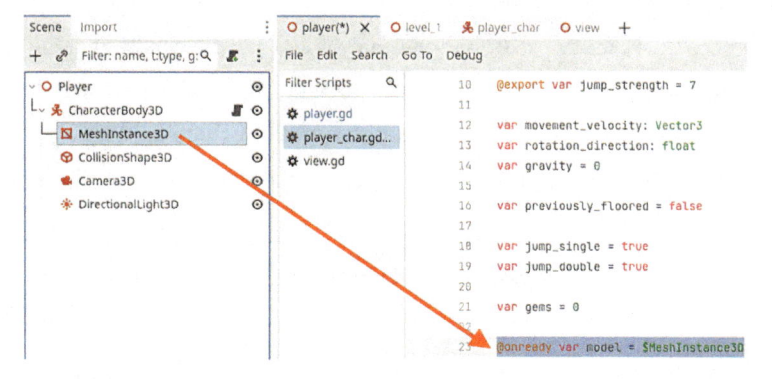

Figure 8.17 – Drag the node into the script and hold down Ctrl as you release it

As our `Player` script grows, it's important to keep things organized and readable. Instead of writing all our logic in one long block, we'll break it into smaller, focused functions. **Functions** allow us to group related lines of code under a single name, making our scripts cleaner, easier to understand, and easier to maintain.

In the next section, we'll start defining functions to handle key parts of our character's behavior. Each function will focus on one specific task, helping us build a well-structured and reusable character controller.

Exploring functions

As mentioned earlier, as our player becomes more interactive, the script that controls it will grow in complexity. To keep our code clean and manageable, we'll break it into functions: reusable blocks of logic that each handle one specific task.

In this section, we'll define functions to control gravity, handle movement input, manage jumping behavior, and track Gem collection. Understanding how to organize code in this way is a key step toward writing scalable and maintainable scripts in Godot.

Let's start by creating a function to handle gravity:

```
func handle_gravity(delta):
    vertical_velocity += GRAVITY * delta
    if vertical_velocity > 0 and is_on_floor():
        jump_single = true
        vertical_velocity = 0
```

Let's break this down:

- `vertical_velocity += GRAVITY * delta`: This gradually increases the gravity over time, simulating the effect of falling
- `if vertical_velocity > 0 and is_on_floor()`: This checks if the player is falling (`vertical_velocity > 0`) and has landed (`is_on_floor()` returns `true`)
- `jump_single = true`: Once the player lands, we allow them to jump again
- `vertical_velocity = 0`: Reset vertical velocity so that the player doesn't continue accelerating downward

This function ensures the player is affected by gravity and can only jump again once they've landed.

Now, let's create a function to handle jumping:

```
func jump():
    vertical_velocity = -jump_strength
    model.scale = Vector3(0.5, 1.5, 0.5)
    
    if jump_single:
        jump_single = false
        jump_double = true
    else:
        jump_double = false
```

Let's look at this in detail:

- `vertical_velocity = -jump_strength`: Reverses gravity to push the player upward and create the jump effect.
- `model.scale = Vector3(0.5, 1.5, 0.5)`: Adds a *squash and stretch* visual effect, compressing the width and exaggerating the height of the player for added game juice. You will learn about game juice in *Chapter 10*.
- `if jump_single:`: Checks if this is the first jump.
- `jump_single = false`: Marks that the first jump has been used.
- `jump_double = true`: Enables a second jump while in the air.
- `else`: Checks if the first jump has already been used.
- `jump_double = false`: Disables further jumping.

This function controls both the physics and visual feedback of jumping while managing single and double jump logic.

At this point, it is good practice to create a custom input map for our control scheme. Let's delve into this in the next section.

Creating an input map

Godot allows us to create our own **input map**, which is a system that lets us define custom actions, such as `jump` or `move_left`, and assign one or more keys, mouse buttons, or gamepad inputs to each action. This helps keep our code clean and flexible because we can refer to actions by name instead of checking for specific key presses directly.

Now, let's look at the steps for creating an input map:

1. First, click on **Project** | **Project Settings** | **Input Map**.
2. Click where it says **Add New Action**, type in the name of the action, such as `left`, and then press *Enter*. Do this multiple times, adding names for `right`, `up`, `down`, and `jump`. Later, we will need actions for moving the camera independently, so add actions such as `camera_left`, `camera_right`, `camera_up`, and `camera_down`.
3. Now, click on the + sign for each new action and then press the key you would like to link to the action. This is shown in *Figure 8.18*.

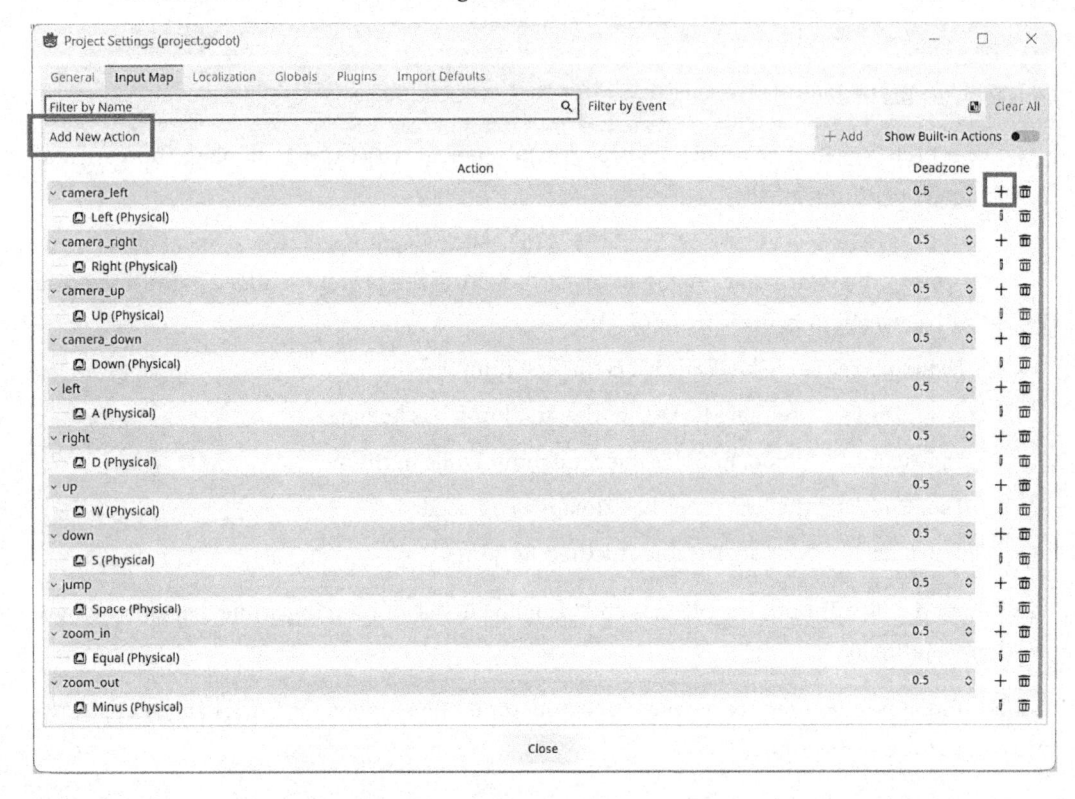

Figure 8.18 – Adding our own action events and keys

Now that we have created our own custom actions to associate with input as shown in *Figure 8.18*, we can go ahead and create a function for player movement.

Implementing player controls and actions

Let's add the `handle_controls` function to handle the controls for player movement:

```
func handle_controls(delta):
    # Movement
    var input := Vector3.ZERO
    input.x = Input.get_axis("left", "right")
    input.z = Input.get_axis("up", "down")

    input = input.rotated(Vector3.UP, view.rotation.z)
    if input.length() > 1:
        input = input.normalized()

    movement_velocity = input * movement_speed * delta

    # Jumping
    if Input.is_action_just_pressed("jump"):
        if jump_single or jump_double:
            jump()
```

The `handle_controls` function stores the player's direction (left, right, up, or down) in the input vector. It then adjusts the player's movement direction (input) to align it with the current view or orientation based on the camera position. Without making this change, movement would always be based on the global x and z position rather than changing based on the perspective of the player camera.

To keep the player's speed the same in all directions (particularly diagonals), we must normalize the input vector (set its length to 1). This ensures that diagonal movement isn't faster than moving along a single axis, which would otherwise give the player an unintended speed boost when pressing two keys at once.

Now we must update the movement velocity based on input and speed.

To handle jumping, we must detect if the jump button has been pressed and then call the `jump()` function if the player is able to jump (i.e., *single* or *double jump*).

Handling game events and feedback

When the player collects Gems, we will increase the gem count and send a signal to alert other parts of the game that the gem count has changed. To do this, we will create our own custom signal at the top of the script.

As the second line of code in the script, add the following:

```
signal gem_collected
```

Now, a new signal will appear in **Inspector**, as shown in *Figure 8.19*:

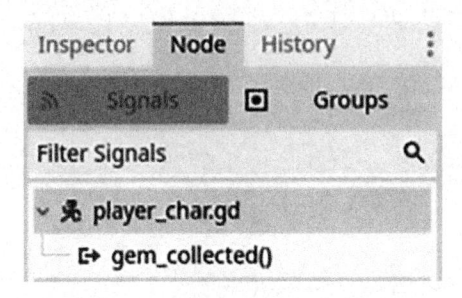

Figure 8.19 – Creating a custom signal

Next, we'll create a new function in our script called `collect_gems()`. This function is shown as follows:

```
func collect_gems():
    gems += 1
    gem_collected.emit(gems)
```

In this function, we will update the current count of the Gems and emit the `gem_collected` signal along with the current Gem count.

Now, create a function to handle the movement of the player called `handle_movement(delta)`, as shown and explained in the following code:

```
func handle_movement(delta):
    var applied_velocity: Vector3
    
    applied_velocity = velocity.lerp(movement_velocity,
    delta * smoothing_factor)
    applied_velocity.y = -gravity
```

```
velocity = applied_velocity
move_and_slide()
```

Here, the local variable `applied_velocity` calculates and stores the velocity of the player in each frame. The calculation is done using the `lerp` function, which uses linear interpolation to slowly move the current velocity (`velocity`) toward the target velocity (`movement_velocity`). This makes the player's movement much smoother.

> **Note**
>
> **Linear interpolation** is a technique used to smoothly or gradually move from one value to another by having the computer calculate and fill in all the values in between.

Setting the vertical part of the velocity to negative gravity makes sure that the player is affected by gravity while the horizontal velocity is being interpolated.

Finally, as shown in the last two lines of the code, we must update the current velocity and call `move_and_slide` to move the character and detect collisions.

Now we need a function to handle the rotation of the player:

```
func handle_rotation(delta):
    if Vector2(velocity.z, velocity.x).length() > 0:
        rotation_direction = Vector2(velocity.z,
        velocity.x).angle()

    rotation.y = lerp_angle(rotation.y, rotation_direction,
    delta * smoothing_factor)
```

In the preceding code, the `handle_rotation` function checks to see if the player is moving and then updates the `rotation_direction` global variable by calculating the angle of the movement direction in radians.

Finally, the character's y-axis is smoothly rotated to face the movement direction using angle interpolation to prevent any abrupt rotation changes.

The final custom function for our player will handle respawning and animation effects upon landing. Create the `handle_respawn()` function as shown in the code:

```
func handle_respawn(delta):
    var border_position_y = -10
    # Threshold below which the player respawns
    if position.y < border_position_y:
        get_tree().reload_current_scene()

    # Animation for scale (jumping and landing)
    model.scale = model.scale.lerp(Vector3(1, 1, 1), delta
    * smoothing_factor)

    # Animation when landing
    if is_on_floor() and vertical_velocity > 2 and
    !previously_floored:
        model.scale = Vector3(1.25, 0.75, 1.25)

    previously_floored = is_on_floor()
```

Let's investigate the `handle_respawn()` function:

- **Scene reload (respawning)**: If the player's `position.y` falls below -10 (meaning they've fallen off the level), we call `get_tree().reload_current_scene()` to reload the current scene and respawn the player at the starting position.
- **Resetting scale (restoring size)**: We use `model.scale.lerp(Vector3(1, 1, 1), delta * smoothing_factor)` to gradually interpolate the player's scale back to normal after any squash-and-stretch effects from jumping or landing.
- **Landing animation (squash effect)**: If the player is currently on the ground (`is_on_floor()`), was falling fast (`gravity > 2`), and was not on the ground in the previous frame (`!previously_floored`), we trigger a squash effect by changing `model.scale` to `Vector3(1.25, 0.75, 1.25)`.
- **Grounded state tracking**: Finally, we update the `previously_floored` variable to keep track of whether the player was on the ground during the last frame.

To keep all these mechanics running smoothly, we need to call our custom functions inside Godot's main physics loop:

```
func _physics_process(delta):
    handle_controls(delta)
    handle_gravity(delta)
    handle_movement(delta)
    handle_rotation(delta)
    handle_respawn(delta)
```

The _physics_process(delta) function is Godot's built-in loop for physics calculations, called every physics frame (by default, 60 times per second). It ensures our game logic runs consistently, regardless of frame rate. By calling our custom functions here, we keep gravity, movement, jumping, camera effects, and respawning in sync with the physics engine.

Now that our character controller is working – handling movement, jumping, and landing animations – it's time to set up the camera so it follows the player correctly in 3D space. A well-configured camera improves the gameplay experience by helping players stay oriented and focused on their surroundings. In the next section, we'll connect the camera to the player and script it to respond smoothly to player movement and rotation.

Implementing a camera controller

To begin configuring the camera, we'll first create a new scene that will act as the camera controller and then link it to the player.

1. Create a new scene and add a **Node3D** node as the root. Rename this to **View**. Now add a **Camera3D** node as a child. The scene tree is shown in *Figure 8.20*:

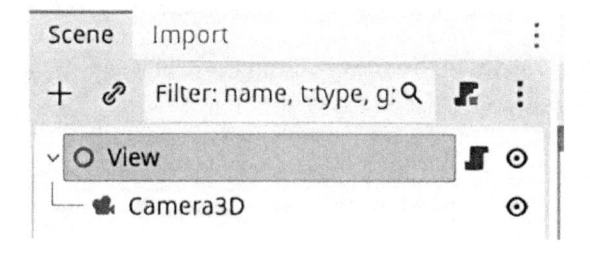

Figure 8.20 – Scene composition for View

2. Select the **Camera3D** node and, in **Inspector**, set the **Current** property to **On** – marking this camera as the one to use. You can also adjust the field of view by setting the **FOV** property to 40. This is shown in *Figure 8.21*:

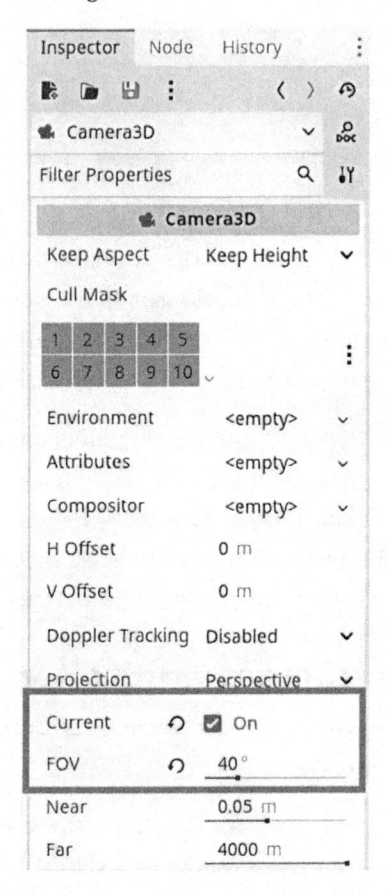

Figure 8.21 – Setting the camera as current and adjusting FOV

3. Now, attach a script to the **View** node and save it as `view.gd`. Make sure that you set the template to **Empty**.

Now we are ready to start building our `Camera Controller` script, which will let the player move the camera and adjust the zoom using the keys on the keyboard, which we defined in the input map.

The camera needs a target node to *look* at or focus on. This will be our **Player** node. We will export this target as a variable shown in the following code:

```
@export_group("Properties")
@export var target: Node
```

This exported `target` variable will appear in **Inspector**, allowing us to drag and drop the **Player** node into it. The camera will then know what it should follow.

Now export variables to control the zoom levels and rotation speed of the camera:

```
@export_group("Zoom")
@export var zoom_minimum = 16
@export var zoom_maximum = 4
@export var zoom_speed = 10
```

These variables define the zoom behavior: `zoom_minimum` and `zoom_maximum` determine how far in and out the camera can zoom. Additionally, `zoom_speed` controls how quickly zooming happens when the input is triggered.

Next, let's define the `rotation_speed` variable:

```
@export_group("Rotation")
@export var rotation_speed = 120
```

This variable sets how quickly the camera rotates around the player when the player rotates or when input is used to turn the camera.

We will use two standard variables to track the current rotation and zoom of the camera:

```
var camera_rotation: Vector3
var zoom = 10
```

Let's explore this further:

- `camera_rotation` will store the current rotation angles (in degrees) of the camera
- `zoom` keeps track of the current zoom value, which we will modify over time based on player input

Finally, we need a reference to the actual **Camera3D** node within this scene so we can manipulate it:

```
@onready var camera = $Camera3D
```

Using `@onready` ensures that this variable is set once the node is added to the scene and ready to be used.

In the built-in `_ready()` function, we will store the initial rotation of the camera:

```
func _ready():
    camera_rotation = rotation_degrees # Initial rotation
```

This initializes the `camera_rotation` variable with the camera's current rotation angles so we can update and modify it from a known starting point.

Much like the player, the camera can be moved around the scene. Let's create a function to handle the camera input:

```
func handle_input(delta):
    # Rotation
    var input := Vector3.ZERO
    input.y = Input.get_axis("camera_left", "camera_right")
    input.x = Input.get_axis("camera_up", "camera_down")
    
    camera_rotation += input.limit_length(1.0) *
    rotation_speed * delta
    camera_rotation.x = clamp(camera_rotation.x, -80, -10)
    
    # Zooming
    zoom += Input.get_axis("zoom_in", "zoom_out") *
    zoom_speed * delta
    zoom = clamp(zoom, zoom_maximum, zoom_minimum)
```

The `handle_input(delta)` function handles camera rotation and zooming based on the input from the player. The horizontal and vertical rotation is stored in the variable called `input` based on the keys the user is pressing.

Next, the camera rotation is updated based on this input. The input is limited to a maximum of `1.0`, which we multiply by the `rotation_speed` variable and `delta` to make everything smooth. Finally, we clamp the vertical rotation to values between `-80` and `-10` degrees. This is to avoid excessive tilting.

For zooming, we update the `zoom` variable based on the player input, which we then multiply by zoom speed and `delta` to ensure smooth zooming. Again, we limit the zoom level between our pre-defined minimum and maximum zoom values.

Next, the _physics_process function needs to be implemented as follows:

```
func _physics_process(delta):
    # Set position and rotation to targets
    self.position = self.position.lerp(target.position, 
    delta * 4)
    rotation_degrees = 
    rotation_degrees.lerp(camera_rotation, delta * 6)
    
    camera.position = camera.position.lerp(Vector3(0, 0, 
    zoom), 8 * delta)
    
    handle_input(delta)
```

Linear interpolation is used again to smoothly move the camera's position towards the target (the player).

We multiply by `delta * 4` to control the speed of repositioning.

Now the current rotation is moved smoothly towards the desired rotation using linear interpolation and multiplying `delta * 6` for the speed.

To make a smooth zooming effect, we move the camera's position along the z axis to match the zoom level. We multiply by `delta * 8` to control the speed.

Finally, we call the `handle_input(delta)` function, which handles the player's input and controls the movements of the camera.

Although we hope that everything will function as expected, we need to test it, correct it, and test it again. This makes game development an iterative process in which we make a change, test to see that the change produces the result that we are expecting and continue in this manner. Therefore, our next step is to test what we have done so far.

Running tests

Return to the **Level 1** scene. Drag the **View** scene into the level. Drag the **Player** scene into the level. Select the **View** node and drag the **Player** scene into the **Target** property of **View**, as shown in *Figure 8.22*:

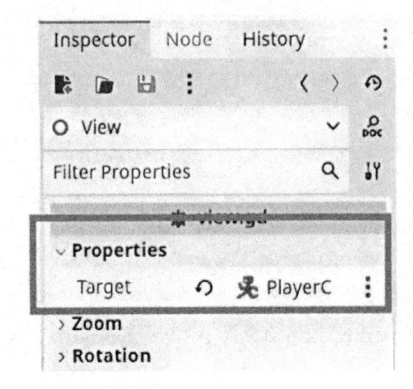

Figure 8.22 – Setting the player as the target for the camera to follow

Now select the **Player** node. In **Inspector**, drag the **View** scene into the **View** property so that the player uses our **View** scene as the Camera Controller. This is shown in *Figure 8.23*:

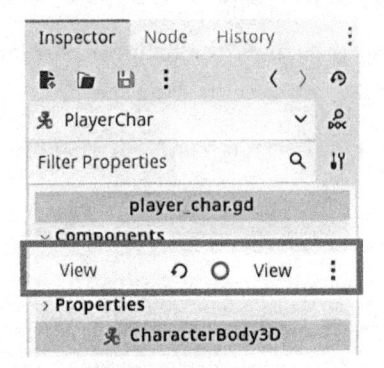

Figure 8.23 – Setting our View scene as the camera controller for the player

Now run the **Level 1** scene and test the game. You can move the player and the camera around the level!

Summary

In this chapter, we explored how to build and organize scenes for a level. We started by creating simple scenes using **StaticBody3D**, **MeshInstance3D**, and **CollisionShape3D** nodes to represent objects in the game world.

Next, we designed a **Player** scene with a script to control movement and added a separate **View** scene featuring a **Camera3D** node that players can control. Finally, we brought everything together by assembling a complex level scene, combining all our individual scene components.

In the next chapter, we will add hazards and collectibles.

Join our community on Discord

Join our community's Discord space for discussions with the author and other readers:

`https://packt.link/godot-4-game-dev`

9

Creating a 3D Mini-Game in Godot – Part 2

Mastering game mechanics and refining player experience are essential steps in creating engaging levels. In this chapter, we'll take a deeper dive into designing interactive and dynamic elements that enhance gameplay and polish the overall feel of your level. You'll learn how to create collectible power-ups that grant temporary abilities, introduce obstacles to challenge the player, and add visual and audio effects that bring the environment to life.

Through practical activities, you will implement a collectible that temporarily boosts the player's jump height, enabling them to reach new platforms. You will design a cannon that shoots cannonballs, providing an exciting challenge for the player to avoid. Finally, you will polish the level by adding audio feedback for actions, background music for atmosphere, and visual effects such as moving clouds to create a more immersive experience.

In this chapter, we're going to cover the following main topics:

- Exploring collectibles
- Introducing obstacles
- Completing our level
- Polishing our level

By the end of this chapter, you'll have a fully playable and visually appealing level with mechanics that balance challenge and reward, preparing you to tackle even more complex designs in the future.

Technical requirements

This chapter's code files are available here in the book's GitHub repository: `https://github.com/PacktPublishing/Godot-4-for-Beginners/tree/main/ch9`

The game assets used in this project are released under a **Creative Commons Zero (CC0)** license by Essssam. Essssam has allowed us to distribute, remix, adapt, and build upon the material in any medium or format, even for commercial purposes.

They can be found here: `https://essssam.itch.io/3d-leap-land`

Visit this link to check out the video of the code being run: `https://packt.link/SDDNS`

Exploring collectibles

Collectibles are a way of adding an objective to a level. By spreading them out, we can encourage the player and reward them for their exploration. Collectibles can also give the player new abilities (either temporary or permanent) or simply add to their score. They could be collected just for fun or as a requirement to complete the level. We will add some Gems to our level for the player to collect.

Creating the Gem scene

Now that we understand the role of collectibles, let's build our first one—a Gem—using a dedicated scene in Godot:

1. Create a new scene with **Node3D** node as the root.
2. Rename this *Gem*. Collectibles in 3D work in a similar way to 2D. In the 2D example, we used **Area2D** node with **CollisionShape2D** node to detect when the **CharacterBody2D** node entered the area of the **Strawberry** node. In 3D, we'll do the same using **Area3D** node with **CollisionShape3D node**, which allows us to detect when the **CharacterBody3D** node (the player) enters the area of the Gem.
3. Add an **Area3D** node as a child of **Gem**.
4. Then add a **MeshInstance3D** node so that we can have a visual model of the Gem itself. Use the `gem.obj` file as the mesh in the **Mesh** property of **MeshInstance3D node**. This is very similar to adding a texture to a sprite in 2D. Remember to drag the `palette.png` texture file onto the Gem mesh in the scene to give it color.

Chapter 9

5. Finally, add a **CollisionShape3D** node as a child of **Area3D**. For the **Shape** property, it is simplest just to contain the Gem in a **BoxShape3D**. All this is shown in *Figure 9.1*:

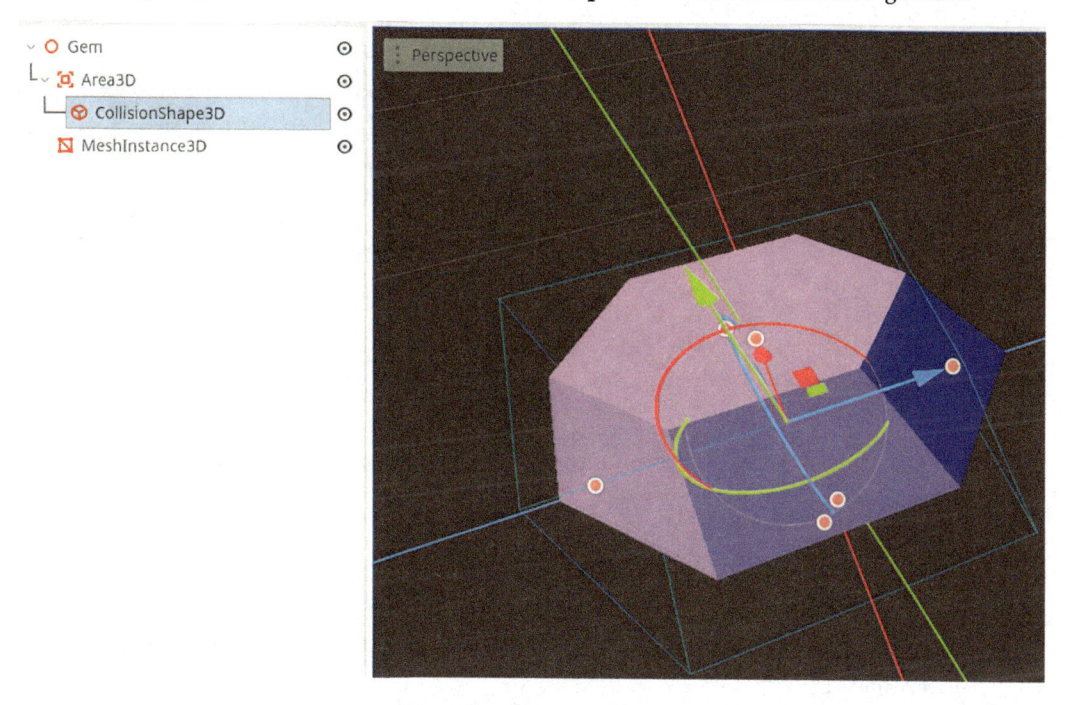

Figure 9.1 – Setting up the components of the Gem scene

As shown in *Figure 9.1*, the Gem can detect when something enters its area. However, we will need to program it to react in the way we intend it to. To do this, we will add a script to the Gem.

Adding the Gem script

You should ask yourself what you want the Gem to do when the player collects it. In our 2D game, we required the player to collect all the strawberries to complete the level. In this game, the Gem will temporarily increase the jump height of the player so that they can reach the highest platform, which will be where the checkpoint flag is.

With the purpose of our Gem defined, let's set it up as a temporary power-up that boosts the player's jump height:

1. Begin by attaching a new script to the **Gem** node.
2. Select the **Area3D** node and connect the body_entered signal as shown in *Figure 9.2*:

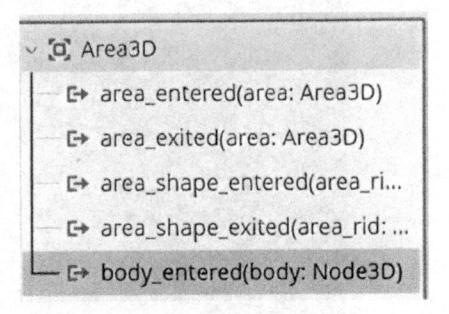

Figure 9.2 – Connect the body_entered signal of the Area3D node

3. We want to check if the body that entered the Gems' area is the player. To do this, we first need to create a group called `player` and add the player to it.
4. Return to the **Player** scene. In the **Inspector**, click on **Node**, then click on **Groups**. Click on **+** and add a group called `player`. Make it a **Global** group. This is demonstrated in *Figure 9.3* as follows:

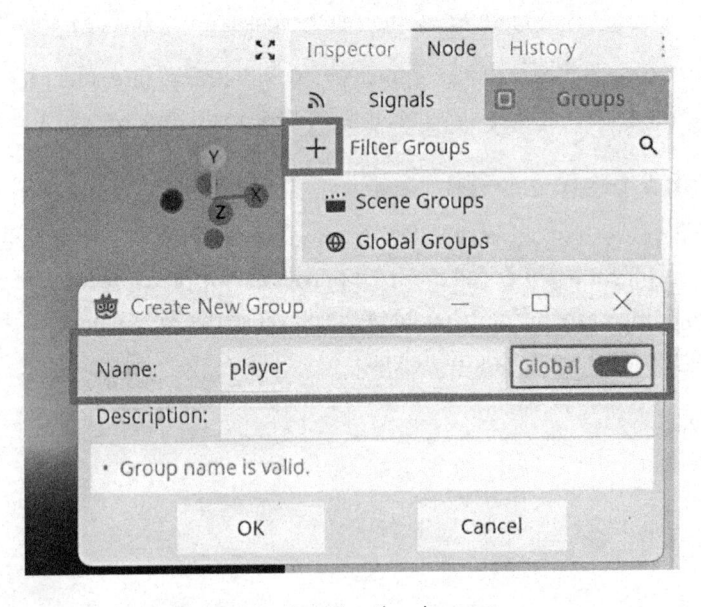

Figure 9.3 – Creating the player group

Chapter 9   227

5. Once you have created the global **player** group, as shown in *Figure 9.3*, you will notice that the **Player** scene is now part of that group because the checkbox for the **player** group is checked.

6. Because we only want to increase the player's jump height temporarily, we will need to add a timer to the player to act as a cooldown mechanism. In the **Player** scene, add a **Timer** node as a child. Rename it to Jump_cooldown_timer, as shown in *Figure 9.4*:

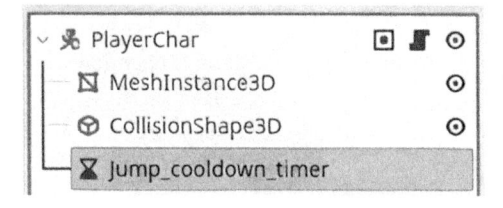

Figure 9.4 – Adding a timer to the player to make jump strength wear off

7. When the player collects the Gem, we will start the timer. If the timer is running, the player can jump higher, but once the timer times out, we return the jump strength to the starting value. In **Inspector**, set the timer to **One Shot** and set **Wait Time** to 3 seconds, as shown in *Figure 9.5*:

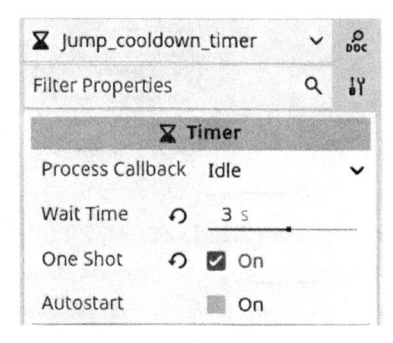

Figure 9.5 – Setting the jump power-up to last 3 seconds

8. As can be seen in *Figure 9.5*, **Wait Time** represents the duration of the boosted jump. If you want the jump power-up to last longer, simply increase this value.

9. Next, connect the **timeout()** signal of **Timer** as shown in *Figure 9.6*:

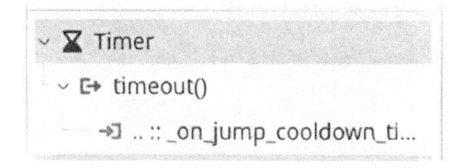

Figure 9.6 – Connecting the timeout signal for the timer

10. Once you have connected the **timeout()** signal of the timer to the Gem script as shown in *Figure 9.6*, add the following code:

    Add a new variable on line **23** called default_jump_strength and set its value to 7:

    ```
    var default_jump_strength = 7
    ```

    Now, code the timeout function as shown:

    ```
    func _on_jump_cooldown_timer_timeout():
        jump_strength = default_jump_strength
    ```

    This code will reset the jump strength to the default value once the timer has reached the duration (wait time).

    > **Quick tip**: Enhance your coding experience with the **AI Code Explainer** and **Quick Copy** features. Open this book in the next-gen Packt Reader. Click the **Copy** button (**1**) to quickly copy code into your coding environment, or click the **Explain** button (**2**) to get the AI assistant to explain a block of code to you.
    >
    > ```
    > function calculate(a, b) {
    >   return {sum: a + b};
    > };
    > ```
    >
    > The next-gen Packt Reader is included for free with the purchase of this book. Scan the QR code OR go to packtpub.com/unlock, then use the search bar to find this book by name. Double-check the edition shown to make sure you get the right one.

11. Before we leave the Player script, we should add a reference variable for the timer so that we can start it from the Gem scene. Underneath the onready variable for **MeshInstance3D**, add one for the timer, as shown here:

    ```
    @onready var model = $MeshInstance3D
    @onready var jump_cooldown_timer = $Jump_cooldown_timer
    ```

12. In the Player script, add a variable for the power-up jump strength:

    ```
    var powerup_jump_strength = 10
    ```

    Now add a function to increase the jump strength and start the timer when the Gem is collected:

    ```
    func on_gem_collected():
        jump_cooldown_timer.start()
        jump_strength = powerup_jump_strength
    ```

13. The **Player** scene is now part of the **player** group. It also has a timer set up to time the duration of the increased jump strength, and we have provided access to the timer. Now return to the **Gem** scene to complete the body_entered() function:

    ```
    func _on_area_3d_body_entered(body):
        if body.is_in_group("player"):
            body.on_gem_collected()
            queue_free()
    ```

    This code will be triggered when a body enters the area of the Gem. If that body is part of the player group, the body (player) will increase jump_strength to 10. The jump_cool_down timer of the body will start and run until it times out, queue_free() ensures that the Gem will be removed from the scene.

14. Instantiate a **Gem** scene into the **Level** scene (in the **Level** scene, hit *Ctrl* + *Shift* + *A*, then choose the **Gem** scene) and test the player can now reach the highest platform once they have collected the Gem. You can now place Gems strategically around the level.

The player has a reward in the form of Gems, which add strength to the jumps. Now we will add an obstacle to the level so that the rewards are not so easy to get.

Introducing obstacles

Obstacles introduce challenge and excitement to a level by creating hazards that the player must navigate around or overcome. They encourage players to strategize, improve their skills, and stay engaged as they progress through the game. Obstacles can take many forms, such as moving platforms, spikes, or environmental traps, and can add variety to the gameplay experience. In this section, we'll add some obstacles to our level to test the player's agility and timing, creating a more dynamic and rewarding experience.

Creating the Cannon scene

A fun and dynamic obstacle to add to the level is a cannon that regularly fires a bullet, which the player will have to avoid before reaching the checkpoint. The cannon is static and purely decorative or set dressing. However, the bullet will move from the cannon, across the level. Set up the **Cannon** scene by following the steps here:

1. Create a new scene with **Node3D** node as the root. Rename this to `Cannon`.
2. Add a **StaticBody3D** node as a child.
3. Add a **MeshInstance3D** node and use `cannon.obj` for the `Mesh` property.
4. Remember to drag `palette.png` to texture the cannon object.
5. Add a **CollisionShape3D** node and use a **New BoxShape3D** property to enclose the cannon.
6. Add a **Timer** node and rename it to `Cannonball_timer`.
7. Add a **Marker3D** node and place it at the mouth/opening of the cannon: **x** position `0.0`, **y** position `0.5`, and **z** position `-1.0`.

Following these steps, the **Cannon** scene tree should look like the one shown in *Figure 9.7*:

- ○ Cannon
  - ▢ StaticBody3D
    - ◩ MeshInstance3D
    - ⊙ CollisionShape3D
  - ⧖ Cannonball_timer
  - -¦- Marker3D

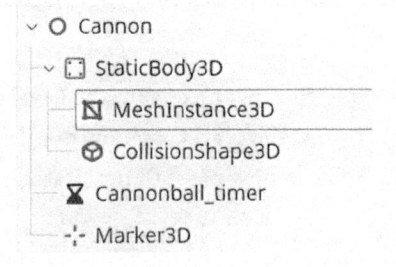

Figure 9.7 – Scene tree for the Cannon scene

Chapter 9

The components in *Figure 9.7* will be used to make the cannon functional. It is a static body because it will not move, but the player can jump onto it and stand on it. The cannonball timer will regularly spawn cannonballs, which move across the level. The marker is used to pinpoint the position at which the cannonballs should appear.

We want the cannon to shoot a ball every three seconds. To do this, adjust the settings of the **Cannonball_timer** node, as shown in *Figure 9.8*:

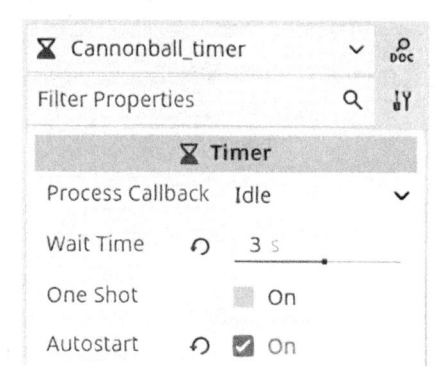

Figure 9.8 – Settings for the cannonball timer

With the settings shown in *Figure 9.8*, the cannon will automatically fire a ball every three seconds. Adjust **Wait Time** if you want to change the firing rate.

The cannon is now ready for scripting; however, we still need a ball or bullet for it to fire. We shall now prepare the **Ball** scene so that there is a projectile to launch from the cannon.

Creating the Ball scene

Create a new scene and use a **CharacterBody3D** node as the root. Rename it to `Ball`.

It's important to note that we would usually use an **Area3D** node for a projectile, since this allows us to detect collisions and trigger events such as applying damage or destroying the projectile on impact. However, in our game, the cannonball is meant to act only as a physical obstacle—it won't damage the player but should simply push them if they come into contact.

Follow these steps to complete the **Ball** scene:

1. You have already created a new scene with **CharacterBody3D** node as the root.
2. You have renamed the root node to **Ball**.
3. Add a **MeshInstance3D** node as a child and use `Bullet.obj` as the `Mesh` property.
4. Apply `palette.png` as the texture of the bullet object.

5. Add a **CollisionShape3D** node and surround the bullet with a new **CapsuleShape3D**.
6. Rotate the **CapsuleShape3D** on the *x* axis and resize it to neatly fit the model.
7. Add a **Timer** node and rename it to `Destroy_timer`.

Following these steps, the **Ball** scene tree should look like *Figure 9.9*:

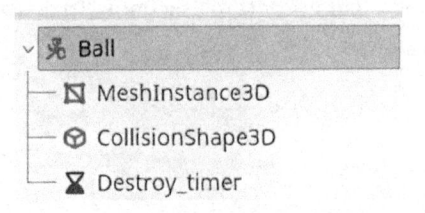

Figure 9.9 – Components of the Ball scene

An important component seen in *Figure 9.9* is the **Destroy_timer** node for the ball. It represents the lifetime of the ball. Once it times out, we destroy the ball and remove the scene from the level. Adjust the settings of the timer to match those shown in *Figure 9.10*:

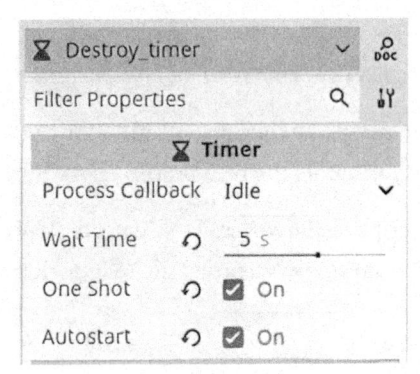

Figure 9.10 – Settings for the timer to destroy the ball

Figure 9.10 sets the lifetime of the ball to 5 seconds; the timer auto-starts but only runs once for each ball. The ball needs to travel across the level and be destroyed. To do that, we will write a script.

Writing the Ball script

A cannon isn't much use without cannonballs—so let's bring them to life with a script that handles their movement and collisions. Follow these steps:

1. Attach a script to the **Ball** node. Set a speed variable and give it the value 3. This is an export variable so that you can change this value while testing the game, so that you can find a value that suits your game best:

   ```
   @export var speed = 3
   ```

2. In the process function, we will move the ball along the z axis. This is the depth axis and represents the ball moving toward or away from us into or out of the screen. To move the ball smoothly, we will change the position by *multiplying* speed by delta, as follows:

   ```
   func _process(delta):
       position.z -= speed * delta
   ```

3. Connect the **timeout()** signal of **Destroy_timer** and in it code the ball to be destroyed once it has reached the wait time of the timer:

   ```
   func _on_destroy_timer_timeout():
       queue_free()
   ```

With this script, the cannonball can do the two tasks we wanted it to. It can move across the level, and it is destroyed after a certain time. Now script the cannon to spawn cannonballs.

Writing the Cannon script

To write the Cannon script, first, we'll attach a script to the **Cannon** node. Throughout the book, I have used @onready var for variables that should be initialized when the scene is first created. This time, I am going to show you an alternative to this shortcut by using the _ready function to initialize variables. Let's see this here:

1. We are going to instance the **Ball** scene (spawn a ball), and so we need a scene variable to store a reference to the **Ball** scene. We also need a variable to represent the ball itself (the ball variable), which will be an instance of the scene. We also need a reference variable (the marker variable) to the **Marker3D** node so that we can position the ball to appear where the invisible marker is:

   ```
   var ball_scene
   var ball_instance
   var marker
   ```

2. None of the variables in the preceding code have been initialized, which is to say that they do not have starting values. We will assign values to them in the _ready() function:

```
# Called when the node is added to the scene tree
func _ready():
    # Load (preload) the Ball scene so we can create a new instance of it
    ball_scene = preload("res://Assets/Scenes/ball.tscn")

    # Load (preload) the Smoke Particle scene for visual effects
    particles = preload("res://Assets/Scenes/smoke.tscn")

    # Create an instance of the Ball from the preloaded scene
    ball_instance = ball_scene.instantiate()

    # Get a reference to the Marker3D node in the scene
    marker = $Marker3D

    # Set the Ball's position to the same location as the Marker3D
    ball_instance.position = marker.position

    # Add the ball instance to the current scene as a child
    add_child(ball_instance)
```

The ready function is called *once* when the cannon is added to the scene to set the initial state of the cannon. Let's go into the line-by-line explanation of the code here:

- The cannonball scene is loaded from the specified path, and we store it in the scene variable. The preload keyword ensures the scene is ready to use when the game runs and offers a performance improvement over the load function when using GDScript.
- An instance of the Ball scene (a copy of the original scene) is stored in the ball variable.
- A reference to the **Marker3D** node is stored in the marker variable.
- The position of the newly created cannonball is set to match the position of marker.
- Finally, the ball instance is added to the **Cannon** node hierarchy (scene tree), making it visible and active in the scene.

3. For the cannon to fire cannonballs at a regular rate, we need to use **Cannonball_timer**. Connect the `timeout()` signal and add the code that follows:

   ```
   func _on_cannonball_timer_timeout():
       ball = scene.instantiate()
       ball.position = marker.position
       add_child(ball)
   ```

   Because we set the **Wait Time** to 3 seconds, the code in the `timeout()` function will run every 3 seconds. A new instance of a cannonball will be created at the position of `marker`, and the scene will be added to the hierarchy of the **Cannon** scene. This timer ensures that a ball is fired repeatedly from the cannon.

4. Instantiate the **Cannon** scene in the **Level** scene and test that everything works as you expect it to.

The level now has collectibles and obstacles. We should focus now on the win condition or objective. For this, we will place a flag that the user must reach to complete the level.

Completing our level

To complete the level, the player must reach the *flag*. The flag is on the highest platform, and the only way to reach it is by getting the Gem to power up the player's jump, avoiding the cannonballs, and racing to the flag.

These are all design decisions, and the assets in the level allow us to consider different options. We could have required the player to obtain a key to unlock the gates to reach the flag. This is why game development is so rewarding! Now we should make a scene for the flag.

Creating the Flag scene

Before creating the **Flag** scene, it would be helpful to decide what a flag should do, as this will help us determine which nodes to use. In our simple case, the only thing the flag needs to do is quit the game when the player touches it. Of course, if we were making more levels, we could just as easily switch levels. Knowing this, an **Area3D** node is the best option for the flag. Follow these steps to set it up:

1. Create a new scene using **Area3D** as the root node.
2. Rename it `Flag`.
3. Add a **MeshInstance3D** node and use `flag.obj` as the `Mesh` property.

4. Apply `palette.png` to texture the flag.
5. Add **CollisionShape3D** node as a child of the flag.
6. Enclose the flag with a **New BoxShape3D**.

After following the steps, your **Flag** scene hierarchy will look like the one shown in *Figure 9.11*:

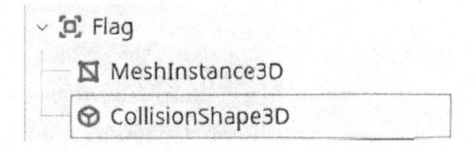

Figure 9.11 – The Flag scene hierarchy

7. Once again, we are utilizing the versatility of the **Area3D** node to detect when a **CharacterBody** node, such as the player, enters its space. Add a script to the **Flag** node and save it as `flag.gd`.
8. Now connect the _on_body_entered signal of the **Flag** node and then code it as follows:

```
extends Area3D
func _on_body_entered(body):
    if body.is_in_group("player"):
        get_tree().quit()
```

This simple code tests whether the body that entered the space of the flag was in the **player** group. If it is, we exit the game.

Changing scenes

It is beyond the scope of this book to create multiple levels; however, if you *had* created another level and wanted to switch to it once the player reaches the flag, it is quite simple to do so.

Firstly, you would need to have your second level created and saved as a scene, such as `level_2.tscn`. Save the path to the scene file in a variable and then use the built-in `get_tree.change_scene_to_file()` function to switch to the next scene. This is shown in the code here:

```
extends Area3D
func _on_body_entered(body):
    if body.is_in_group("player"):
        var next_scene_file =
        "res://scenes/level_2.tscn"
        get_tree().change_scene_to_file(next_scene_file)
```

This code checks whether the player has entered a specific area. If so, it loads the next level of the game. It uses groups to ensure that only the player triggers the action. It uses the scene path to determine what level to load. This is explained line by line here:

- When a body enters the area of the **flag**
- The code checks whether that body is in the "player" group
- Store the path to the level 2 scene file in a variable called next_scene
- Use the change_scene_to_file method to change to the scene saved

Now that the player has a power-up to collect, an obstacle to avoid, and an objective to reach, the level is minimally playable. Let's now work on adding polish to the level in the form of things such as particles, movement, and color.

Polishing our level

Creating a functional level is an important first step in game development, but making it visually appealing and engaging for players requires an extra layer of effort—this is where level polish comes in.

Polishing a level means enhancing its look and feel with elements such as dynamic visuals, smooth animations, and vibrant effects. These additions not only make your game more immersive but also help convey mood, add personality, and make gameplay more satisfying.

In this section, we'll explore how to add movement, color, and particle effects to breathe life into your level, turning it from a basic design into an experience that players will enjoy.

Godot provides a node called **WorldEnviornment**, which is used to set the default environment properties for the entire scene, including post-processing effects, lighting, and background settings.

In the **Level 1** scene, add a WorldEnvironment node. In **Inspector**, find the Environment property and choose New Environment. This is shown in *Figure 9.12* as follows:

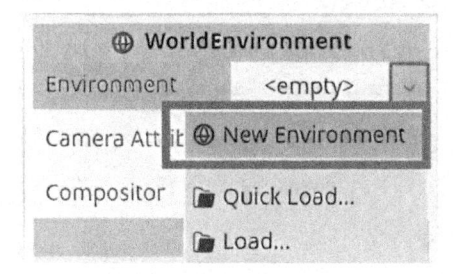

Figure 9.12 – Adding a new environment to the world

Once we have loaded a new environment, as shown in *Figure 9.12*, we now have access to many more properties and settings.

Setting the background color

Change the background color of the level to *sky blue* by clicking on **Environment**, choosing **Background**, then **Custom Color**, and finding sky blue. This is shown in *Figure 9.13*:

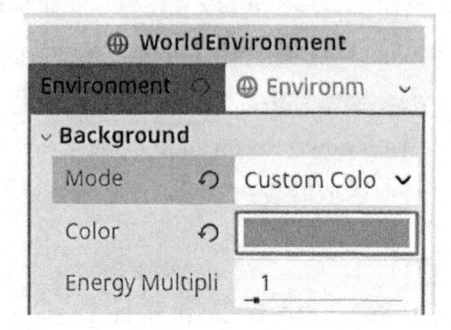

Figure 9.13 – Setting a custom background color for the level

Now that we have added background color to the level, as shown in *Figure 9.13*, we should add some smoke effects to the cannon after each shot fired.

Adding particle effects

Particle effects are a powerful tool in game development for adding visual flair and enhancing the atmosphere of your game. They can simulate various natural phenomena such as fire, smoke, rain, or explosions, as well as creating abstract effects such as sparkles, trails, or magical glows. By incorporating particle effects, you can make your game feel more dynamic and engaging, helping players better connect with the world you've created. In this section, we explore how to create and customize particle effects to bring your scenes to life.

Creating the smoke scene

As mentioned earlier, we are going to create a little puff of smoke that rises into the sky after each cannon shot. We will make use of one of the cloud models, which we will scale down and rotate. Follow these steps to create the smoke scene:

1. Create a new scene using **CPUParticles3D** as the root node.
2. Rename the node to Smoke.
3. Expand the **Drawing** section and find the **Mesh** property.

Chapter 9

4. Drag the `cloud_1.obj` file into the **Mesh** property. This is shown in *Figure 9.14*:

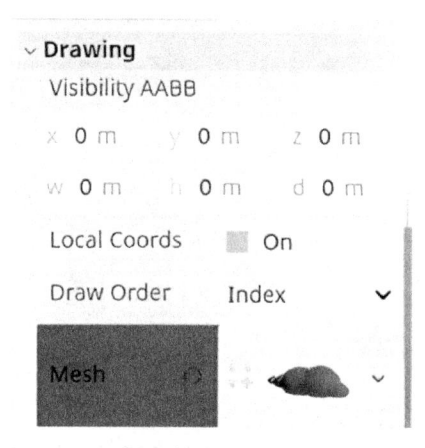

Figure 9.14 – Using one of the clouds as Mesh to represent smoke

5. Remember to texture the mesh by applying the `palette.png` texture.
6. Expand the **Gravity** section and make the **y** value positive. Once you do this, the smoke rises.
7. Reduce the **Amount** property to 1, so that a puff of smoke will rise from the cannon.
8. Set the **One Shot** property to **On**. This is shown in *Figure 9.15*:

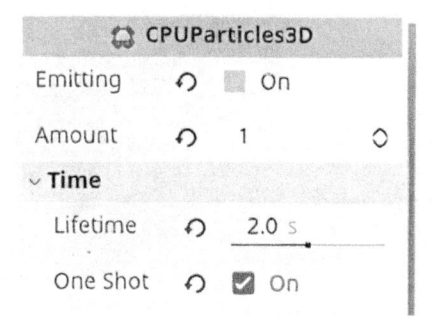

Figure 9.15 – Changing the amount and setting One Shot to On

9. Orient the cloud vertically by expanding the **Transform** section of **Node3D** and rotating the **z** axis by `90` degrees. This is shown in *Figure 9.16*:

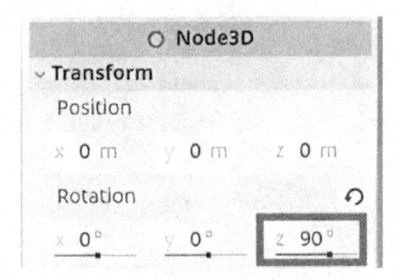

Figure 9.16 – Rotating the model on the z axis to make it vertical

10. Adjust the scale of the cloud over time, from `0` to full size (`1`). Do this by expanding the **Scale** section and setting **Scale Amount Minimum** to `0` and **Scale Amount Maximum** to `1`.
11. Create a **Scale Amount** Curve by clicking on **New Curve** and adjusting the scale over time, as shown in *Figure 9.17*:

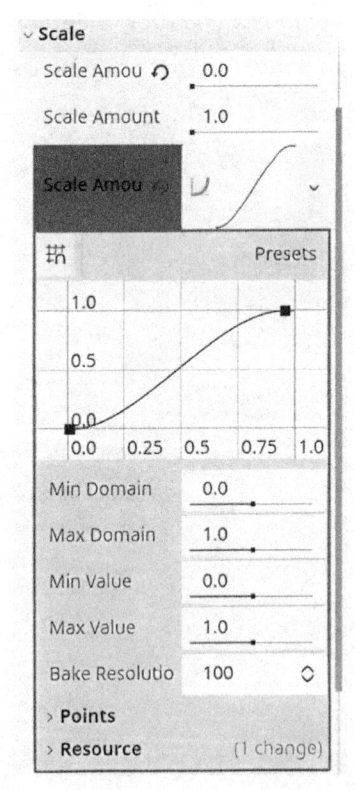

Figure 9.17 – Setting min, max, and scale curve

This sets the scale from 0 to 1; however, I recommend experimenting with the curve values until you find a result that you are happy with.

The **Smoke** scene is complete and ready to be instanced in the Cannon script. When we instance a cannonball from within the Cannon script, we should instance the smoke just afterward. Now, let's return to the Cannon script.

12. Add two new global variables called particles (to reference the particles scene file) and smoke (to be an instance of the scene):

```
extends Node3D
var ball_scene
var ball_instance
var marker
var particles
var smoke
```

13. Adapt the _ready function so that we also preload the smoke particles scene. The new lines are commented in the following code. Create an instance of the smoke, position it at the marker, make it a child of the **Cannon** scene, and set the emitting property to true:

```
func _ready():
    scene = preload("res://scenes/ball.tscn")
    particles = preload("res://scenes/smoke.tscn")
    ball = scene.instantiate()
    
    # Create an instance of the smoke particles
    smoke = particles.instantiate()
    
    marker = $Marker3D
    ball.position = marker.position
    
    # Also place the smoke effect at the Marker3D position
    smoke.position = marker.position
    
    add_child(ball)
    
    # Add the smoke effect to the current scene as a child
    add_child(smoke)
```

```
            # Start the smoke particle effect so it emits immediately
            smoke.emitting = true
```

14. Finally, we must create new instances in the `timeout` function so that a puff of smoke appears each time the cannon fires:

```
    func _on_cannonball_timer_timeout():
        ball_instance = ball_scene.instantiate()
        smoke = particles.instantiate()
        smoke.position = marker.position
        Ball_instance.position = marker.position
        add_child(ball_instance)
        add_child(smoke)
        smoke.emitting = true
```

With these adaptations to the script for the cannon, you can test the level again. You will notice now that each time a cannonball is fired, two little clouds of smoke trail into the air. This is a simple way to add some dynamism to the level.

Another way to make a level more engaging is to add audio, such as sound effects and background music. In the next section, we will learn how to work with audio.

Adding audio to our level

It would be fun if the player character made a noise when it jumped. Let's add some audio!

1. To do this, we need to record a sound ourselves or find one that is in the public domain with a Creative Commons license. Here's one we can use for this project: https://opengameart.org/content/jump-sound-16bit.

2. Download the jump.wav file. In **FileSystem**, go to the assets folder, and create a subfolder called audio. Drop the sound file in there as shown in *Figure 9.18*:

Chapter 9   243

Figure 9.18 – Adding the jump.wav file to our audio folder

3. Open the **Player** scene and add an **AudioStreamPlayer** node as a child. In the **Stream** property, drag and drop the audio file. Leave the rest of the properties unchanged. This is shown in *Figure 9.19*:

Figure 9.19 – Giving AudioStreamPlayer a sound file to play

4. Open the Player script and add a reference variable for `AudioStreamPlayer` to your list of onready variables:

```
@onready var model = $MeshInstance3D
@onready var jump_cooldown_timer = $Jump_cooldown_timer
@onready var audio_stream_player = $AudioStreamPlayer
```

5. We only want to play the jump sound effect when the player jumps. To do this, we tell **AudioStreamPlayer** to play the file when the `jump` function runs. Add that request as the first line in the `jump` function:

```
func jump():
    audio_stream_player.play()
```

6. That is all that is required to play a sound effect when the player jumps.

But what if we wanted to play an effect when the player lands?

1. Grab another CC0-licensed sound effect from **Open Game Art** (https://opengameart.org/content/jump-landing-sound) and add it to the audio folder.
2. To play the right sound at the right time, the code must be adjusted to first load the corresponding audio file into **AudioStreamPlayer** before attempting to play it.
3. Add another line as the first line in the `jump` function to first load the file before playing it:

```
func jump():
    audio_stream_player.stream =
    preload("res://assets/audio/jump.wav")
    audio_stream_player.play()
```

4. Similarly, when the player lands, we must load the corresponding audio file and then play it. Do so by adding these lines after scaling the player when it lands, in the `handle_respawn()` function:

```
if is_on_floor() and gravity > 2 and !previously_floored:
    model.scale = Vector3(1.25, 0.75, 1.25)
    audio_stream_player.stream =
    preload("res://assets/audio/jumpland.wav")
    audio_stream_player.play()
```

Chapter 9

5. Using the technique in the code, we ensured that we loaded the correct audio file into the player before we played it. The next step is to add background music to the level. Start by downloading the background music (https://opengameart.org/content/background-music-2-the-ice-caves) and adding it to the audio folder.

6. This time, we will add an **AudioStreamPlayer** node to the **Level 1** scene. We will drag and drop the Background Music 2.ogg file into the **Stream** property. Set the **Autoplay** property to **On**. This is shown in *Figure 9.20*:

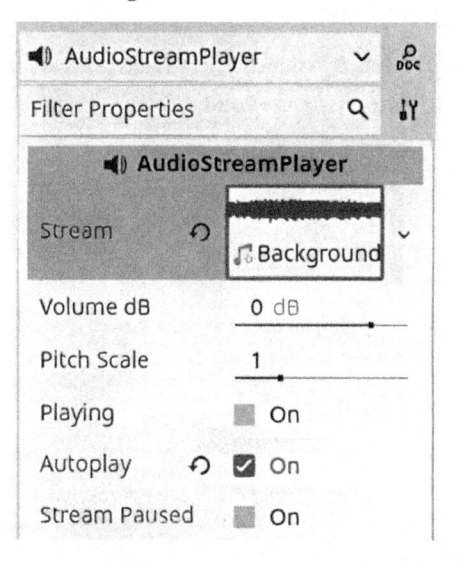

Figure 9.20 – Setting the Autoplay property of the Stream player

7. There is one more step, and that is to ensure that the track is looping. Expand the **Parameters** section and turn on looping as shown in *Figure 9.21*:

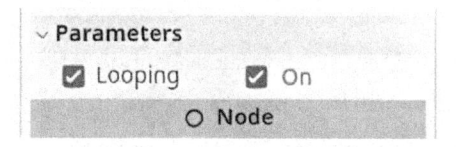

Figure 9.21 – Turning looping on for the background music

As shown in *Figure 9.21*, by turning on looping, we can have a background music track that plays repeatedly in the level.

In game design, repetitive movement is often used to create dynamic and lifelike effects, such as clouds drifting across the sky, waves lapping at the shore, or power-ups slowly rotating or hovering up and down. This type of movement is typically achieved by adjusting an object's properties (such as position, size, or angle) back and forth in a smooth and natural way using the oscillations of a sine wave. In our final section, we will use the `sine` function to move our clouds slowly back and forth in our level.

Using the sine function

As mentioned earlier, rather than having the clouds sitting still in the sky, we will drift them back and forth using a *sine wave*. Return to the **Cloud** scene and attach a script to the root node (**Cloud**).

The entire code to make the clouds drift is given here and then explained line by line afterward:

```
extends Node3D
@onready var mesh_instance_3d: MeshInstance3D = $MeshInstance3D
var time: float
func _process(delta):
    time += delta
    mesh_instance_3d.position =
    vector3(get_sine(),get_sine(),get_sine())

func get_sine():
    return sin(time * 0.5) * 0.5
```

Let's break down this code here for a better understanding:

- A variable called `time` is declared as a float to track the elapsed time. It is used to calculate the sine wave for movement.
- A reference is created for the `StaticBody3D` node of the cloud since this is essentially the cloud object that we will be moving.
- In the `process` function, we increase the `time` variable for each frame. This ensures that the sine wave animation progresses smoothly over time.
- Next, update the `position` property of the cloud (`StaticBody3D`) in every frame.
- The *x*, *y*, and *z* coordinates are set using the `get_sine()` function, which produces a smooth oscillating value.
- The `get_sine()` function calculates a smooth oscillation based on the `time` variable.

- `time * 0.5` is the **frequency** of the wave, and this slows down the oscillation.
- Multiplying the result by `0.5` outside the brackets is the **amplitude** of the wave. Here, we are reducing it, making the movement less extreme.
- The entire result is returned for use in updating the `position` in the transform property.

In essence, this script creates a smooth, oscillating movement for the cloud. The sine wave makes the movement more natural.

Summary

In this chapter, you transformed your level into a dynamic and engaging experience by adding key gameplay elements and refining its overall presentation. You created a collectible power-up that temporarily boosted the player's jump height, allowing them to access higher platforms and complete the level. We introduced a cannon obstacle, which added a layer of challenge as the player had to avoid its cannonballs.

To complete the level, you implemented a flag mechanic, giving the player a clear and satisfying objective. Finally, you polished the level by adding sound effects for feedback, background music for atmosphere, and moving clouds for visual appeal.

At the end of this chapter, you've not only developed the essential mechanics of a fun and interactive level but also enhanced its presentation, making it more immersive and enjoyable for players. These skills will serve as a solid foundation for creating even more intricate and polished levels in the future.

Unlock this book's exclusive benefits now

Scan this QR code or go to `packtpub.com/unlock`, then search this book by name.

Note: Keep your purchase invoice ready before you start.

10
Adding Game Juice

Game development isn't just about mechanics and level design—it's also about how the game feels to play. This is where game juice comes in. *Game juice* refers to all the little enhancements that make a game more satisfying and responsive, from visual effects and sound design to UI feedback and animations. Adding game juice can turn a basic game into a polished, engaging experience that players love.

In this chapter, we'll explore what game juice is and why it's important. You'll learn how to make your game feel more polished and responsive by adding dynamic effects that provide feedback to the player. We'll implement several juicy elements to enhance the experience: a confetti cannon that bursts when the player reaches a checkpoint, a **heads-up display** (**HUD**)-based health bar where hearts gray out as health decreases, and immersive background audio and sound effects that bring the level to life.

In this chapter, we're going to cover the following main topics:

- Understanding game juice
- Implementing a health bar HUD
- Adding a hit animation
- Creating a confetti cannon effect
- Adding audio and sound effects

By the end of this chapter, you'll understand how small changes can dramatically improve the feel of your game. You'll have practical experience in implementing visual and audio feedback that enhances player immersion, making your game more enjoyable and satisfying to play.

Let's begin to give your game that extra polish it deserves!

Technical requirements

By this point in the book, you should know how to do the following:

- Create nodes and scenes (see *Chapter 2*)
- Work through the `Pixel Adventure` project from *Chapter 7*

You should also know about variables and functions (see *Chapter 8*) for use in GDScript.

This chapter's code files are available here in the book's GitHub repository: `https://github.com/PacktPublishing/Godot-4-for-Beginners/tree/main/ch10`

Visit this link to check out the video of the code being run: `https://packt.link/W1K5s`

Understanding game juice

When a game feels good to play, we now know that it's usually thanks to something called **game juice**. This refers to small but impactful enhancements—such as subtle animations, particle effects, or sound design—that make the gameplay more responsive, satisfying, and polished.

Juice doesn't change the mechanics of the game, but it transforms how the player experiences them. Hence, adding *juice* to a game involves taking a working game and adding layers of satisfaction to improve its feel. For the player, satisfaction is created by the senses, and so we need to feed those senses. Creating visual effects and adding audio will enhance the player's experience. You can imagine this as if you are squeezing every drop of juice out of a delicious orange.

Some examples of using game juice to improve the player experience are the following:

- A standard jump can feel more impactful with *squash and stretch* animation
- Collecting a coin feels more rewarding with a *flash effect* and *a satisfying sound*
- Taking damage in combat is more engaging with *screen shake* and *a brief pause* for impact

In the next section, we'll explore the foundational aspects of juicing.

Foundations of juicing: animation and audio

This section will introduce you to the foundational techniques of juicing, which we'll soon apply in practical ways, such as a hit animation, health bar HUD, confetti cannon, and audio feedback. These basics are just as useful in 3D as they are in 2D, and they'll elevate your game no matter the genre or perspective.

Visual feedback (animation and particle effects)

Visual feedback plays a key role in making actions feel impactful. Two common techniques used in game juicing are as follows:

- **Squash and stretch**: Slightly deforming your character's scale when they land, jump, or change direction gives them a bouncy, lively appearance. This animation technique makes movement feel more expressive.
- **Particle effects**: Adding dust trails when the player runs or jumps makes movement more dynamic and grounded. Even small bursts of particles can communicate energy and motion clearly.

You'll soon be implementing these ideas in your own game, including the following:

- A *hit animation* that makes enemies react visually to player attacks
- A *confetti cannon* that celebrates success with an explosion of particles

Audio feedback (music and sound effects)

Audio is just as important as visuals when it comes to creating a juicy experience. It reinforces player actions, adds personality, and builds atmosphere. Consider the following:

- **Sound effects**: A satisfying squish when landing or a crunchy impact when hitting enemies can bring a scene to life
- **Background music**: A well-chosen track can set the emotional tone of your level, guiding how players feel as they explore

We'll be exploring how to implement both ambient music and character sound effects later in this chapter.

Implementing a health bar HUD

A common **user interface** (**UI**) element in a game that visually represents the player's health is a **health bar** as part of the HUD. Its purpose is to provide immediate feedback on how much damage the player has taken and how close they are to death.

Three examples of how health is displayed to the user are shown in *Figure 10.1*:

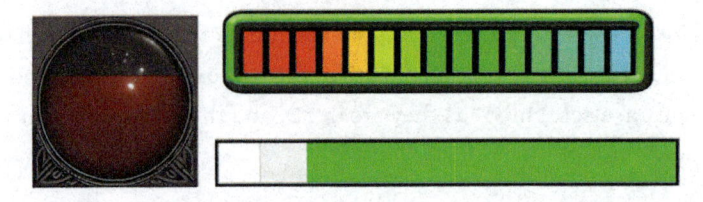

Figure 10.1 – Three different ways to display health in a game

In the subsequent section, we'll implement a heart-based health system, where *each heart* represents a portion of the player's health, and hearts become *grayed out* as damage is taken. This approach makes the information easy to read at a glance while adding a bit of visual appeal to the UI.

Developing a heart-based health system

To implement our heart-based health system, we'll set up the UI, write the logic to update the hearts based on the player's health, and ensure the system reacts dynamically as damage is done. Let's walk through the steps to bring it to life.

Let's begin by opening the `Pixel Adventure` Godot project and adding a new scene with an `AnimatedSprite2D` node as the root node. Rename the node to `HUD` and save the scene as `hud.tscn`, as shown in *Figure 10.2*:

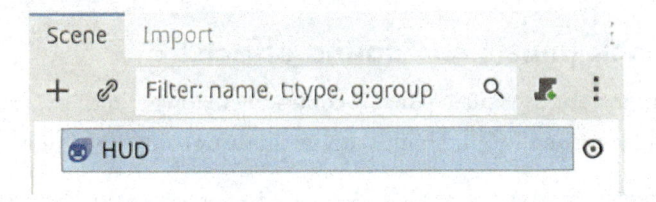

Figure 10.2 – The HUD scene to represent player life

We are going to use a simple technique to indicate the loss of health. The health bar will begin with three full red hearts. Each time the player is injured, we will change one of the hearts from red to gray.

You can use free and open source image editing software, such as **LibreSprite** (https://libresprite.github.io/#!/), to draw your own hearts and create four frames representing the changing health, as I have done in *Figure 10.3*:

Chapter 10

Figure 10.3 – Frames of hearts representing the changing health of the player

> **Resources**
>
> If you don't feel comfortable drawing your own hearts, you can use the one created by Shlok Gupta. However, you will still need to modify it in order to have hearts at different levels of health. It is available on their **Itch** page here: `https://gamedevshlok.itch.io/heartpack`.

When the images of your hearts are ready, go to the **Sprite Frames** property of the **AnimatedSprite2D** node named **HUD**, and select **New SpriteFrames**, as shown in *Figure 10.4*:

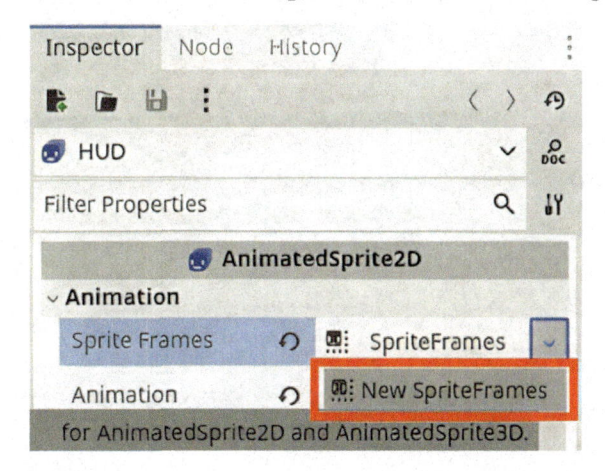

Figure 10.4 – New SpriteFrames for the AnimatedSprite2D node

Now, click on the word **SpriteFrames** in the property to open the **Animation Frames** window. Rename the default animation to `idle` and add the four frames, as shown in *Figure 10.5*:

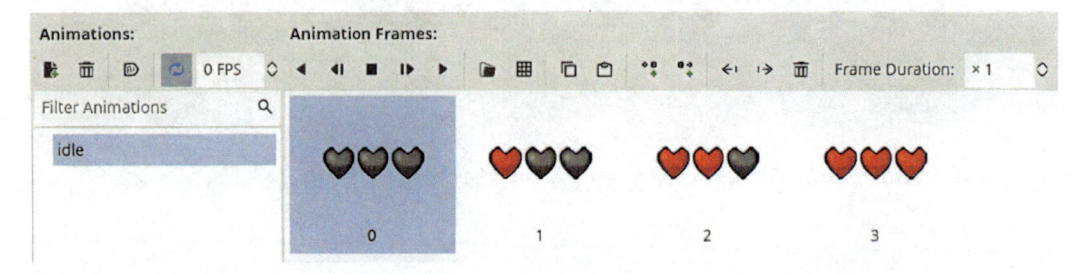

Figure 10.5 – The idle animation for the health bar has four frames for the health total

As you can see in *Figure 10.5*, whenever the player loses health, we will change the animation frames to match. We don't need to add a script to the health bar; all we need is a reference to it in the script attached to `level1.tscn`.

In the **Level1** scene, drag your newly created `hud.tscn` into your level and place it toward the top left, as shown in *Figure 10.6*:

Figure 10.6 – A good spot for the HUD

Chapter 10   255

Once you have placed the HUD in the scene, your scene tree for **Level1** should include the **HUD** scene and look like the scene hierarchy shown in *Figure 10.7*:

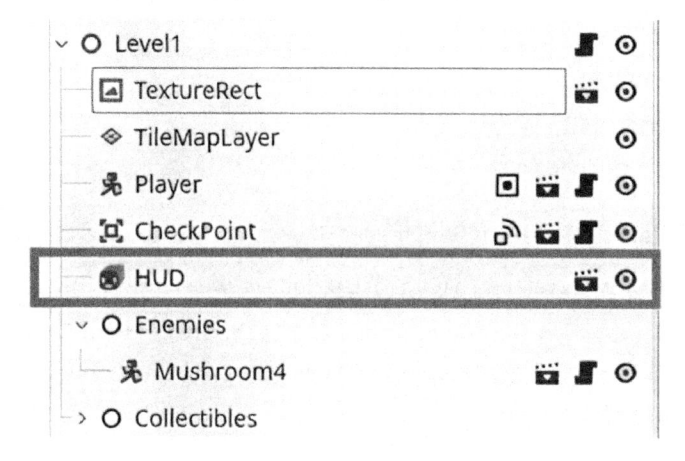

Figure 10.7 – The scene hierarchy for level 1

With the scene in place as shown in *Figure 10.7*, it is time to open the script attached to **Level1** and make some additions so that the HUD will update the hearts according to how much health the player has.

Updating the HUD in the Level script

Now that our heart-based health system is in place, we need to make sure the player's current health is reflected on the screen. To do this, we'll update the HUD from the Level script. The HUD will visually change depending on how many hearts the player has left, graying out hearts as damage is taken.

We'll begin by adding an @onready variable to reference the HUD scene. In the _process() function, we will update the HUD's frame property to match the player's current health. This determines how many hearts are displayed as active (*red*) versus inactive (*gray*). For example, if the player has three hearts, we'll set the HUD frame to 3 to show three red hearts.

Here's the updated Level script:

```
extends Node2D

@onready var update_health_hud = $HUD
@onready var player = $Player
```

```
@onready var strawberries = $Collectibles

func _ready():
    player.level_strawberries = strawberries.get_child_count()

func _process(delta):
    update_health_hud.frame = player.get_hearts()
```

Let's break down the code to understand it better:

- update_hud stores a reference to the **HUD** node so we can easily access and update it.
- In _process(), which runs every frame, we set the HUD's frame to reflect the player's current number of hearts. This means the HUD will visually update in real time as the player gains or loses health.

The line player.get_hearts() relies on a new function we need to create inside the Player script. This function simply returns the current number of hearts the player has:

```
func get_hearts():
    return hearts
```

To support this, add a new variable at the top of the Player script to store the player's health:

```
var hearts = 3
```

The question is: why do we add this variable?

The hearts variable tracks how much health the player has. We initialize it to 3, meaning the player starts with full health. As the player takes damage, this value will decrease.

Next, let's create a hurt() function to reduce the player's health when they are injured:

```
func hurt():
    hearts -= 1
    if hearts <= 0:
        death()
```

This function subtracts one heart whenever the player is hurt. If hearts reaches 0, we trigger the death() function, which we'll now create in the following code:

```
func death():
    #shoot the player upward upon death
    velocity.y = -600
```

```
    #disable collisions so the player falls through the level
    set_collision_mask_value(2, false)
    set_collision_mask_value(3, false)
```

Here's a breakdown of the preceding code:

- `velocity.y = -600` shoots the player upward when they die, adding a bit of *juice* to make the death feel more dramatic
- We disable collisions with the environment by turning off the level's collision layers, allowing the player to fall off the screen

Another bit of game juice that provides great visual feedback to the player—helping them quickly recognize when they've taken damage—is a *hit flash effect*. This common technique briefly changes the player's appearance (often to *white* or *red*) to signal that they've been hurt, making the experience feel more responsive and polished.

Adding a hit animation

In this section, we'll create a simple animation that causes the player to flash white for a short time when they're injured. This effect not only makes the moment of taking damage more dramatic but also helps the player stay aware of their current health status, especially in fast-paced moments.

In your file explorer, locate the `Pixel Adventure/Main Characters/Ninja Frog` folder (you can download all the assets here: `https://pixelfrog-assets.itch.io/`) and drag the `Hit.png` file into the Godot **FileSystem**.

In the **Player** scene, select the **AnimatedSprite2D** node and add a new animation called `hit`. Now, click on the **Add Frames from Sprite Sheet** button and set it to 7 horizontal frames and 1 vertical frame. Then, select all frames and import them. Set the animation speed to 16 **FPS** and not looping. The `hit` animation will look as it does in *Figure 10.8*:

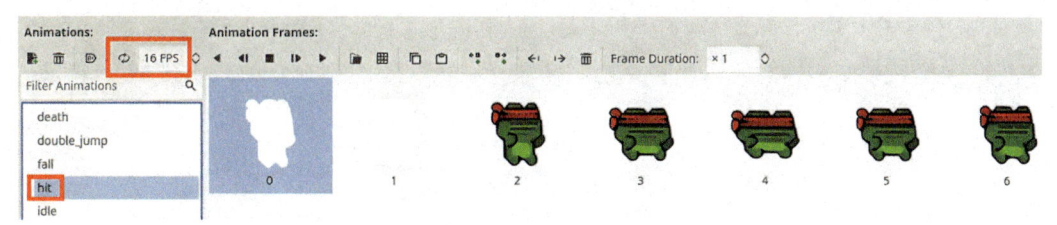

Figure 10.8 – The new hit animation

> **🔍 Quick tip:** Need to see a high-resolution version of this image? Open this book in the next-gen Packt Reader or view it in the PDF/ePub copy.
>
> 📕 **The next-gen Packt Reader** and a **free PDF/ePub copy** of this book are included with your purchase. Scan the QR code OR visit packtpub.com/unlock, then use the search bar to find this book by name. Double-check the edition shown to make sure you get the right one.

To ensure that our animation runs when it needs to, add a helper variable called `isHit` to our group of vars at the top of the `Player` script. It will be a Boolean, which is set to `false` by default:

```
var isHit = false
```

Now, modify the `hurt()` function so that `isHit` is set to `true` when the player takes damage:

```
func hurt():
    isHit = true
    hearts -= 1
    if hearts <= 0:
        death()
```

Now, we can modify our `animate()` function to include checks on the number of hearts the player has, as well as whether they have been hit or not:

```
func animate():
    if isHit:
        animations.play("hit")
        await animations.animation_finished
        animations.play("idle") # transition back to idle
        return # Prevent further changes this frame
    if hearts == 0:
        return # Dead, don't animate further
    
    # Stationary player
```

```
if velocity.x == 0 and velocity.y == 0:
    animations.play("idle")

# Player moving right
elif velocity.x >= 0 and velocity.y == 0:
    animations.play("run")
    animations.flip_h = false

# Player moving left
elif velocity.x <= 0 and velocity.y == 0:
    animations.play("run")
    animations.flip_h = true

# Player is falling
elif velocity.y > 0 and !is_wall_sliding:
    animations.play("fall")

# Player is jumping (initial jump)
elif velocity.y < 0 and jump_count == 0:
    animations.play("jump")

# Player is double-jumping
elif !is_on_floor() and jump_count > 0 and
!is_wall_sliding:
    animations.play("double_jump")

# Player is wall sliding on the right
elif is_wall_sliding and
Input.is_action_pressed("ui_right"):
    animations.flip_h = false
    animations.play("wall_slide")

# Player is wall sliding on the left
elif is_wall_sliding and
Input.is_action_pressed("ui_left"):
    animations.flip_h = true
    animations.play("wall_slide")
```

The `animate()` function is responsible for switching between different animation states based on the player's movement, health, and whether they've been hit. Let's walk through each condition to understand what's happening.

First, let's look at the code for the `idle` state:

```
if velocity.x == 0 && velocity.y == 0 && hearts > 0 && isHit == false:
    animations.play("idle")
```

If the player is not moving (`velocity.x == 0` and `velocity.y == 0`), still alive (`hearts > 0`), and hasn't just been hit (`isHit == false`), we play the `"idle"` animation.

Next, let's examine the `hit` state:

```
elif isHit:
    animations.play("hit")
```

If the player has been hit, we play the `"hit"` animation to show a reaction. This usually plays for a short time before reverting to other animations.

This is how we detect *running to the right*:

```
elif velocity.x >= 0 && velocity.y == 0 && hearts > 0:
    animations.play("run")
    animations.flip_h = false
```

If the player is moving horizontally to the right (positive x-velocity), not moving vertically, and still alive, we play the "run" animation and make sure the sprite is facing right (`flip_h = false`).

The code for *running left* is similar:

```
elif velocity.x <= 0 && velocity.y == 0 && hearts > 0:
    animations.play("run")
    animations.flip_h = true
```

This will be the same as the previous condition, but for moving left. We flip the sprite horizontally (`flip_h = true`) to face the left direction.

Here's how *falling* is handled:

```
elif velocity.y > 0 and !is_wall_sliding && hearts > 0:
    animations.play("fall")
```

If the player is moving downward (velocity.y > 0), not sliding on a wall, and still alive, we show the "fall" animation.

The *jumping* logic looks like this:

```
elif velocity.y < 0 and jump_count == 0 && hearts > 0:
    animations.play("jump")
```

This condition checks whether the player is jumping upward (velocity.y < 0) and it's their first jump (jump_count == 0), which triggers the "jump" animation.

Here's the check for *double jumping*:

```
elif !is_on_floor() and jump_count > 0 and !is_wall_sliding:
    animations.play("double_jump")
```

If the player is in the air (not on the floor), has used at least one jump, and isn't sliding on a wall, we show the "double_jump" animation.

This handles *wall sliding* on the right:

```
elif is_wall_sliding and Input.is_action_pressed("ui_right"):
    animations.flip_h = false
    animations.play("wall_slide")
```

If the player is sliding on a wall and holding the right movement key, we play the "wall_slide" animation and face the sprite to the right.

And, finally, this is what we use for *wall sliding (left)*:

```
elif is_wall_sliding and Input.is_action_pressed("ui_left"):
    animations.flip_h = true animations.play("wall_slide")
```

It is the same as for *wall sliding (right)*, but for the left side.

Everything is working almost as we want it to. However, you will notice that the player gets stuck in the hit animation, and that is because there is no event that sets the isHit variable back to false. The final step is to return to the **Mushroom** scene, select the **HurtPlayerZone** node, select the **Node** tab, then the **Signals** tab, and connect the body_exited() signal. Code the signal function as shown here:

```
func _on_hurt_player_zone_body_exited(body: Node2D):
    if body.is_in_group("Player"):
        body.isHit = false
```

To be consistent, we should also call the `isHit` function from the `Mushroom` script:

```
func _on_hurt_player_zone_body_entered(body):
    if "Player" in body.name:
        body.hurt()
        body.isHit = true
```

The preceding code ensures that if the body that exited the `HurtPlayerZone` **Area2D** node is part of the group called `"Player"`, the `hit` variable is reset to `false`. This means that when the player stops colliding with the Mushroom, the `hit` animation will also stop.

Now, everything is in place to provide satisfying visual feedback to the user when they are playing the game to alert them that they are in danger.

Our next step is to add a fun visual effect to the checkpoint flag. We will fire off a confetti cannon as a small celebration of finishing the level.

Creating a confetti cannon effect

To reinforce the feeling of achievement and as an extra reward for completing the level, when the player touches the checkpoint flag, we will fire some multi-colored confetti from the flagpole. This will take the form of a particle effect, which we will set up as its own scene. Let's get started!

We'll begin by creating a new scene with **Node2D** as the root node. Rename the node to `Confetti_Cannon`, add a **GPUParticles2D** node as a child, and rename this to `Blue`, as this will represent the blue confetti. This is shown in *Figure 10.9* as follows:

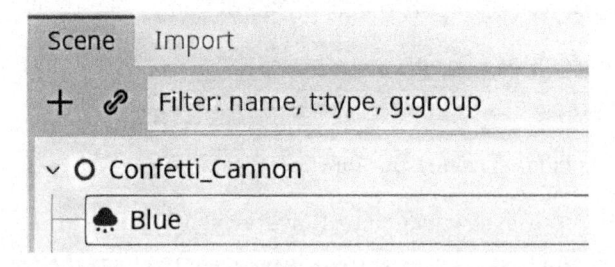

Figure 10.9 – The Confetti_Cannon node and confetti particles

Now, select the **Blue** confetti particles node. In **Inspector**, find the setting for **Process Material** and then add **New ParticleProcessMaterial**, as shown in *Figure 10.10*:

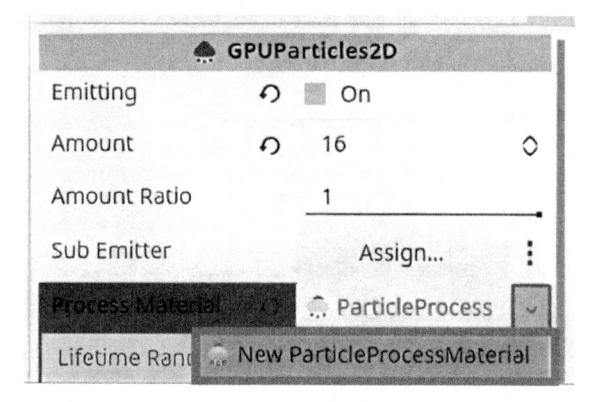

Figure 10.10 – Creating a new particle process material

Next, click on **ParticleProcessMaterial** (the word) to expand the menu of settings for the particle.

The confetti should spin (rotate) as it flies, but it shouldn't move away from the player. Enable **Rotate Y** and **Disable Z** in the **Particle Flags** settings, as shown in *Figure 10.11*:

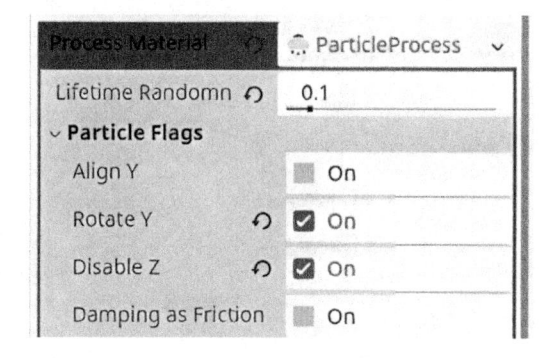

Figure 10.11 – Particle Flags settings

The confetti should move in an arc to mimic the way confetti behaves in real life. To achieve this, adjust the angle at which the confetti spawns. You can adjust the numbers to suit yourself—I have set the minimum angle to 209 and the maximum to 327, as shown in *Figure 10.12*:

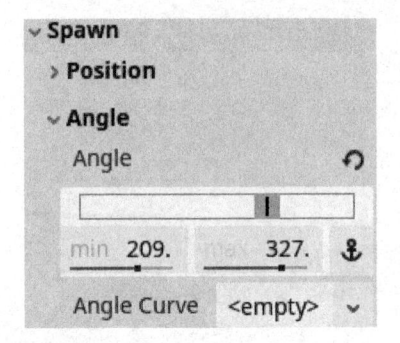

Figure 10.12 – Setting the min and max spawn angles for the confetti

Make sure to set the **Direction** variables as x = 0.0, y = -1.0, and z = 0.0, as shown in *Figure 10.13*.

The confetti particles should also spread out, and not all head off on the same path. To spread them out along a range of angles, I chose a **Spread** value of 100, which will pick an angle between –100 and 100 degrees for each new particle.

Additionally, since confetti is usually an explosive event, we want to vary the **Initial Velocity** values of the particles. Both changes are shown in *Figure 10.13*:

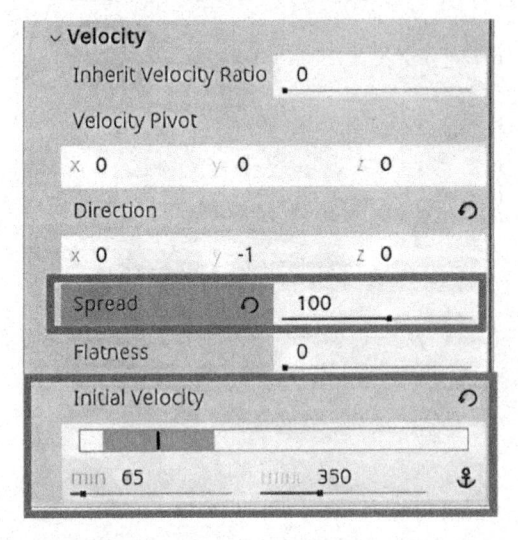

Figure 10.13 – Varying the Spread and Initial Velocity settings of the confetti particles

To make the effect even more impressive, we can change the rate at which each particle spins as it moves through the level. This can be done by varying the **Angular Velocity** values. I've locked the rate at 280, as shown in *Figure 10.14*:

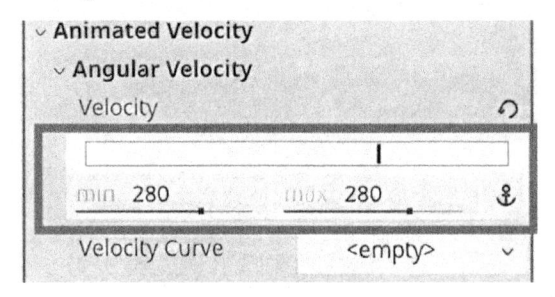

Figure 10.14 – Setting the variable rate of angular velocity for the particles

The confetti should also accelerate away from the center at a steady rate, and we can easily set this in the linear acceleration setting (that is, **Linear Accel**) as shown in *Figure 10.15*:

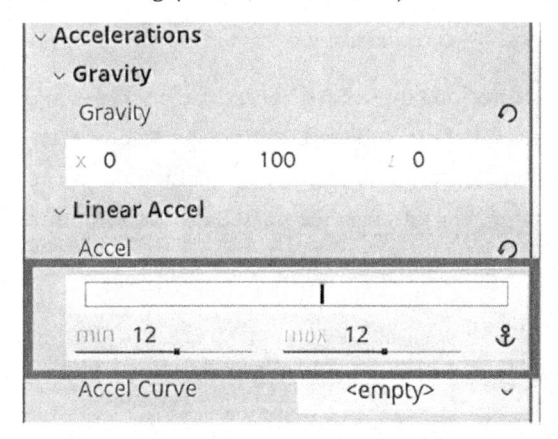

Figure 10.15 – Setting the linear acceleration for the particles

To prevent the confetti from getting too far away from the flag, we should increase **Gravity** in the **Accelerations** section, as shown in *Figure 10.16*:

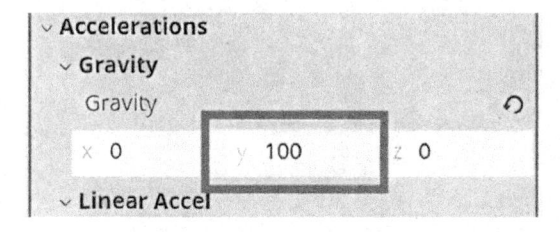

Figure 10.16 – Increasing the gravity in the y direction for the particles

To control what the confetti particles look like, we head to the **Display** properties of **ParticlesProcessMaterial**. Now, vary the **Scale** values of the confetti particles—I have set the minimum size to 5 and the maximum to 20. For **Color**, I chose *sky blue*. These changes can be seen in *Figure 10.17*:

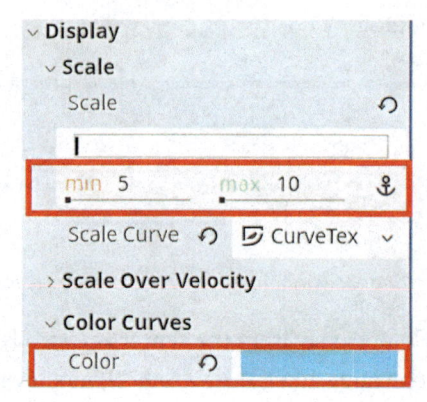

Figure 10.17 – Setting the scale variety and the color for the particles

The next step is to control how long these particles remain on screen and how they behave while they are alive. The settings for this can be found in the **Time** property. The default lifetime is **1** second, which is fine; however, we must turn on **One Shot** so that the confetti only fires once and does not keep spawning. You can vary **Explosiveness** and **Randomness**, or use the values shown in *Figure 10.18*:

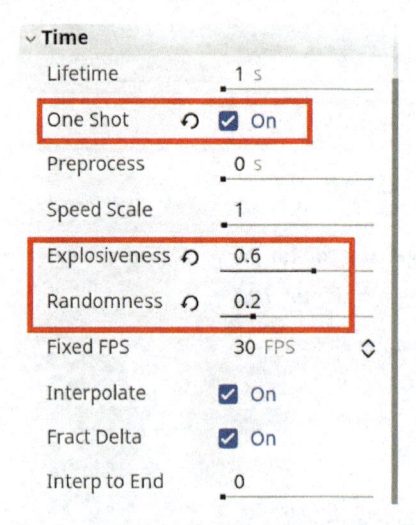

Figure 10.18 – Adjusting the Time properties for the particles

Chapter 10

The final step is to head to the **Drawing** property and tick the box to use **Local Coords**. This just ensures that the particles follow their own path and not the path of any parent nodes to which they may be attached. It keeps the particles in the place where we put them in the scene. This is shown in *Figure 10.19* as follows:

Figure 10.19 – Setting the particles to use local coordinates in the Drawing property

To preview this confetti particle effect, scroll up to the very top of the **Inspector** and turn on the **Emitting** checkbox. Each time you check it, you should see the blue confetti particles fire in the scene, as shown in *Figure 10.20*:

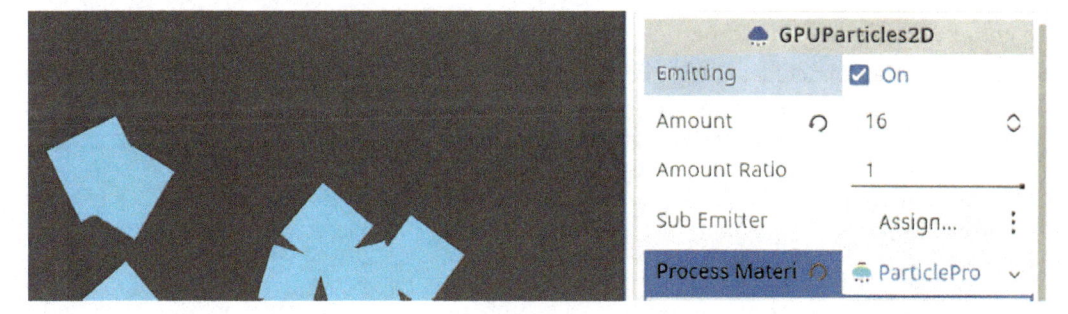

Figure 10.20 – Turning Emitting on fires the particles

We now have a scene for a sky-blue confetti particle, but a confetti cannon should shoot a rainbow of colored particles into the sky.

To achieve this, duplicate the blue particle, then *right-click* on **ParticleProcessMaterial** and choose **Make Unique**, then change the color under the **Display** properties (as we did in *Figure 10.17*) and rename the particle node to match. This is shown in *Figure 10.21*:

```
∨ O Confetti_Cannon
    ● Blue
    ● Orange
    ● Green
    ● Yellow
    ● Red
    ● Pink
```

Figure 10.21 – The confetti cannon scene tree

Note that not all the confetti particles are emitting. We'll fix this in the next section.

Scripting the confetti cannon

To ensure that all the confetti particles fire at the right time, we attach a script to the **Confetti_Cannon** node and define a `fire()` function as follows.

```
extends Node2D
func fire():
    $Blue.emitting = true
    $Orange.emitting = true
    $Green.emitting = true
    $Yellow.emitting = true
    $Red.emitting = true
    $Pink.emitting = true
```

This `fire()` function turns on all the confetti particle emitters at once by setting their `emitting` property to `true`. Each line targets a different colored particle node—`Blue`, `Orange`, `Green`, `Yellow`, `Red`, and `Pink`—and activates them simultaneously. This creates the effect of a celebratory burst of colorful confetti when the `fire()` function is called.

By keeping all the emitters inside the **Confetti_Cannon** node and triggering them through this one function, we keep our code organized and make it easy to fire all the confetti with a single command.

Recall that the cannon fires confetti as a small visual reward for the player when they complete the level and touch the checkpoint flag. It makes sense, then, that the cannon should be attached to the checkpoint. We can do this quite easily in Godot by dragging the confetti_cannon.tscn file into the scene tree of the **CheckPoint** scene, as shown in *Figure 10.22*:

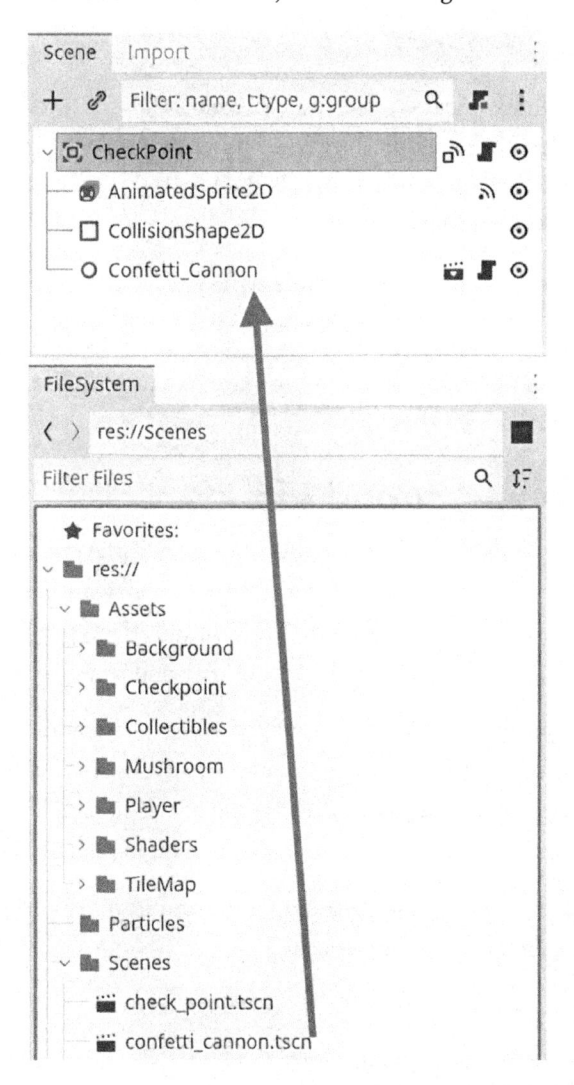

Figure 10.22 – Adding the confetti cannon to the CheckPoint scene

Once the confetti cannon is part of the **CheckPoint** scene, we will need to add some code to check_point.gd to call the fire method once the level is complete.

Click on the **CheckPoint (Area2D)** node to select it in the scene tree. Now, click on the **Node** tab and then the **Signals** tab. Connect the on_body_entered() signal and code it as follows:

```
func _on_body_entered(body):
    if level_complete:
        $Confetti_Cannon.fire()
```

The preceding code is called when the _on_body_entered() signal is received. This means that the player has collided with the checkpoint flag. Then, if the level_complete Boolean is set to true, the fire() method of the confetti cannon is called. The fire() method then sets the emitting property of all of the confetti in the cannon to true.

With everything now in place, when you complete the level and touch the checkpoint flag, you will be rewarded with a delightful burst of confetti.

In the final section, we will learn how to add sound effects and audio to our levels to add another layer of polish and atmosphere.

Adding audio and sound effects

Sound is a powerful tool in game development, shaping the player's experience in ways that visuals alone cannot. A well-crafted soundtrack sets the mood, whether it's a fast-paced action sequence or a calm exploration scene. Along with this, sound effects provide immediate feedback for player actions, making the game world feel more alive and responsive.

In this section, we'll explore how to enhance our game's feel with audio. We'll add background music to create an atmosphere and introduce sound effects for key interactions, such as collecting items, taking damage, or completing a level. By the end of this section, you'll understand how to implement and fine-tune audio to make your game more immersive and engaging.

So, let's make the level more enjoyable by adding some entertaining background music. A good resource for royalty-free music is **Incompetech**:

https://incompetech.com/music/royalty-free/music.html

I have chosen the track *Adventures in Adventureland* by Kevin MacLeod from this website. The track is licensed under Creative Commons: By Attribution 4.0 license (http://creativecommons.org/licenses/by/4.0/).

Chapter 10

Let's begin by making a new sub-folder in the `Assets` folder called `Audio` and drag and drop the `Adventures in Adventureland.mp3` file into it, as shown in *Figure 10.23*:

```
v   res://
L v   Assets
    L v   Audio
            ♪ Adventures in Adventur...
```

Figure 10.23 – Adding background music to our audio folder

To play audio, Godot has a special node called **AudioStreamPlayer**. It is ideal for playing background music as it does not play audio positionally. If you want audio to play from different sources on the screen, then you use the **AudioStreamPlayer2D** or **AudioStreamPlayer3D** node.

Since the level will have background music, add a new **AudioStreamPlayer** node to the level scene, as shown in *Figure 10.24*:

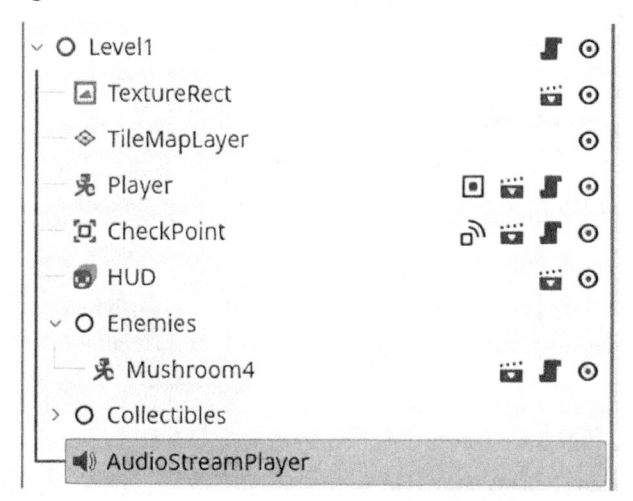

```
v  O Level1
   ▣ TextureRect
   ◈ TileMapLayer
   ⚡ Player
   ▣ CheckPoint
   🍄 HUD
   v O Enemies
       ⚡ Mushroom4
   > O Collectibles
   ◀)) AudioStreamPlayer
```

Figure 10.24 – Adding an AudioSteamPlayer node to the level scene

With **AudioStreamPlayer** selected, look at its properties in **Inspector**. Here, the **Stream** property is the audio source that it will play. Drag and drop the MP3 file into **Stream**. Lower the volume to -20 dB and set **Autoplay** to **On**. All these changes are reflected in *Figure 10.25*:

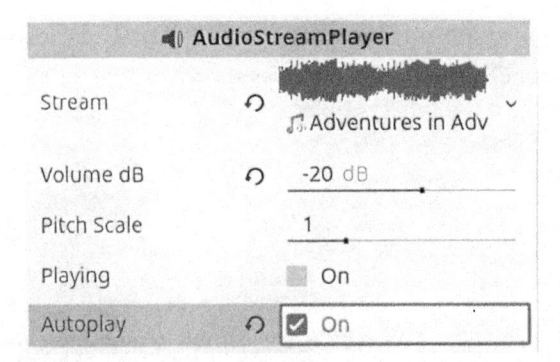

Figure 10.25 – Setting up the stream for our audio player

Because **Autoplay** is set to `true`, the track will begin playing as soon as the level loads. If you want to stop the music, all these settings can be changed from the script attached to the level, and playing can be set to `false`.

Now that we've got background music up and running, let's move on to adding sound effects to the game.

Implementing a sound effect

Sound effects do not play automatically and continuously. Instead, they are triggered by or paired with an event. A good example of this is when the player jumps or collects something.

First, you will need to download a sound effect of your choice. You can visit **Open Game Art** (`https://opengameart.org/`) and search for a jump sound and a coin or collectible sound. This website is an excellent resource for free game assets, all made available under a Creative Commons CC0 license.

Once you have a suitable jump sound and a collection sound, add your files to the `Audio` folder in the Godot **FileSystem**. This is shown in *Figure 10.26*:

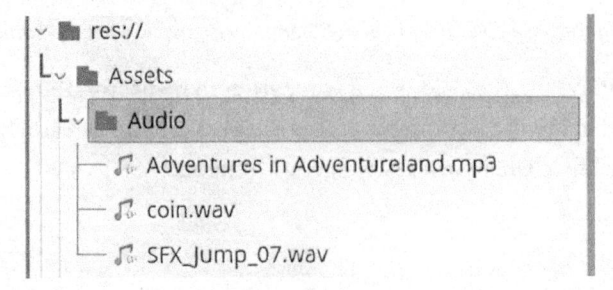

Figure 10.26 – Adding sound effects to our Audio folder

Since things are simple in our game and we only have two sound effects, one for *jumping* and one for *collecting*, we will add two **AudioStreamPlayer** nodes to the **Player** scene to handle this. Rename the **AudioStreamPlayer** nodes to reflect the sound effect they will play, as shown in *Figure 10.27*:

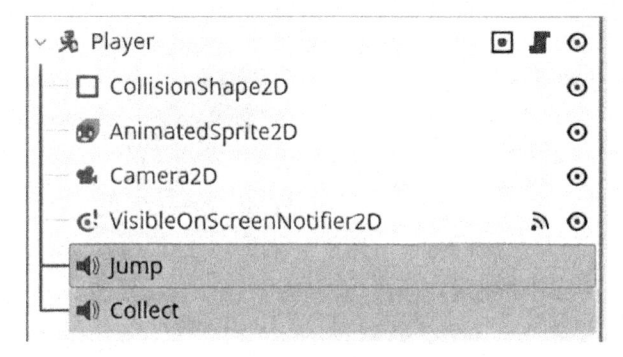

Figure 10.27 – Adding multiple audio streams to the Player scene

For more complex games with multiple overlapping sound effects, adding multiple **AudioStream** nodes is not the optimal solution, and you would consider a **Sound Manager** scene or setting up some audio buses for music and sound effects.

Each **AudioStreamPlayer** node should play the associated sound effect, so make sure that you drag the correct file to each **Stream**, as shown in *Figure 10.28*:

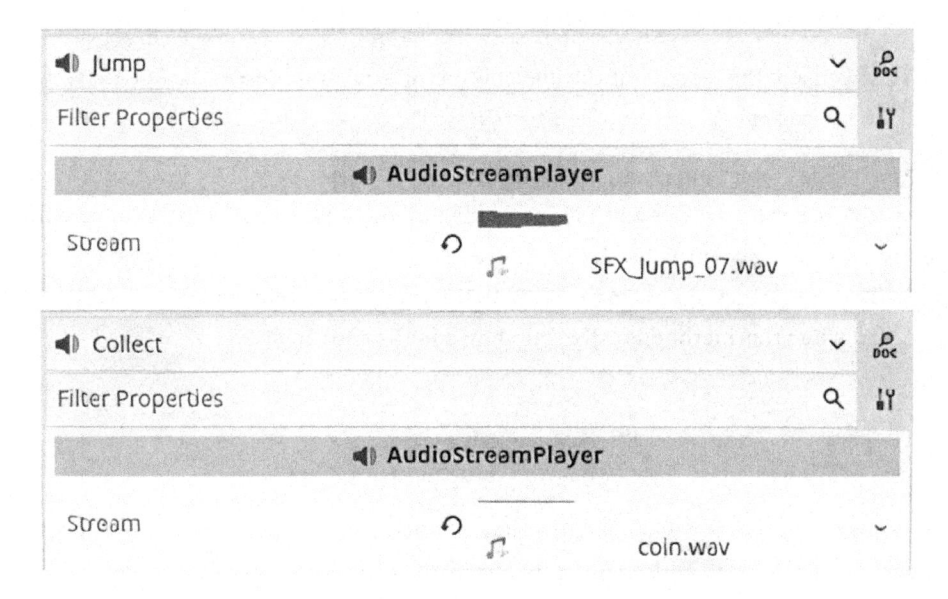

Figure 10.28 – Two audio streams for the two different sound effects

With the two audio streams set up with the right sounds and the default settings, open the player.gd script and add two references to the **AudioStreamPlayer** nodes as onready variables. You can do this by dragging the nodes into the script and then, before releasing them, holding *Ctrl*. This code is shown as follows:

```
extends CharacterBody2D

@onready var animations = $AnimatedSprite2D
@onready var jump = $Jump
@onready var collect = $Collect
```

Now that a reference to each of the nodes is available, we can find the right point to trigger the stream to play. Jumping should be triggered when the player presses the *jump* key.

In the standard_player_movement() function, the jump is handled through a specific if statement.

Just after the condition that checks whether the *spacebar* is pressed and the player is on the floor, call the play() function of the jump **AudioStreamPlayer** node, as shown here:

```
func handle_jump():
    # Handle jump.
    if Input.is_action_just_pressed("ui_accept") and is_on_floor():
        jump.play()
```

This code will ensure that each time the player is on the floor and presses the *jump* key, the jump sound effect will also play.

Moving on to the collection sound effect, it should play whenever the player collides with a Strawberry. Fortunately, we already have a function in the Player script that is called when this happens: add_score(amount). Recall that this function is called whenever a player collides with a Strawberry to keep track of how many Strawberries have been collected. We can call the sound effect to play when this method is called, as shown in the code here:

```
func add_score(amount):
    collect.play()
    strawberry_count += 1
```

The preceding code is called whenever the player collects a Strawberry in the level. It plays the collection sound effect and adds one Strawberry to the count of Strawberries collected.

With just a single line of code, we've added satisfying audio feedback to the Strawberry collection, helping to make the moment feel more rewarding for the player.

Summary

Game development isn't just about mechanics and level design—it's also about how the game *feels* to play. In this chapter, we explored the concept of game juice and how small enhancements can make a game more engaging, polished, and satisfying.

We implemented several key elements to improve player feedback and immersion. First, we introduced a health bar HUD using hearts that gray out as the player loses health, providing clear and intuitive feedback on player status. To further enhance responsiveness, we integrated hit animations to make taking damage feel impactful.

Next, we added a confetti cannon effect at the checkpoint to celebrate level completion, reinforcing player achievement with a burst of visual excitement. Finally, we brought the level to life with background music and sound effects, making the game world more immersive and dynamic.

By applying these techniques, we've demonstrated how small visual and audio improvements can dramatically enhance the player's experience. Game juice transforms a basic game into one that feels polished, responsive, and fun to play, helping to keep players engaged and invested in the game world.

In the next chapter, we'll take a step back from hands-on coding to explore the bigger picture of game development: game design. Now that you've experienced how small touches can enhance gameplay through polish and feedback, it's time to understand how those elements fit into a well-planned design. You'll learn how to structure your ideas, define gameplay mechanics, and shape the player's experience through thoughtful planning. This foundation will help you make better design choices and avoid costly rework as your projects grow in scope.

Join our community on Discord

Join our community's Discord space for discussions with the author and other readers:

https://packt.link/godot-4-game-dev

11
Understanding Game Design

Until now, the focus of this book has been to provide hands-on and practical guidance on how to develop a game in Godot. However, games are rarely made by opening a game engine and creating something with no plans. **Game design** is the first step in game development. It is the blueprint for crafting enjoyable, engaging, and memorable games.

This chapter will explore how game design acts as a guiding force, shaping gameplay mechanics, narrative structure, and player experiences.

In this chapter, we're going to cover the following main topics:

- Understanding the foundations of game design
- Exploring the game design document
- Detailing the key elements of the GDD

By the end of this chapter, you'll understand the value of thoughtful game design in streamlining development, reducing costly errors, and improving player satisfaction. Whether you aspire to design your own games or work effectively as part of a development team, these lessons will equip you with a clearer perspective on how great games are made.

Technical requirements

No prior experience or knowledge of game design is required.

Understanding the foundations of game design

Games are a form of entertainment, and successful games are often described as *fun*. But what does that actually mean? What elements come together to create a fun, rewarding experience? These are the questions that game design seeks to answer.

Hyper-realistic visuals and optimized programming alone don't guarantee that a game will be enjoyable. In fact, some of the most beloved games succeed not because of how they look or how technically advanced they are, but because of how they make the players feel. A game that is engaging, satisfying, and memorable—regardless of graphics or performance—is a product of thoughtful game design.

Let's look at some examples:

- **Stardew Valley (initially released in 2016)**: This indie farming simulator became a global hit not because of cutting-edge graphics but because of its satisfying gameplay loop, sense of progression, and meaningful interactions with characters. Its game design focuses on player choice, routine, and community-building—all of which contribute to a deeply engaging experience.
- **Celeste (initially released in 2018)**: *Celeste* is a challenging 2D platformer that combines tight controls with emotionally resonant storytelling. The design encourages perseverance, rewarding players for mastering difficult sections, while also offering accessibility options that respect different skill levels. It's a perfect example of how game design can support both gameplay and emotional impact.
- **Among Us (initially released in 2018)**: This social deduction game exploded in popularity thanks to its clever design that encourages communication, deception, and collaboration. Despite its simple art style, the core loop—figuring out who the impostor is—keeps players engaged and coming back.

These examples show that great game design doesn't always mean complexity or realism. Instead, it means creating systems and experiences that connect with players.

It is during the design process that these experiences are crafted, and it's important to be as detailed and thoughtful as possible. After all, you're laying out the foundation on which your entire game will be built.

Game design might feel more abstract than programming, and that's because it leans toward the arts and storytelling. As you've already experienced, making a game is difficult; there are many moving parts that all need to work together. Game design may be even more challenging because there's no strict formula for success. Unlike programming, there are no hard rules—just principles, patterns, and a deep understanding of what players find meaningful and enjoyable.

Introducing the game design document

There are some established frameworks for documenting your design. Once you have an idea for a game, capturing it using these industry-accepted frameworks, such as a **game design document (GDD)** or a feature checklist, will help you develop your idea more clearly and get you closer to game design gold.

When working in Godot, having a solid design plan can make a huge difference. For example, clearly defining your game mechanics early on allows you to decide what nodes, scripts, and scenes you'll need. If your design includes character upgrades, level transitions, or specific interactions, you can structure your Godot project with that in mind from the start.

Linking your design decisions directly to Godot's scene system, input handling, and scripting with GDScript will help you avoid guesswork and rework and build a game that's not only fun but also cleanly built and easier to maintain.

In the next section, we'll look at how to document your game design effectively. This is a crucial step that helps you turn your ideas into clear, actionable plans and ensures your development process in Godot stays focused, efficient, and aligned with your original vision.

Why is documentation necessary for your game design?

You might think that because the game you're making is small, or since you're the only person working on it, there's no real need to write anything down. However, this might be a short-sighted decision. Even the simplest game projects benefit from clear documentation—it helps you stay organized, think through your ideas more thoroughly, and avoid costly missteps later in development.

It is essential to document your design so that you—and anyone else working on the game—understand everything about the game and what needs to be done to finish it. Games are complex and have many interactive features. Often, you only figure out how to solve a problem while solving it. A few months down the line, you might not even remember why something was included or how it works. That's where documentation becomes invaluable.

Developing documentation for your game design is especially helpful when working in Godot, as it allows you to plan the structure of your game more efficiently, deciding what nodes you'll need, how different objects will interact, and how to organize your scripts in GDScript. This up-front clarity reduces the risk of confusion or messy rewrites and helps you stay focused as your project grows in complexity.

Creating a GDD helps you do the following:

- Reduce rework and avoid duplicating effort by clearly outlining decisions already made
- Remember the *why* behind your design choices when returning to your project after a break
- Track changes and ideas throughout the development process
- Identify interdependencies between mechanics, features, and systems
- Stay consistent with your vision and scope
- Make collaboration easier if you ever bring in additional team members or contributors

Your game design documents do two important jobs: they look back to capture all the decisions you've made so far, and they look forward, guiding the game's development. They serve as both a *record of your thinking* and a *roadmap* for building your game.

Therefore, your GDD becomes your project's single source of truth, keeping you grounded, focused, and efficient throughout development.

Understanding the guiding principles for the GDD

Firstly, it is important to note that GDDs are *living documents*. This means that they can change often, and they should be continually looked at and referred to during the development of the game. This is because, although the core idea of the game may not change, many elements around it should evolve, and the documentation should reflect that through adaptation.

> Additional reading
>
> You can see how commercial games were made by reading their GDD on **Gamescrye** and **Roobyx's** GitHub repositories:
>
> - `https://gamescrye.com/resources/game-design-documents/`
> - `https://github.com/Roobyx/awesome-game-design`

To prepare the GDD, any good collaborative documentation and design software, such as **Notion** (https://www.notion.com/), **Obsidian** (https://obsidian.md/), or **OneNote** (https://www.OneNote.com), will work well here. However, there are also solutions tailored to the game development industry, such as **CodeDecks** (https://www.codecks.io/) and **HacknPlan** (https://hacknplan.com/).

To make your game design documentation truly effective, it should follow a few best practices. These principles will help ensure your ideas are communicated clearly and can actually be used to guide development. Let's look at these in the subsequent sections.

Think visually

Use a mix of text, systems diagrams, flowcharts, wireframes, and other visuals to communicate your ideas. Visuals act as a universal language that transcends barriers, making complex concepts easier to grasp. They improve communication and make ideas more accessible, actionable, and adaptable for everyone involved.

Keep it brief and clear

Clarity and brevity are key. Your document should be the following:

- **Short and to the point**: Use bullet points to convey ideas efficiently
- **Accurate**: Be specific—include exact values for things such as speed or jump height, and always write in the present tense
- **Prioritized**: Make it clear which features are essential for your **minimum viable product (MVP)**, which are nice-to-have, and which are purely optional

Stay organized

A well-organized document is far more usable. Best practices include the following:

- **Use a web-based format**: This makes it easy to access and update, and allows for sections to be broken into separate, focused pages
- **Structure information logically**: Start with general overviews and move on to specific details only as needed

Learn by example

There is not a single *correct* way to write a design document. A helpful way to get started is to study examples from real-world games. The **Game Docs** website (https://gamedocs.org/documents/) offers a curated collection of design documents from commercial releases. Explore these to see how others structure their ideas and adapt what works for your own project.

Now that you understand the key principles behind effective documentation, let's take a closer look at what goes into creating a GDD.

Exploring the Game Design Document

By now, we know that the GDD is a highly descriptive, living software design document for a video game. For developers using Godot (or any game engine), a well-prepared GDD helps streamline the development process by clearly outlining gameplay systems, scene structures, and script logic, making it easier to translate ideas into Godot's node-based architecture and GDScript.

The first page or home page of the GDD should be a high-level overview of the game concept, which would give you the main idea behind the game. This is also sometimes referred to as a **pitch document**. In the following sections, we'll look at the sections to include on this page.

Title: what will you call your game?

The *title* is often a working title, which is subject to change as the game evolves. The title should represent the main idea of the game, so it is worth spending some time thinking about this.

As an example, our working title could be SILENT STATION. Let's develop this in the following subsections.

Team: who will build or develop the game?

List the people working on the game and what exactly they are responsible for. Don't worry about designations; concentrate on exactly which aspects of the project they will make functional.

Status: what is the status of the project?

This is best described using a traffic light system or a kanban board. Create color-themed headings: **TO DO** (*yellow*), **DOING** (*orange*), **DONE** (*green*), and **BLOCKED** (*red*). List the features of the game under each of these headings. Anything blocking the progress of the game or any major issues should fall under the red category. An example of this is shown in *Figure 11.1*:

Figure 11.1 – An example of a simple Kanban board for development tasks

Statement of concept: what is your game about in one sentence?

Describe the core features of your game in a *single sentence*. Try to include the setting, main character, primary objective, and obstacles to overcome.

Here is an example from *SILENT STATION*:

A lonely astronaut must navigate a derelict alien space station (setting) *using only a flashlight to find missing crewmates* (objective) *while avoiding hostile creatures that react to sound* (obstacles).

Expanded concept paragraph and USP: what makes your game unique, and how can you describe it in more detail?

In this section, we expand on the statement of concept and describe the gameplay. Keep in mind that this is a paragraph that briefly expands on the core loop and progression of the player. Highlight the games' **unique selling points (USPs)**, which are sometimes called the **hook**—this is what will keep the player invested.

Here is an example from *SILENT STATION*:

The player must explore pitch-dark, claustrophobic corridors with only a limited beam of light, managing both visibility and sound. The game's unique mechanic is its sound-reactive enemies combined with real-time voice input that can attract danger, making the microphone part of the gameplay loop.

Genre: what type of game are you making?

These are categories of video games that share similar gameplay characteristics. While single-genre games still exist, it's likely that these markets are oversaturated, and you will have more success in mashing together multiple genres to create new gameplay styles and mechanics.

Here is an example from *SILENT STATION*:

Survival horror with light puzzle-solving and exploration elements.

Audience: who is this game for?

This is the market you are targeting. Here, you might list the age range and the **Entertainment Software Rating Board (ESRB)** rating. You will look at the types of games this audience plays and perhaps even link to a more detailed page of player profiles and how the game will appeal to them.

Here is an example from *SILENT STATION*:

Mature players (ESRB 16+) who enjoy narrative-driven sci-fi horror games such as Alien: Isolation or Dead Space.

Experience: what should the player feel or experience while playing?

What will the player's experience in the game be? How will the game make them feel? How long does the experience last? This heading can link to a detailed page on player progression and objectives, and the details can be revealed there.

Here is an example from *SILENT STATION*:

The game is designed to create a sense of dread and tension, with brief moments of relief. It encourages slow exploration, attention to audio cues, and emotional connection through rescuing survivors.

Anchor points: what are the core ideas, inspirations, or reference points?

These are experiences in the game that tie the players to the character, invest them in the story, and keep them playing. These could be opening scenes, important boss battles, or major item discoveries that unlock narrative development. Highlighting some of these here and then linking to a page that gives more detail of the story arc is key here.

Here is an example from *SILENT STATION*:

- *The initial moment the astronaut loses contact with base*
- *Discovering the first survivor in a cryo pod*
- *First encounter with a sound-reactive enemy*
- *Turning on the power to an entire sector using a stealth route*

Platform: which platforms will the game be released on?

This is the platform you are targeting. It could be PC, mobile, or console. It could be one or all of them or something else entirely. Usually, you will narrow your scope and focus on a single platform.

Here is an example from *SILENT STATION*:

PC (initial), with future potential for console.

Review competition: what similar games exist, and how will yours stand out?

List some games that are similar or even directly competing with yours. Then, link to a page on which you analyze the competition in depth. Highlight what sets your game apart.

Here is an example from *SILENT STATION*:

Like Alien: Isolation and Observation, but differentiates with unique microphone input and sound as a core mechanic.

Assets: what art, sound, and other resources will your game need?

You might include some concept art that establishes the general tone of the game and link to a more detailed document that lists all the known sound and image assets needed for the game. This would include the interface, animations, world, and characters in detail.

Here is an example from *SILENT STATION*:

- *Audio: environmental ambience, voice lines, creature sounds*
- *Visuals: modular sci-fi interior tileset, dynamic lighting assets*
- *UI: oxygen meter, flashlight battery icon, sound detection meter*

Monetization: how will the game generate revenue, if at all?

Here, you explain how the game will generate revenue. It might be that the game is a one-time purchase or is free-to-play, or has in-game purchases. Whatever the case may be, it needs to be expanded on the linked page on the systems and features.

Using these as the main headings on the first page of your GDD and linking them to other pages in the GDD, which contain further detail, will provide a great overview of the concept for your game and give everyone reading it a clear idea of what type of game this is and who it is aimed at.

The next step in the design process would be to focus on the key elements of the game that now require more detail.

Here is an example from *SILENT STATION*:

Premium model – one-time purchase. Future DLC (Downloadable Content) could add new storylines or challenge modes.

Describing game elements of the GDD in detail

This section will highlight the parts of the GDD that require more detail. The reason these sections need so much detail is that they are the fundamental elements without which there would be no game.

Therefore, you and other team members need to have a very clear idea of what is going into the game and how it works and affects other systems in the game. Use the guidance in the subsequent sections to add as much detail as possible to your game idea. Note that each heading represents a new page or pages in the GDD.

Player progression and objectives

In this section, you should answer the following questions about the *player*:

- Who are they?
- What do they know?
- What is their narrative arc?

- What are their goals?
- How do they progress?
- What is the core loop?
- What is the outer loop?

The *Player progression and objectives* page links to anchor points on the main page. As a web-based document, this would typically be a hyperlink, but these points also connect conceptually, guiding how the game unfolds over time.

To define progression clearly, it's helpful to break it down into two layers:

- **Core gameplay loop**: The core gameplay loop represents the fundamental actions the player repeats to play the game. For example, in a platformer, this might involve running and jumping to traverse a level, attacking enemies, and avoiding hazards.
- **Outer loop**: The outer loop, on the other hand, describes the broader progression system—how players are rewarded for engaging with the core loop. This could include unlocking new levels, gaining upgrades, or progressing through a story.

The core loop should feed into the outer loop, and vice versa, creating a satisfying and reinforcing gameplay experience.

Here is an example from *SILENT STATION*:

Player Progression & Objectives:

- *Start: Wake up in medical bay*
- *Mid-game: Repair communication array*
- *Late-game: Evacuate remaining crew*
- *Core loop: Explore → Find tools → Avoid noise → Progress*
- *Outer loop: Unlock new zones, backtrack with new tools, piece together story*

Game world and background

In this section, you should answer questions about the world:

- **World lore**: Is there a back story that sets the scene for the game?
- **World physics**: Can you run, fly, fall, float, and so on?
- **World points**: How does the player progress through the game, locations, and so on?
- **Easter eggs**: Do you have any hidden surprises for the player to find?

This page can link to a new document on world fiction if required.

Here is an example from *SILENT STATION*:

Game World and Background:

- *Space station lore: abandoned research facility on a rogue moon*
- *Gravity and oxygen are managed room by room*
- *Hints at secret government experiments via environmental storytelling*

The overworld map shown in *Figure 11.2* is an example of how a game's world can be visually represented, helping to convey the structure, scale, and key locations within your game's setting:

Figure 11.2 – The overworld (Credit: https://kenney.nl/)

This map gives a bird's-eye view of the game world, showing how different areas are connected and where key events or challenges might occur. Including visuals like this in your GDD helps both you and your team stay aligned with the spatial layout and narrative flow of the game.

User interface

This section should detail all the ways in which the player interacts with the game world and receives information about the world and their own status. Also, be sure to focus on the look and feel. You should answer these questions:

- What is the control scheme?
- What is required to move from one screen to the next? (Consider providing wireframes.)

Chapter 11

- What help or hint system do you provide, and what does it look like?
- How do you present the controls on screen?
- What does the **Options** menu look like?
- What does the **Pause** menu look like?

Here is an example from *SILENT STATION*:

Minimal UI, primarily diegetic (flashlight glow, sound bars integrated into helmet visor)

Figure 11.3 shows a UI mock-up demonstrating elements, such as buttons and sliders:

Figure 11.3 – A UI mockup (Credit: https://kenney.nl/)

Audio and visual style

This page provides details on the atmosphere and ambience of the game. It should clearly define how the game should look and sound. This all contributes to the overall mood of the game, and you should answer questions such as the following:

- What is the color palette?
- What is the musical style?
- What is the art style?
- Include references, examples, and concept art
- Give an idea of the environment, characters, enemies, objects, and so on

This page should link to your complete game asset list.

Here is an example from *SILENT STATION*:

- *Art style: stylized realism*
- *Sound: layered ambient tones, positional audio, player breathing*

Figure 11.4 shows an example of a color palette. For more examples, check out **Lospec** (https://lospec.com/).

Color	Hex	RGB
	#365655	(54,86,85)
	#4d3451	(77,52,81)
	#581929	(88,25,41)
	#b26245	(178,98,69)
	#d6c376	(214,195,118)

Figure 11.4 – An example of a color palette

Game systems and features

Games are never really finished—there's always the temptation to add new, cool features that could make the game even better. So, how do you decide which features to include in this section?

The answer is to list all systems and features required for either an MVP or a **vertical slice** of the game to be playable:

- An MVP is the simplest version of your game that includes just enough core features to be functional and testable. It's what you would show to get initial feedback or confirm that the basic concept works.
- A vertical slice is a small, fully polished portion of the game that represents the final look, feel, and gameplay. It's typically used to showcase the game to others, such as in a pitch or trailer, and helps clarify the quality and scope of the finished product.

Essentially, you are listing critical components without which the game would not be playable. Consider answering these questions:

- Why is this feature required?
- How does this feature interact with any other features?
- How does each feature contribute to gameplay?
- How does each feature contribute to monetization or not?

Here is an example from *SILENT STATION*:

Flashlight system:

- *Why required: The flashlight is the player's only way to navigate the dark environment, creating tension and visibility control*
- *Feature interaction: Integrates with power management and stealth systems; has limited battery life, requiring strategic use*
- *Contribution to gameplay: Controls how much the player sees, influences exploration, pacing, and adds vulnerability*
- *Contribution to monetization: Not directly, but critical for the emotional tone and market appeal*

Figure 11.5 illustrates how individual systems and features in a game function like building blocks. Each block represents a different system, such as movement, physics, UI, or level design. On their own, these systems may seem simple, but when carefully connected, they support and enhance each other to create a cohesive, engaging experience.

Figure 11.5 – How systems and features work together to create a bigger experience

(Credit: https://kenney.nl/)

Just like in *Figure 11.5*, it's the combination and interaction of these blocks that form the full structure of a game.

Software requirements

This section should be dedicated to listing the software tools required to develop the game and the assets, too, if necessary. It should also outline the purpose of each tool. You should answer these questions:

- What game engine will be used?
- What will be used for world creation and level design?

Chapter 11

- What will be used for dialogue trees and narrative structure?
- What will be used for mission and quest design?
- What other tools are needed for the development of the game?

Here is an example from *SILENT STATION*:

- *Godot 4 for the game engine*
- *Blender for modeling*
- *Reaper for sound editing*

Figure 11.6 shows a screenshot of the Godot engine interface:

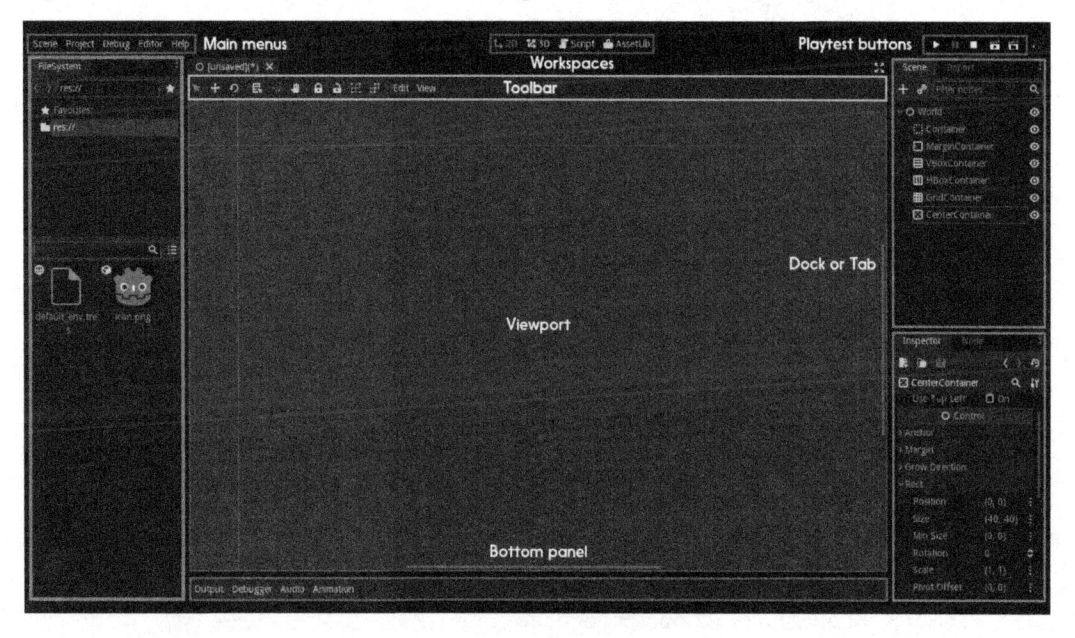

Figure 11.6 – The Godot engine interface

> **Quick tip:** Need to see a high-resolution version of this image? Open this book in the next-gen Packt Reader or view it in the PDF/ePub copy.
>
> **The next-gen Packt Reader** and a **free PDF/ePub copy** of this book are included with your purchase. Scan the QR code OR visit `packtpub.com/unlock`, then use the search bar to find this book by name. Double-check the edition shown to make sure you get the right one.

Game objects

This page should list the details of all the objects defined in your game. You should list the details of these elements, including the following:

- All **non-player characters (NPCs)** and enemies
- The story regarding NPCs and enemies
- Dialogue of NPCs and enemies, including links to dialogue files
- All NPC and enemy properties, such as abilities, special attacks, and so on
- All the attributes and values of other game objects, such as moving platforms, and so on
- All the functions, methods, or behaviors of the game objects
- This page should link to the asset list page
- This page should link to the asset attribute and property list page

Here is an example from *SILENT STATION*:

- *Enemies: "Echo Wraiths" – blind but highly reactive to sound*
- *Survivors: Have dialogue trees and scripted events*

Figure 11.7 demonstrates the assets linking to the world map:

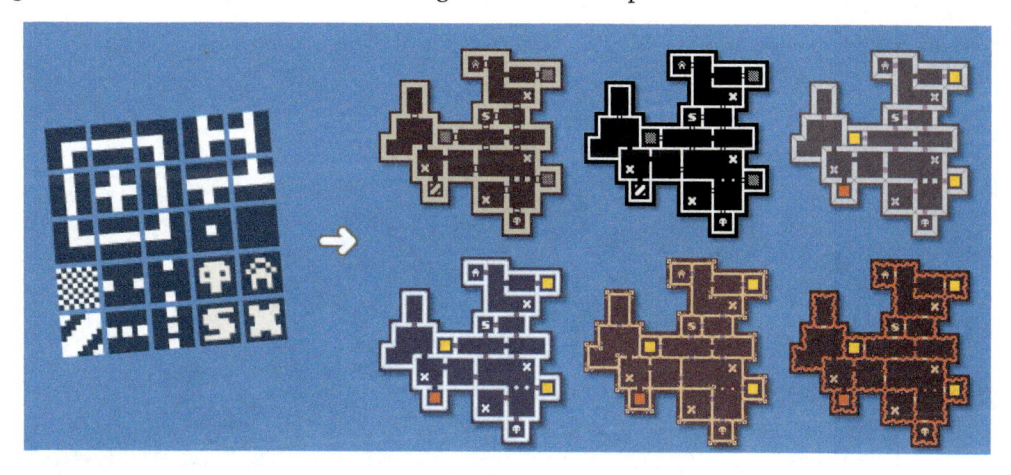

Figure 11.7 – Assets linking to the game world map (Credit: https://kenney.nl/)

Detailed asset list

This is the page on which your design documents should be linked. It could be a spreadsheet that is continually updated as it contains the entire asset list, which defines each object and its properties. This would include every object: all text, graphics, and audio content used in the game.

You should start this list as soon as you begin *prototyping* and *testing* gameplay. This is because the number of assets you need will give you a good indication of the scope of the game and an estimate of how long it will take to make. If you do not create an asset list and keep it updated, it will be very hard to keep track of the game development.

Here is an example from *SILENT STATION*:

You would link to the spreadsheet showing model names, file types, poly count, and usage tags

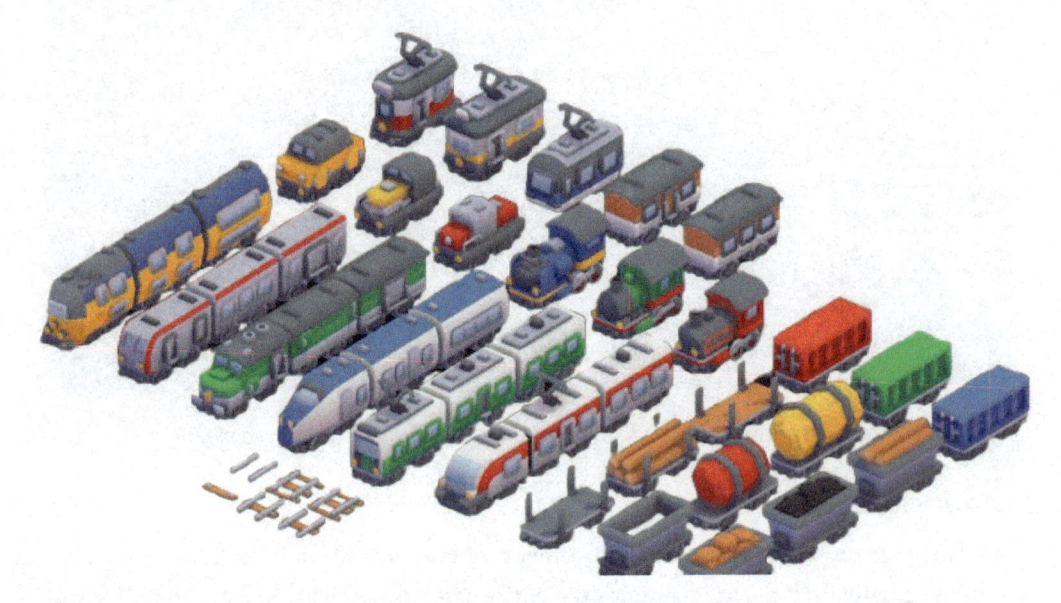

Figure 11.8 – It is essential to keep a list of all assets in the game (Credit: https://kenney.nl/)

Prototypes

Often, you will want to test ideas, features, and mechanics. When you develop prototypes to test these ideas, you should link them to your GDD. Provide as much detail as you can about the prototype, including the date it was made, the purpose of the prototype, and what it was testing. You should also include how this changed the design of the game.

Here is an example from *SILENT STATION*:

- *Prototype 1: enemy AI sound detection test*
- *Prototype 2: flashlight battery depletion vs. level pacing*

Playtesting

While you are developing the game, you will conduct a lot of play tests. This is an essential step in game development because it is an incremental process. You should have links in your document to the outcomes of each test you conduct.

The page should contain an overview of the following:

- What were you testing?
- Why were you testing it?
- What did you learn from the test?
- How did it affect the development of the game?

Here is an example from *SILENT STATION*:

Playtest 1 revealed players didn't understand how sound affected enemy behavior → added subtle audio tutorial in early level

Figure 11.9 demonstrates the concept of gray boxing, a technique used during early testing phases of game development. In **gray boxing**, simple shapes and placeholder graphics are used to build a level layout before adding final art or assets. This allows developers to focus on testing core gameplay mechanics such as movement, collision, level flow, and challenge balance without being distracted by visuals.

Figure 11.9 – Record all the results of every test (Credit: https://kenney.nl/)

Gray boxing is a vital part of the broader testing and playtesting process, helping teams identify design issues early, refine the player experience, and ensure the game is fun and functional before committing to polished visuals.

Archive

Over time, you will try many different ideas and test several different features as you develop your game. Not all these ideas will work, and so, instead of throwing them out, create an archive and store them there.

Further down the development road, parts of those ideas and features may be useful. The archive will also give you a sense of how your design has developed over time, and you can get a good perspective on just how much progress you have made.

Here is an example from *SILENT STATION*:

Original idea for two-player co-op archived but may return in expansion

Figure 11.10 – Take ideas from the archive and use them elsewhere in your design (Credit: https://kenney.nl/)

Current concerns and considerations

Because you will be deliberately limiting your scope, usually to just what is required for an MVP or vertical slice, many of your ideas and features will not make it to production. However, they can be marked for a future expansion of the game.

Similarly, you may have concerns about implemented features, and they might not currently be resolved or working just the way you want them to. You should list these here, and once they are resolved, you should move them to a new page or section for resolved issues with a detailed description of what the issue was and how it was resolved.

Here is an example from *SILENT STATION*:

Uncertainty about microphone support on all platforms

Implementation details

Every feature, system, and mechanic in the game will need documentation that details the technicalities of its implementation. They should demonstrate in detail exactly how each element can be achieved by the developers. This is the least design-focused page and instead is development-focused. It should answer the following questions:

- What algorithms and data structures are required?
- How are features such as navigation, resources, and dialogue implemented?
- What procedural systems are needed?
- How does the game's economy function?
- What network architecture is required?
- What hardware is being targeted?
- Are there any game cheats for testing purposes?
- What is the project folder structure, and what are the file naming conventions?

Here is an example from *SILENT STATION*:

- *Sound detection system uses raycasting and dynamic decibel thresholds*
- *Enemies use a state machine switching between patrol, alert, and chase*

With the implementation details in place, the design document shifts from conceptual ideas to practical execution.

This section ensures that developers have a clear blueprint for building the game's systems effectively. With the groundwork laid, the next step is to consider how all these elements come together during production, testing, and iteration.

Summary

In this chapter, we explored the critical role of game design within game development, with a specific focus on the structure and purpose of the GDD. We broke down each section of the GDD in detail, covering everything from the title and team composition to monetization strategies, game systems, prototypes, and playtesting.

By walking through the key headings—such as the statement of concept, audience, USPs, assets, player progression, and audio-visual style—we laid out a clear framework for documenting every important aspect of a game. This structured approach ensures that ideas are well-communicated, feasible, and aligned with the project's goals.

Creating a design document, even for a small single-screen game, is not just a formality—it's an essential step in bringing your vision to life. It provides a roadmap for development, helping you stay focused and consistent while also anticipating potential challenges. Additionally, a clear and well-organized GDD acts as a valuable tool for collaboration, whether you're working solo or in a team, ensuring that everyone involved understands the core ideas and direction of the game.

Ultimately, investing time in a GDD streamlines the development process, reduces costly revisions, and lays the foundation for a polished, engaging player experience. Whether you're building a simple game or a complex multi-level adventure, thoughtful design planning is what transforms creative ideas into a playable reality.

Now that you've seen how to plan and document your game in detail, the next chapter will guide you through what happens after your design is complete. You'll explore educational resources, ways to practice your skills, connect with the game development community, find useful tools and assets, and begin building your portfolio. You'll also learn how to come up with compelling game ideas and follow a design process for your future projects.

Unlock this book's exclusive benefits now

Scan this QR code or go to `packtpub.com/unlock`, then search this book by name.

Note: Keep your purchase invoice ready before you start.

12
Where to Next?

Congratulations on reaching the final chapter of *Godot 4 for Beginners*! You now have a solid foundation in using the Godot Engine to create games, and you've developed practical skills to bring your ideas to life. But the journey doesn't end here—this chapter is designed to help you take the next step in your game development career.

This chapter will introduce you to a variety of resources and opportunities that will support your continued growth as a developer. From YouTube channels and blogs to game jams and asset marketplaces, you will discover valuable tools, communities, and experts that can inspire, teach, and elevate your projects.

In this chapter, we're going to cover the following main topics:

- Utilizing educational resources
- Exploring opportunities for practice
- Community and networking
- Utilizing tools and assets
- Building your portfolio
- Developing game ideas
- Design guide for your next project

By the end of this chapter, you'll have a curated list of resources to deepen your knowledge, expand your skills, and connect with other developers. You'll also have discovered how to stay motivated, stay informed about the latest trends, and build your presence in the game development community.

Wherever your game development journey takes you next, these resources will be your foundation for continued learning and success. Let's explore what is out there!

Technical requirements

No technical setup is needed—just a willingness to explore, experiment, and take the next step in game development.

Utilizing educational resources

Learning how to develop games in Godot doesn't stop with a single project or tutorial; it's an ongoing process. This section introduces a variety of trusted educational resources, such as YouTube channels, blogs, and books, that can help you deepen your knowledge, stay up to date with the engine's evolution, and find inspiration from experienced developers.

Whether you prefer watching video tutorials, reading step-by-step guides, or learning from community insights, these resources will support your journey as you grow your skills and take on more ambitious game projects.

YouTube

There are many free game development learning resources available on YouTube. Because Godot itself is open source, the community around the engine has a philosophy of sharing and helpfulness. There is a belief among the community that *we should not gatekeep knowledge and instead that we all learn more through openness and sharing.*

Some of the best Godot game development YouTube channels are the following:

- **GDQuest** (`https://www.youtube.com/@Gdquest`): Arguably the best resource for learning how to create games with the Godot Engine, GDQuest is a professional and well-established group of Godot educators. This means that you will get the cumulative knowledge of those highly experienced in the Godot Engine. I have personally used their channel for the bite-sized explanations of various nodes since they explain everything succinctly and get straight to the point.

    All the material on their YouTube channel is free, and if you respond well to their teaching style, then it would be wise to explore their paid courses, which I will discuss later in this chapter.

Chapter 12	303

- **Heartbeast** (https://www.youtube.com/@uheartbeast): Another fantastic resource for anything Godot-related is the YouTube channel Heartbeast. Benjamin was an early adopter of Godot, and his tutorials are some of the most thorough, detailed, and yet beginner friendly that I have ever seen. He has a great way of explaining why things are done the way they are, and I highly recommend his channel.

  If you are looking for the full experience of creating a game in Godot from start to finish, with careful and detailed explanation along the way, then Heartbeast is the channel for you. Benjamin also has paid courses if you want to go beyond the basics discussed on his YouTube channel.

- **Godot Tutorials** (https://www.youtube.com/@GodotTutorials): If you want to focus more on coding in the Godot Game Engine, then check out the Godot Tutorials channel. This channel takes a detailed approach to making games with Godot and includes elements of game design in its teaching, too. The channel concentrates on coding principles using GDScript within the Godot Engine, making it a great place to visit for a deeper understanding of how to implement things in Godot.

  The channel has an accompanying website with text-based versions of all the video tutorials. I really appreciate this as I learn better from text, so if this is your learning style too, then check out https://godottutorials.com/.

- **GameDev Journey** (https://www.youtube.com/@GameDevJourney): Finally, if you enjoyed the way that the materials were presented to you in this book, then you will enjoy the tutorials on my personal YouTube channel. It also has an accompanying website with the same tutorials presented in text format, which you can visit at https://www.gamedevjourney.co.uk/home.

  The tutorials are modular and focus on individual game mechanics. Beyond tutorials, there are also developer diaries, discussions around game assets and resources, and encouraging videos with advice to keep you motivated.

Now, let's move on to some blog recommendations.

Blogs

Game development is an area that is always evolving, and there is always more to learn. There are some amazing blogs online covering game design and the theory behind making games.

To stay up to date and remain aware of the current best practices, the following blogs are useful:

- **Deconstructor of Fun** (https://www.deconstructoroffun.com/blog): This blog analyzes the design of popular, free-to-play games, with a critical eye on what works and what doesn't in terms of engagement, retention, and monetization. Written by a team of developers who also play games extensively, the content is especially valuable for aspiring game makers who want to understand the balance between fun and profitability. If you're planning to build games for a living, this blog offers real-world insights into what makes games successful in a competitive market.
- **Game Design Skills** (https://gamedesignskills.com/blog/): This blog offers a rich and steadily growing library of articles focused on the practice of game design, particularly around how players interact with game systems. It dives deep into mechanics, controls, progression, and balancing, making it a great resource for aspiring and experienced designers alike. Whether you're learning the fundamentals or refining your skills, this site is a valuable place to explore real examples and practical design thinking.
- **Game Developer** (https://www.gamedeveloper.com/): Game Developer is a go-to hub for anyone working in or studying the games industry. It features detailed postmortems, developer insights, and behind-the-scenes articles on released games, alongside regular updates on industry trends and news. Ideal for students, indie devs, and professionals alike, it's a place to learn from real-world experiences and stay informed about the evolving landscape of game development.

Whether you prefer quick insights or in-depth articles, these blogs are a great way to stay current with evolving design trends and industry practices. For a more structured and comprehensive approach to learning, see which books are recommended at the end of this chapter in the further reading section.

Exploring opportunities for practice

In my conversations with many game developers, there is one piece of advice that comes up repeatedly: *start small* when making a game. The benefits of this approach are as follows:

- Starting with a small game allows you to learn the core concepts, such as movement, collisions, and basic mechanics, without being overwhelmed by the scope of a larger game.
- A smaller project can be completed faster. This gives you the satisfaction of finishing something and seeing it in action. It also gives you the experience of the process of making a game from start to finish, which boosts confidence and motivation. Having a game that others can play also gives you the chance to get feedback, which you can learn from.

- Having a small game provides a safe space for you to make mistakes and learn from them. Trial and error is a great way to learn in the beginning. In larger projects, your mistakes will compound and are difficult to fix.
- When you work on smaller games, you get the chance to develop essential problem-solving skills without needing to balance multiple systems at once.
- Making many small games lets you build a portfolio gradually. A collection of small but polished projects is better than having many rough and unfinished large projects. This is a good way to showcase your work.
- Once you have completed some smaller games, you will have a better understanding of game development workflows and will have laid a foundation for yourself to undertake more ambitious projects.

A great way to practice your skills is to take part in game jams. We'll discuss this in the next section.

Participating in game jams

Game jams are time-limited events in which individuals or teams create a game from beginning to end based on a given theme and set of constraints. They usually last anywhere from 48 hours to a week and are open to participants of all skill levels.

For beginners, game jams are a fantastic way of getting hands-on experience. You'll have the chance to practice everything from designing mechanics to writing code, creating art, and composing sound—all in a short burst of focused creativity. Don't worry if you're not confident in every area—game jams often attract a wide range of people, and many participants team up and learn from each other.

Additionally, you'll also experience the full game development cycle: brainstorming, prototyping, testing, and finishing a playable project. This can be a huge confidence boost and a great portfolio piece. More importantly, it's a fun and welcoming way to connect with others who share your passion for games. You can find a game jam to enter that suits your skill level and time requirements on **itch.io** (`https://itch.io/`). They have a calendar of jams, and you can sign up for one that suits you at `https://itch.io/jams`.

The other big jams are the following:

- **Godot Wild Jam**: `https://godotwildjam.com/`
- **Ludum Dare**: `https://ldjam.com/`
- **The Global Game Jam**: `https://globalgamejam.org/`

Game jams are just one example of how powerful it can be to learn alongside others. Whether you're collaborating in a team, sharing feedback, or simply seeing how others approach the same theme, these events highlight the importance of community in game development.

In the next section, we'll explore how getting involved in the wider game development community, and building a professional network, can open doors, provide support, and help you grow even further as a developer.

Community and networking

One of the most inspiring things about game development is its encouraging and supportive community. Every game developer knows how difficult it is to make a game, and they know what it is like to be starting out and to feel that you don't know how to do even the simplest things. This is why they are always willing to help others learn. Game developers also rely on each other for gameplay testing and feedback.

Why networking matters

Networking with fellow game devs can open doors and allow you to form collaborations and gain mentorships, job offers, and gigs. Many game developers find their first job in the industry or meet future collaborators through the connections that they have built.

Networking also gives you visibility. By engaging with the community and networking at events such as game jams, conferences, and meetups, you can start to become noticed. This visibility can be crucial for landing jobs, securing funding, or gaining traction for a game release.

Where to build your network

You can build your network and connect with the community on platforms such as **X**, **Reddit**, and **Discord** servers. Participating in game jams will get your name out there and may even give you the opportunity to be part of a team.

Attending industry events and conferences, such as the **Game Developers Conference (GDC)**, and smaller local meetups can provide opportunities to network in person and to learn from industry veterans.

You can also offer value to others even if you are new to game development. It's not all about asking for help; it is also about offering it! If someone is looking for feedback or needs someone to play test their game, don't hesitate to volunteer.

People to follow

Some of the best professionals to follow on LinkedIn are the following:

- Sergei Vasiuk (https://www.linkedin.com/in/sergeivasjuk/)
- Gökhan Üzmez (https://www.linkedin.com/in/gkhnuzmez/)
- Jakub Remiar (https://www.linkedin.com/in/jakubremiar/)
- Amir Satvat (https://www.linkedin.com/in/amirsatvat/)
- Mayank Grover (https://www.linkedin.com/in/mayankgrover/)
- Mirko Minenza (https://www.linkedin.com/in/mirko-minenza/)
- Anton Slashcev (https://www.linkedin.com/in/aslashcev/)

By building a network and becoming part of a game development community, you can grow your skills, learn, and foster a passion for creating games. Surrounding yourself with like-minded individuals who share your interests will allow you to find inspiration, guidance, and camaraderie, which will make your game development journey more rewarding.

Utilizing tools and assets

When working in game development, and especially when starting out, it is so important that you have the right tools and assets to bring your ideas to life. Game development is such a complex process and involves many disciplines, including art, audio, programming, and design. Let's have a look at some tools and resources to help you with these aspects.

Tools

In this section, we'll look at some essential tools across key areas of game development:

- **Game engine**: Our game engine of choice is Godot (https://godotengine.org/) due to it being free and open source. It is beginner-friendly, lightweight, and perfect for both 2D and 3D projects.
- **Graphic tools**: Here are a few recommended tools for creating graphics:
    - **GIMP** is a free and open source alternative to Photoshop: https://www.gimp.org/
    - **Krita** is also a free and open source tool for creating digital paintings and 2D art: https://krita.org/en/
    - **LibreSprite** is a free and open source alternative to Aseprite for creating pixel art: https://libresprite.github.io

- **Blender** is a free and open source tool for creating 3D models and animations: https://www.blender.org/
- **Audio tools**: Here is a list of free tools to get you started:
  - **Audacity** is a free tool for recording and editing audio: https://www.audacityteam.org/
  - **LMMS** is free and open source software for composing music: https://lmms.io/
  - **Bosca Ceoil: The Blue Album** is a free and open source tool for making retro game music: https://yurisizov.itch.io/boscaceoil-blue
  - **Bfxr** is a free tool for creating retro sound effects: https://www.bfxr.net/
- **Version control**: To track changes to your project and collaborate with others, Git (https://git-scm.com/) is great. Usually, Git is paired with GitHub or GitLab.

Resources

Asset marketplaces exist that provide a variety of assets, including sprites, 3D models, music, and sound effects. Mostly, you need to purchase assets; however, some vendors provide assets for free. Here is a list of such vendors:

- **itch.io** has an assets section that contains free and paid resources created by indie developers: https://itch.io/game-assets
- **Kenney** offers many game assets for free, and he has a clean and simple style: https://kenney.nl/
- **Quaternius** also offers free game assets focusing largely on low-poly 3D: https://quaternius.com/
- **OpenGameArt** is a repository of free art and sound assets: https://opengameart.org/
- **Freesound** is a community-driven database of sound effects: https://freesound.org
- **ZapSplat** is a collection of royalty-free sound effects and music tracks: https://www.zapsplat.com/
- The **BBC** has released an archive of sound effects for personal use: https://sound-effects.bbcrewind.co.uk/
- **Lospec** is an amazing resource for color theory and color palettes: https://lospec.com/
- **Pixabay** and **Unsplash** are great resources for placeholder or background imagery:
  - https://pixabay.com
  - https://unsplash.com/

- **BlenderKit** is a good resource for free and premium 3D models that are integrated with Blender: `https://www.blenderkit.com/`
- **Google**, **DaFont**, and **Font Squirrel** all provide excellent fonts for you to use in your projects:
    - `https://fonts.google.com/`
    - `https://www.dafont.com/`
    - `https://www.fontsquirrel.com/`

When creating your first games or prototypes, it is always best to start with free resources or create your own. This will let you learn without spending money. If you are using resources from elsewhere, you must remember to check the license for any asset you download. This is even more important if you plan to publish your game.

When developing, make use of placeholders or basic shapes in the early stages. This frees you to focus on mechanics and gameplay rather than visuals.

Finally, join communities where you can share resources and advice. By using the right tools and knowing where to find assets, you can focus on learning and building games.

Building your portfolio

A **portfolio** is a must-have for any aspiring game developer. This is because game development is a fundamentally practical skill and not another theoretical discipline. Of course, it is important to understand the underlying concepts of design, programming, and art; however, the true demonstration of a game developer's ability is in their application of these skills.

A portfolio of your work provides evidence of your mastery of these concepts, and it showcases your experience with game development tools, techniques, and workflows. Your ability to create functional, engaging, and entertaining games will be clearly demonstrated. Include your completed projects and prototypes to highlight your hands-on experience and problem-solving skills, to show that you are familiar with industry-standard tools such as game engines and asset creation software.

A great place to start with a game's portfolio is **itch.io** (see the *Participating in game jams* section for website). You can create an account on itch and host your games there for free just by signing up. Every itch page can be completely customized, and you can follow their handy guide for doing so here: `https://itch.io/docs/creators/design`.

Game developers are always learning, and your portfolio will reflect that. You are on a lifelong journey as a developer. Your portfolio traces that journey, proving that you have put theory into practice and that you can turn ideas into playable realities.

Developing game ideas

Now that you have all this information, you might be keen to begin working on a game for your portfolio. It can be daunting not knowing where to begin. Creativity is not easy, and often a prompt is extremely helpful in lighting the spark of inspiration, which can quickly turn into wildfire!

If you are struggling to come up with a game idea for your next project, you can use a game idea generator: `https://letsmakeagame.net/game-idea-generator/`.

If a random idea doesn't appeal to you, then you can try out these tried and tested techniques for coming up with creative starters:

- **Mash-up hit games**: Have a look at the core mechanics in at least two hit games and then come up with a way to combine them into one mechanic in your game. This can lead to some interesting and emergent gameplay.
- **Simplify**: Look at some complex games for inspiration and think creatively about how you could simplify the experience into a casual game for mobile. Think about adding constraints such as only using a single screen or having gameplay last no longer than a minute.
- **Polish**: There are so many games released daily on various digital storefronts. This is a goldmine of ideas as many of these games are rushed to market and are decidedly lacking in polish. You don't have to come up with a totally new idea; you need only execute a popular idea well.
- **Surprise people**: Take an idea to ridiculous levels. Often, the key to a great game is the unexpected and the element of surprise.
- **Feeling is fun**: Appeal to the player's emotions. Your audience may well forget what your game was about, but they will never forget how it made them feel. This will encourage word-of-mouth advertising.
- **Use new tech**: With the rise of generative AI, everyone has access to a sounding board for ideas and an infinite well of feedback and assistance. Make use of this technology.
- **Personal inspiration**: Your game will be unique and relatable if it is inspired by your own real-life experiences.

- **Reversals**: Inverting familiar concepts can be a good source of interesting ideas. For example, instead of playing as the hero saving the world, what if you played as the villain trying to avoid being stopped? *Overlord* (initially released in 2007) and *Untitled Goose Game* (initially released in 2019) both play with this idea—letting the player cause chaos instead of preventing it.
- **Reverse engineer**: You can deconstruct and rebuild well-known and successful games and add a new twist to them. Take *Tetris* (initially released in 1984), for example. What if instead of fitting blocks together, your goal was to break apart a complete structure? Or imagine a farming game such as *Stardew Valley* (initially released in 2016) but set on an alien planet where you must adapt your crops to strange biomes and manage oxygen levels.

Now that you've explored different ways to generate unique and engaging game ideas, it's time to take the next step—turn those ideas into a fully planned project. In the next section, you'll find a practical design guide to help you shape your concept into a game you can start building.

Design guide for your next project

Once you have the idea, the following design principles can help to make your game a rewarding experience:

- **Curiosity should be rewarded**: Players should be encouraged to explore the levels that game developers have spent so much time planning and designing. If they do stray from the main path, then it should be worth that time investment. Bonus story content, hidden treasures, rare items, or power-ups will keep players exploring and make gameplay fresh.
- **Clear separation between win and lose conditions**: Do not confuse the player with ambiguous win-and-lose conditions. Players need accurate and immediate feedback on why they have failed and how they can succeed. Visual cues can help a lot here. Using things such as progress bars, health bars, danger symbols, and color references will give the player confidence.
- **Consistency is key**: Teach the players the rules of your game and then stick to those rules. Patterns build trust for players and create a consistent game world that the player will enjoy exploring.
- **Show don't tell**: A tutorial level can be extremely dull, and since it's often the first level a player experiences, it has the potential to put someone off the game entirely. The best tutorials subtly guide the player to discover the solutions and gameplay mechanics on their own, without breaking immersion.

One excellent example of this is *Portal* (first released in 2007) by Valve, which introduces each new mechanic through cleverly designed puzzles that gradually increase in complexity. The player learns by doing, not by reading instructions. This kind of interactive learning keeps players engaged and makes the tutorial feel like a natural part of the game.

- **Fair is fun**: Humans have a strong sense of justice, and they want things to be fair. Don't increase the difficulty by allowing the enemies to break the rules that apply to the player. By this, I mean enemies that can teleport and defy the in-game physics—basically, cheat.
- **Avoid negative reinforcement**: If a player has worked hard to earn a reward, don't take it away from them. If something is taken away from the player without their input, it can feel unfair. Allow the player to give up an item by choice, usually through selling or swapping.
- **Clear objectives**: One of the most frustrating things for a player is not knowing what to do next. Even in open-world exploration games, the player should always have a clear sense of what they can do next. This can be a completely linear path or a choice between multiple goals. The journey can be challenging, but the objective must be obvious.

  A great example of this is *The Legend of Zelda: Breath of the Wild* (initially released in 2017). While the game gives players the freedom to explore, it consistently provides gentle guidance through environmental cues, map markers, and subtle NPC dialogue to help players orient themselves and choose what to tackle next.

- **A foundation of fun**: Fun is a nebulous term. Essentially, what we mean when a game is fun is that the player is always incentivized to continue playing. The core gameplay must be fun; it must incentivize the player to continue the journey because if not, then no amount of rewards, content, or story will matter.
- **Player knows best**: Listen to feedback and implement changes and suggestions early on. Are players bored, frustrated, or confused? Players will point out the real issues, things that prevent them from wanting to continue playing. Player feedback can save your game.
- **Respect the player**: If you offer the player a choice, then you must honor their decision. Do not provide false choices to force the player into a *correct* decision. This can ruin immersion. Your game's outcomes should match the player's expectations.

Now that you have a solid foundation for designing your game, you are ready to explore specific areas of game development. The following resources have been curated to help you continue learning and growing as a developer.

Further reading

- Vanhove, S. (2024). *Learning GDScript by Developing a Game with Godot 4: A fun introduction to programming in GDScript 2.0 and game development using the Godot Engine.* Packt Publishing Ltd. (https://www.packtpub.com/en-in/product/learning-gdscript-by-developing-a-game-with-godot-4-9781804616987?srsltid=AfmBOorONDSKsGBPgQdezH_3z6R8z1cQn57-bahYjmhfNzjd4JT3EP3t)

  "Sander Vanhove is a seasoned game developer with over 20 games to his credit. This book will serve as your entry point into game development, showing you how to leverage the powerful features of the open source, versatile GDScript 2.0 to develop your ideas, from simple platformers to complex RPGs.

  Whether you're an aspiring game developer, a hobbyist seeking a creative outlet, or simply someone intrigued by the world of game programming, this book will guide you through the intricacies of the Godot 4 game engine. Starting with a primer on the fundamentals of programming, you'll cover everything from data to logic, while familiarizing yourself with Godot's built-in tools such as the physics engine, navigation, and cameras. As you progress, you'll unlock deeper insights into more advanced tools that will take your programming to the next level. Aided by easy-to-follow step-by-step tutorials, examples, exercises, and experiments, you'll seamlessly integrate this newfound knowledge to create a vampire survivor-like game from scratch.

  By the end of this book, you'll have become proficient in leveraging the Godot 4 game engine to bring your gaming visions to life."

- Campos, H. (2025). *Game Development Patterns with Godot 4: Create Resilient Game Systems Using Industry-Proven Solutions in Godot.* Packt Publishing Ltd. (https://www.packtpub.com/en-us/product/game-development-patterns-with-godot-4-9781835880296?srsltid=AfmBOoo26F6O5FFeCa5HioxsnGU9jrLlGrs8DHGUhT6ho3YN5r77i6Gj)

  "Henrique "Ludonaut" Campos is an indie game developer and game designer working in the industry for years. He began as a university teacher in 2015 in the computer graphics and artificial intelligence chairs and worked in the GDQuest team from 2018 to 2022. Henrique is also an independent consultant for studios and schools. Under the alias of Ludonaut, Henrique creates game development content on his YouTube channel, making games, assets, e-books, and courses that can be found on his itch.io profile. As the author of The Essential Guide to Creating Multiplayer Games with Godot 4.0, *Henrique paved the way for Godot users to make reusable and scalable code libraries for Godot Engine projects.*

If you are a game developer, game designer, technical artist, or solo developer with programming experience in Godot Engine and the GDScript programming language, this book is for you. It is perfect for professionals looking to create solid, reusable, and reliable architecture that can adapt and grow with their creative vision."

- Bradfield, C. (2023). *Godot 4 Game Development projects: Build five cross-platform 2D and 3D games using one of the most powerful open source game engines*. Packt Publishing Ltd. (https://www.packtpub.com/en-cy/product/godot-4-game-development-projects-9781804610404)

"Chris Bradfield has worked in the internet technology space for over 25 years. He has worked in the online gaming space for several MMO and social gaming publishers in South Korea and the United States. In his game industry career, he served as a game designer, developer, product manager, and team leader. In 2012, he discovered a love for teaching and founded KidsCanCode to provide programming instruction and curriculum to young students. He is a member of the Godot Engine documentation team and works to provide learning resources for game development students around the world.

This book is for game developers at all levels, from beginners seeking an introduction to experienced programmers aiming to delve into the intricacies of Godot Engine 4.0. It is a valuable resource for newcomers and a treasure trove of insights for experienced developers. Prior programming experience is a prerequisite."

- Obuz, K. (2022). *Game Development with Blender and Godot: Leverage the combined power of Blender and Godot for building a point-and-click adventure game*. Packt Publishing Ltd. (https://www.packtpub.com/en-us/product/game-development-with-blender-and-godot-9781801816021)

"Kumsal Obuz is a self-taught but veteran web developer with more than 15 years of experience in two different countries, leading teams and projects of various sizes. After several years of preparation and transition, he started his own game studio in August 2020. He launched a small puzzle strategy game at the end of 2020 and is currently working on an ambitious farming simulation game. He also likes to mentor (perhaps due to his genetic background, since both of his parents are teachers!). Because of his love for Godot, he founded and still organizes the Godot Toronto Meetup group.

This book is for game developers who are looking to make the transition from 2D to 3D games. Readers should have a basic understanding of Godot, being able to navigate the UI, understand the Inspector panel, create scenes, add scripts to game objects, and so on. Previous experience with Blender is helpful but not required."

- Johnson, J. (2023). *Godot 4 Game Development Cookbook: Over 50 solid recipes for building high-quality 2D and 3D games with improved performance.* Packt Publishing Ltd. (https://www.packtpub.com/en-mx/product/godot-4-game-development-cookbook-9781838826079?srsltid=AfmBOorXABpX5GKKuUDe8VzCkqBkVdbBV6aClIAg1A0VunYHftfrI_Nq)

"Jeff Johnson is a game developer who started using Unity 4.0 in 2014 and released a couple of games on itch.io. In 2018, he created 999 Dev Studio. Toward the end of developing Escape From 51, *he changed engines to Godot 3.0.2 and ported almost the whole game to Godot from Unity. He released* Escape From 51 *on itch.io as well as some mobile games on Google Play.*

Godot 4 Game Development Cookbook is for seasoned game developers who want to acquire skills in creating games using a contemporary game engine. It is an invaluable resource for indie game developers and Godot developers who are familiar with Godot 3 and have some level of expertise in maneuvering the interface."

Summary

You've reached the end of *Godot 4 for Beginners*, but your journey as a game developer is just beginning. In this final chapter, you explored the next steps you can take to continue growing your skills, from educational resources and communities to asset marketplaces and game jams. You saw just how important networking, participating in industry events, and building a strong portfolio to showcase your work are.

Game development is a continuous learning process, and by engaging with these resources, you can refine your craft, stay inspired, and connect with like-minded creators.

It has been a pleasure for me to provide some stepping stones for you on your game dev journey. Keep experimenting, keep creating, and, most importantly, keep making games!

Join our community on Discord

Join our community's Discord space for discussions with the author and other readers:

https://packt.link/godot-4-game-dev

13
Unlock Your Book's Exclusive Benefits

Your copy of this book comes with the following exclusive benefits:

- Next-gen Packt Reader
- AI assistant (beta)
- DRM-free PDF/ePub downloads

Use the following guide to unlock them if you haven't already. The process takes just a few minutes and needs to be done only once.

How to unlock these benefits in three easy steps

Step 1

Have your purchase invoice for this book ready, as you'll need it in *Step 3*. If you received a physical invoice, scan it on your phone and have it ready as either a PDF, JPG, or PNG.

For more help on finding your invoice, visit https://www.packtpub.com/unlock-benefits/help.

> **Note:** Did you buy this book directly from Packt? You don't need an invoice. After completing Step 2, you can jump straight to your exclusive content.

Step 2

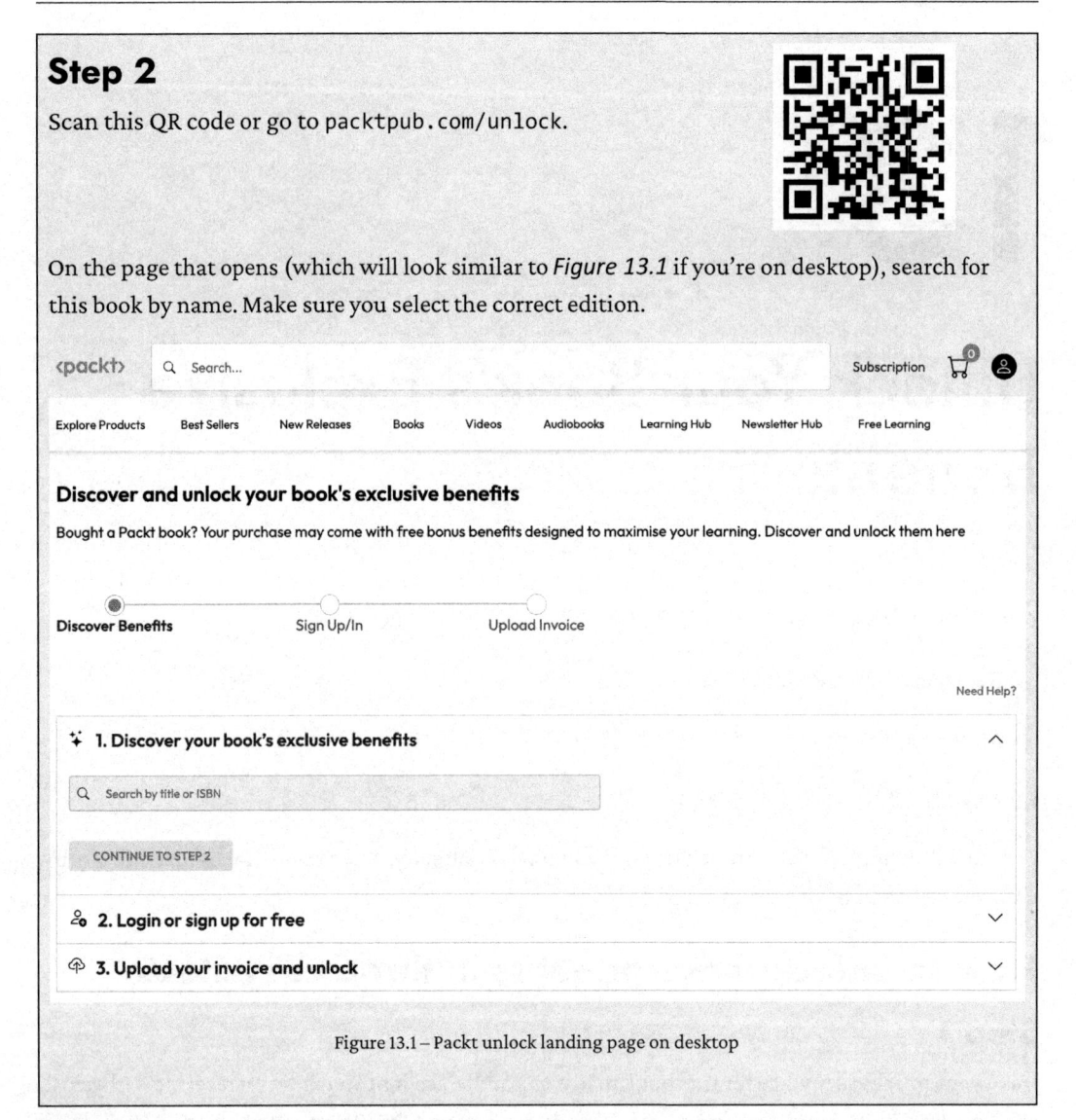

Scan this QR code or go to packtpub.com/unlock.

On the page that opens (which will look similar to *Figure 13.1* if you're on desktop), search for this book by name. Make sure you select the correct edition.

Figure 13.1 – Packt unlock landing page on desktop

Step 3

Once you've selected your book, sign in to your Packt account or create a new one for free. Once you're logged in, upload your invoice. It can be in PDF, PNG, or JPG format and must be no larger than 10 MB. Follow the rest of the instructions on the screen to complete the process.

Need help?

If you get stuck and need help, visit https://www.packtpub.com/unlock-benefits/help for a detailed FAQ on how to find your invoices and more. The following QR code will take you to the help page directly:

> **Note:** If you are still facing issues, reach out to customercare@packt.com.

‹packt›

packtpub.com

Subscribe to our online digital library for full access to over 7,000 books and videos, as well as industry leading tools to help you plan your personal development and advance your career. For more information, please visit our website.

Why subscribe?

- Spend less time learning and more time coding with practical eBooks and Videos from over 4,000 industry professionals
- Improve your learning with Skill Plans built especially for you
- Get a free eBook or video every month
- Fully searchable for easy access to vital information
- Copy and paste, print, and bookmark content

At www.packtpub.com, you can also read a collection of free technical articles, sign up for a range of free newsletters, and receive exclusive discounts and offers on Packt books and eBooks.

Other Books You May Enjoy

If you enjoyed this book, you may be interested in these other books by Packt:

Game Development Patterns with Godot 4

Henrique Campos

ISBN: 978-1-83588-028-9

- Create reusable and scalable code that follows SOLID principles
- Identify common game development issues and apply industry-standard solutions
- Understand feature requests and how to turn them into concrete solutions leveraging design patterns
- Analyze game development pathologies to figure out underlying issues
- Architect reliable systems that are understandable, intuitive, and scalable
- Structure professional, collaborative game systems that are easy to maintain

Learning GDScript by Developing a Game with Godot 4

Sander Vanhove

ISBN: 978-1-80461-698-7

- Develop your GDScript 2.0 programming skills from basic to advanced, emphasizing code cleanliness
- Harness Godot 4's integrated physics engine to control and manipulate in-game objects
- Design a vibrant and immersive game world by seamlessly integrating a diverse array of assets
- Master the art of processing input from various sources for enhanced interactivity
- Extend the reach of your game by learning how to export it to multiple platforms
- Incorporate simple multiplayer functionality for a dynamic gaming experience

Packt is searching for authors like you

If you're interested in becoming an author for Packt, please visit `authors.packt.com` and apply today. We have worked with thousands of developers and tech professionals, just like you, to help them share their insight with the global tech community. You can make a general application, apply for a specific hot topic that we are recruiting an author for, or submit your own idea.

Share your thoughts

Now you've finished *Godot 4 for Beginners*, we'd love to hear your thoughts! Scan the QR code below to go straight to the Amazon review page for this book and share your feedback or leave a review on the site that you purchased it from.

`https://packt.link/r/1836203098`

Your review is important to us and the tech community and will help us make sure we're delivering excellent quality content.

Index

Symbols

2D Mini-Game
  background, adding to level 136-138
  collisions, detecting 142, 143
  level, building with TileMap 132-136
  physics layer 146, 147
  player animations, setting up 139-141
  player, controlling 136
  player, creating 136
  TileMap collisions 143, 144
  tiles, painting 148, 149

3D character
  building 192-196

3D dimension
  working 192

3D Mini-Game
  audio, adding to level 242-245
  background color, setting 238
  Ball scene, creating 231, 232
  Ball script, writing 233
  Cannon scene, creating 230, 231
  Cannon script, writing 233-235
  Flag scene, creating 235, 236
  Gem scene, creating 224, 225
  Gem script, adding 225-229
  level, completing 235
  level, polishing 237
  particle effects, adding 238
  scenes, modifying 236, 237
  sine function, using 246, 247
  smoke scene, creating 238-242

3D objects
  creating 56-58
  material, applying 65, 66
  material, creating 62-65

3D scene
  moving around 59-61

A

albedo 64
animate function 163, 165, 260
argument 105
assignment operator 93
Audacity
  URL 308
audio effect
  adding 270, 271
audio tools 308
  Audacity 308
  Bfxr 308
  Bosca Ceoil 308
  LMMS 308

B

Ball scene
　creating 231, 232
Ball script
　writing 233
BBC
　URL 308
Bfxr
　URL 308
Blender
　URL 308
BlenderKit 309
blog recommendations
　Deconstructor of Fun 304
　Game Design Skills 304
　Game Developer 304
Bosca Ceoil
　URL 308
built-in method 50

C

camera controller
　implementing 215-219
Cannon scene
　creating 230, 231
Cannon script
　writing 233-235
CharacterBody2D template
　adding, for Player script 149-153
Character Controller script
　working with 203, 204
clean code concept 154, 155
CodeDecks
　URL 281

collectible items 166
　strawberry scene 166-170
collectibles 224
collision layers 144
collision masks 144
community 306
comparison operators 101, 102
　equality 101
　greater than 101
　greater than or equal to 101
　less than 101
　less than or equal to 102
　not equals 102
confetti cannon effect
　creating 262-270
　scripting 268
constants 152
coordinates 118, 119
Creative Commons Zero (CC0) 158, 192
cross product 129
custom functions
　using 104

D

DaFont
　URL 309
delta 25, 27
design principles 311, 312
directional light 73, 74
direction vector 117
dot notation 121
dot product 129
double-jump animation 159, 160
double-jump function 160, 161

Index

E

educational resources
  blogs 303, 304
  utilizing 302
  YouTube 302, 303
Entertainment Software Rating Board (ESRB) 284
exported variables 204

F

fall animation 158
fire() function 268
Flag scene
  creating 235, 236
Font Squirrel
  URL 309
foundational techniques, game juice
  audio feedback 251
  visual feedback 251
FreeFont
  URL 309
Freesound
  URL 308
friction 161
functions 89, 208
  exploring 208
  game events and feedback, handling 212-215
  input map, creating 209, 210
  _physics_process(delta) 91
  player controls and actions, implementing 211
  _process 90
  _process(delta) 90
  _ready 89, 90
  return values 107, 108

G

game design 277
  documentation, significance 279, 280
  examples 278
  foundations 278, 279
game design document (GDD) 279
  anchor points 285
  assets 285
  audience 284
  elements, describing 286
  expanded concept paragraph and USP 283
  exploring 282
  genre 284
  guiding principles 280-282
  monetization 286
  platforms 285
  player's experience 284
  project, status 282
  review competition 285
  statement of concept 283
  team 282
  title 282
game design document (GDD), elements
  archive 298
  audio and visual style 290
  current concerns and considerations 298
  detailed asset list 295
  details, implementation 299
  game objects 294
  player progression and objectives 286, 287
  playtesting 297, 298
  prototypes 296
  software requirements 292, 293
  systems and features 291, 292

user interface 288
world and background 287, 288
Game Developers Conference (GDC) 306
game development
practice opportunities, exploring 304
Game Docs
reference link 282
game engine 6, 307
game ideas
developing 310, 311
game jams 305
Godot Wild Jam 306
Ludum Dare 306
participating in 305
The Global Game Jam 306
game juice 250
examples 250
foundational techniques 251
game loop 90
Gamescrye
reference link 280
GDScript 56, 84
Gem scene
creating 224, 225
Gem script
adding 225-229
GIMP
URL 307
Git
URL 308
Godot 6
features 7
URL 8
Godot 4
setting up 8-11

Godot 4.0 3
Godot Project Manager 12
graphic tools 307
Blender 308
GIMP 307
Krita 307
LibreSprite 307
gray boxing 297
grouping 203

H

HacknPlan
URL 281
handle_controls function 211
handle_respawn() function
grounded state tracking 214
landing animation 214
resetting scale 214
scene reload 214
heads-up display (HUD) 249
health bar HUD
heart-based health system, developing 252-255
HUD, updating in level script 255-257
implementing 251, 252
helper variables 159, 160
hit animation
adding 257-262
hook 283

I

idle animation 158
input map 209
creating 209, 210
instance 38

Index

irregular collision shapes
   handling 199-201
itch.io
   URL 309

J

jump animation 158

K

Kenney
   URL 308
Krita
   URL 307

L

LEGO model 34
level completion
   implementing 183-186
level component
   creating 197
   grass platform, creating 197-199
level design 196
   creating 196
   irregular collision shapes, handling 199-201
   level component, creating 197
   level layout, creating 201, 202
level layout
   creating 201, 202
   level scene, organizing 202
LibreSprite
   URL 307
lighting 72
   directional light 73, 74
   omni light 74-78
   spotlight 78-80

linear algebra 129
linear interpolation 213
LMMS
   URL 308
Lospec
   URL 308

M

Material Maker
   reference link 65
materials 62
   applying 65, 66
   creating, for object 62-65
   replicating 67
   shiny metal material 68, 69
   texture, adding 71
   transparent pink capsule 70
mathematical operators
   addition 98
   division 98, 99
   multiplication 98, 99
   subtraction 98, 99
mesh 59
MeshInstance3D 59
minimum viable product (MVP) 281
movement 122
mushroom stomping 180-183

N

networking 306
   professionals 307
   with community 306
nodes 30, 34
   working 30
non-player characters (NPCs) 294

normalized vector 117, 125, 129
Notion
   URL 281

O

Obsidian
   URL 281
obstacles 230
omni light 74-78
OneNote
   URL 281
OpenGameArt
   URL 308
operators 98
   comparison 101, 102
   mathematical 98, 99
   order of operations 100

P

parameter 105
particle effects 238
PascalCase 96
pass-through platforms
   setting up 165, 166
patrolling enemy
   adding 175-179
PEMDAS 100
Pixabay 308
Pixel Adventure 1
   reference link 158
Pixel Adventure 2
   reference link 158

player animations
   controlling, with code 158, 159
player input
   player reactions, scripting to 49
   reacting to 39-48
player reactions, to player input
   input handling 50-52
   label, hiding 49
Player script
   CharacterBody2D template, adding for 149-153
point 114
portfolio 309
   building 309
positioning 122
position vectors 118
project
   additional scene, adding 38
   creating 12-22
   editing 31-33
   Label node, removing from Main scene 35-37

Q

Quaternius
   URL 308

R

RayCast2D 179
resources 7, 34, 308, 309
return values 106, 107
Roobyx
   reference link 280
run animation 158

Index

S

scalar 125
scene 31, 34
  dynamic, making 23, 24
SCREAMING_SNAKE_CASE 96
scripts 31
  creating 84-88
shortcut operator 99
sine function
  using 246, 247
smoke scene
  creating 238-242
snake_case 96
sound effect
  adding 270, 271
  implementing 272-274
spotlight 78-80
sprite 39
sprite sheet 139, 167
StaticBody3D node 197
  using, for stationary elements 197
strawberry scene 166-170
Strawberry script
  implementing 170-173
String 97
stub testing 181

T

tests
  running 220
TileMap 157
  level, building 132-136

tools 307
  audio tools 308
  game engine 307
  graphic tools 307
  version control 308

U

unique selling points (USPs) 283
Unsplash 308
user interface (UI) 251

V

variables 93
  creating 93, 94
  data types 95
  naming conventions 96, 97
  Player script, linking with camera 205-207
  reference variables method,
    adding 207, 208
  using 204
variable scope 101
vector addition 123, 124
vector length 127
vector multiplication 125, 126
vectors 114, 115
  distance, calculating to object 128
  normalization 128
  using 119-122
vector subtraction 124
velocity 116
velocity vector 116

W

wall-slide animation 159, 160

wall-slide function 161, 162
   conditions, checking 162
   download speed, limiting 162, 163
   input, detecting 162
   resetting 162

Y

YouTube channels
   GameDev Journey 303
   GDQuest 302
   Godot Tutorials 303
   Heartbeast 303

Z

ZapSplat
   URL 308

Printed in Dunstable, United Kingdom